# Examples of GE's Major Nuclear Weapons–Related Work
## Federal Tax Dollars Paid to GE for Nuclear Weapons*
### Fiscal Years 1984–1988

| Nuclear Weapons–Related Systems and Parts | GE's Contracts *(in Millions)* |
|---|---|
| Aegis Missile | $1,655.71 |
| Minuteman Missile | $104.60 |
| MX Missile | $660.86 |
| Poseidon Missile | $11.66 |
| Tomahawk Cruise Missile | $37.79 |
| Trident Missile | $1,312.71 |
| A-6 Intruder Attack Aircraft | $50.01 |
| B-1 Bomber | $95.13 |
| F-4 Phantom II Fighter Aircraft | $16.17 |
| F-15 Eagle Fighter Aircraft | $49.55 |
| F-18 Hornet Fighter Aircraft | $2,488.94 |
| F-111 Fighter Aircraft | $276.58 |
| Aircraft Engines (e.g., F-110, F-101, F-104) | $5,846.24 |
| Trident Nuclear Submarine | $584.45 |
| SSN-688 Nuclear Submarine | $564.46 |
| AN/SQS-53 Sonar | $303.90 |
| Defense Satellite Communication System (DSCS III) | $705.28 |
| Strategic Army Communication System (STARCOM) | $71.10 |
| Naval Nuclear Reactor Program (Knolls Atomic Laboratory) | $1,063.91 |
| Pinellas Plant (Neutron "Trigger" for Nuclear Bombs) | $603.59 |
| Other Nuclear Weapons–Related Work | $1,770.32 |
| **Taxpayer Money Grossed by GE for Nuclear Weapons–Related Work Fiscal Years 1984–1988*** | **$18.3 Billion ($18,272,969,000)** |
| **Nuclear Weapons–Related Work* as a Percentage of GE Annual Revenues** | 10.4% |

\* Data from public information sources for prime contracts.
  (Does not include, for example, subcontracts and classified programs.)

# Bringing GE to Light

## How General Electric Shapes Nuclear Weapons Policies for Profits

**Researched and Compiled by INFACT**

**New Society Publishers**
**Philadelphia, PA and Santa Cruz, CA**

First published by INFACT in 1988
Copyright © 1990 by INFACT

INFACT and New Society Publishers grant permission to reprint properly credited quotations of up to 2000 words. INFACT asks that a complimentary copy of all works in which quoted material appears be sent to:

INFACT
256 Hanover Street
Boston, MA 02113

(617) 742-4583

For permission to reprint longer extracts, please contact:

New Society Publishers
4527 Springfield Avenue
Philadelphia, PA 19143

ISBN 0-86571-170-4 Hardcover
ISBN 0-86571-171-2 Paperback
Library of Congress Catalog Card Number: 88-80296

Typesetting by Resolution Graphics, Boston, MA.
Layout by Resolution Graphics and New Society Publishers.
Printed in the United States of America on partially recycled paper.

New Society Publishers is a project of the New Society Educational Foundation, a nonprofit, tax-exempt, public foundation. Opinions expressed in this book do not necessarily represent positions of the New Society Educational Foundation.

# Table of Contents

# Acknowledgements

This exposé of General Electric would not have been possible without the help and inspiration of many friends and allies. Through all the excitement, the frustration, the laughter and cooperation, *together* we made this book happen. And *together* we can and will stop GE's production and promotion of nuclear weapons.

For those before us who understood the importance of focusing on GE to stop the company's nuclear weapons work—you have been an inspiration: AFSC/GE Project; Brandywine Peace Community, Philadelphia; Cincinnati CARE and Polly Brokaw; the Good Things Committee, Fairfield, Connecticut; the Immanuel House, St. Petersburg, Florida; the Interfaith Center for Corporate Responsibility (ICCR); the Knolls Action Project, Albany, New York; the GE Stockholders' Alliance Against Nuclear Power and Weapons; and John Woodmansee.

For those before us whose books and research focused on the workings of the military-industrial complex and the power of U.S. transnational corporations—your information has been invaluable: Gordon Adams (*The Politics of Defense Contracting: The Iron Triangle*); Dick Barnet (*Roots of War*); G. William Domhoff (*Who Rules America* and other books); William Hartung (*The Economic Consequences of the Freeze*); Investor Responsibility Research Center (IRRC) (*The Nuclear Weapons Industry*); NARMIC (a project of the American Friends Service Committee); the Natural Resources Defense Council (*The Nuclear Weapons Databooks*); Harvey Wasserman (co-author of *Killing Our Own*); and John Woodmansee (*The World of a Giant Corporation*).

For all those who helped edit the drafts and final manuscript—your careful work and helpful comments moved us forward: Diane Bratcher, Crosby Milne, and John Woodmansee.

For those who provided other valuable assistance for the book—thanks: for research and other special help—Rosalee Anders (Council for a Livable World), Miriam Boucher, June Casey, Janet Gordon (Citizens' Call, Utah), Paul Murphy (Military Spending Research Service), Erik Pratt, Mark Sharwood, and Bill Whistler; for photography, Ruth Carmichael; and for technical illustration, Bruce Sesnovich.

For those who gave permission to use their materials in our book—thanks: from our allies—Center for Defense Information (CDI), Council on Economic Priorities (CEP), Common Cause, Jobs with Peace, World Priorities, Inc.; and from publicly available materials of the federal government—Department of Defense (DOD), Department of Energy (DOE), Government Accounting Office (GAO), and Government Service Administration (GSA).

For typesetting and production services above and beyond the call of duty—your patience and friendship have made this all possible: Sara Arrand and Ed Perlmutter of Resolution Graphics, with assistance from Robin Eldridge.

And finally, this book is dedicated to those hundreds of thousands of INFACT activists and supporters, who day in and day out use their energy and creativity, their financial resources, their consumer power, and their hard work to build a more secure world, free from nuclear weapons.

# Prologue: A Call to Action

## The Issue Is Global Survival

There are now 50,000 nuclear warheads poised around the globe. And every day, the U.S. builds five more nuclear bombs. Each one of these bombs is massively more destructive than the bomb that devastated Hiroshima; each bomb costs an average of $40 million; each bomb increases the likelihood of global nuclear war.

The human costs of this spiraling arms build-up are drastic, as resources are diverted to weapons and basic human needs go unmet. Globally, $2 million is spent on the military every minute—*and every minute of every day, 30 children die from lack of food or inexpensive vaccines*. In this country, our children are suffering, and our children's future has been sacrificed to the most massive military expansion in the nation's history. Radiation from the nuclear weapons production cycle is killing atomic veterans, plant workers, uranium miners, and people in communities near bomb factories, test sites, and waste dumps. Yet the nuclear arms race escalates.

One reason for the insane build-up is clear. Nuclear weapons are big business. Transnational weapons corporations like General Electric first promote the nuclear weapons build-up and then produce these weapons of mass destruction at public expense for private profit.

The chief executives of weapons corporations have now assumed significant decision-making roles in issues of national security. Corporations do not simply make the weapons, nor do they passively respond to government requests. Rather, the weapons corporations *create both the supply and the demand for ever more costly and deadly nuclear weapons*. Yet these corporate interests operate hidden from public view, accountable not to the public interest and safety but to the corporate bottom line.

## The American People Have the Right to Know

This country's national security is guided in large part by the interests of weapons corporations, not by what the American people and our elected representatives have determined is in our best interests. The power of these corporations represents an unprecedented threat to democracy. Yet the nuclear weapons corporations insist that they merely do what the government asks of them. It is now time to expose to public scrutiny what the nuclear weapons industry has worked so hard to conceal.

**The American people have a right to know** that the impetus for new, more complicated, and more expensive nuclear weapons systems comes principally from corporate R & D labs and not from a reasoned military assessment of what is needed to defend the country.

**The American people have a right to know** that public fears about the Soviet Union are purposefully fanned by the nuclear weapons corporations.

**The American people have a right to know** that one of our most basic democratic institutions, Congress, is being dangerously undermined by lobbying, PAC contributions, and jobs extortion.

In a democracy, the people and their elected representatives should make the life and death decisions about national security—free from powerful conflicts of interest. This is a serious responsibility requiring an informed and knowledgeable populace. The people have the right to timely and accurate information about how the current system works and how it is being undermined by corporate interests. From this position of knowledge, rational options for change can then be identified and acted upon.

## Boycott GE!

A grassroots action organization is now challenging this threat to democracy and global survival. INFACT runs corporate responsibility campaigns to stop corporate abuses that endanger people's health and survival.

Nuclear weapons pose the ultimate threat to global survival, and the unwarranted influence of the weapons contractors must be challenged and reduced. The American people cannot vote corporate heads out of office but other strategies are available.

Massive grassroots pressure on General Electric—the leader of the nuclear weapons industry—challenges GE to live up to its public claim to "bring good things to life." Because the root of the problem is economic, consumers have a very powerful tool. Consumers can "vote" with their pocketbooks by choosing to withhold business from GE until the company stops endangering our lives.

You can make a difference. Help stop the production and promotion of nuclear weapons. Join the GE Boycott!

# PART I. SETTING THE STAGE

# The Saga of the B-1 Bomber

*The fact is that among intelligent defense experts, the B-1 is a joke. It is a public works project for the aerospace industry rather than a needed weapon for the defense of the United States.*
— Senator William Proxmire (1971)[1]

The B-1 bomber has a long and controversial history. And General Electric has been shaping this history from the very beginning. The development and production of the B-1 has been opposed by congressional committees, presidential administrations, and military experts for close to three decades; yet it has survived to become one of the most well funded weapons in the U.S. arsenal. The B-1 is a striking symbol of the power the weapons industry maintains over military strategy and federal spending decisions.

To understand why this obsolete, unnecessary, extremely costly, and deadly nuclear weapon system is still being built, it is illuminating to look closely at the bomber's proponents in the military and the industry. Often they are one and the same.

## Mission of the B-1 Bomber

The forerunner of the B-1 was first conceptualized as a long-range, supersonic bomber, and in 1955 this bomber was supported with federal research funds. Rockwell received the research and development money to build the airframe, and General Electric received the R & D money to build the engine prototypes. This bomber, however, never got past the R & D stage. After another false start, studies for the final concept design of the new long-range bomber began in 1963. This design became known as the B-1.[2]

The B-1 bomber was designed "...to cross the Arctic or the Atlantic like a javelin, befuddle Soviet air defenses with sophisticated electronics, thunder over Soviet treetops to drop nuclear bombs on strategic targets and then return home."[3] The B-1's main mission is described as a "ground-hugging racer." It was intended to "...penetrate a defensive network of radar, anti-aircraft missiles and fighter planes by streaking through valleys and around hills at 650 miles an hour, which is nearly the speed of sound, at 200 feet above ground."[4]

Over time, the B-1 was modified to launch cruise missiles and was intended to be serviceable for more conventional warfare bomber missions. The B-1 is now capable of carrying 24 nuclear bombs, 8 nuclear-tipped cruise missiles, or 64,000 pounds of conventional bombs.[5]

## The Watershed Year for the B-1 and GE—1968

Since the time of its earliest forerunners, the B-1 has been steeped in controversy, and its continued existence has been constantly in question. The long-range bomber program has been plagued by excessive expense and charges of obsolescence.

In retrospect, 1968 was the watershed year for the B-1, and accordingly, for its main contractors, GE and Rockwell. It was not until 1968 that the B-1 became solidly entrenched as the third leg of this country's "strategic triad"—the triad being those nuclear weapons that could be launched by land, by sea, or by air.

### The GE Connection

As part of the 1968 presidential elections, the Republican National Party looked to two men to develop its platform plank on national security: Neil McElroy and Thomas Gates. Both men were well placed in powerful business circles and experienced in the military hierarchy.

Neil McElroy, President of Procter and Gamble, sat on General Electric's board of directors from 1950–1957. He then interrupted his GE board service to spend two years as secretary of defense. After his term in the government, McElroy was back on GE's board for another 13 years, from 1959 to 1972.[6]

Throughout these years, revolving back and forth between GE and the Pentagon, McElroy consistently upheld GE's financial interests in areas of military strategy and foreign policy. In 1969, for example, intense public and congressional debate centered on the issue of anti-ballistic missile systems (ABM). At that time, GE held a $45 million contract for the ABM. As the controversy raged, a group called Citizens for Peace with Security entered the debate by placing full page ads in favor of the ABM in the *Washington Post* and six other newspapers. GE director McElroy signed the ad as a "citizen," not mentioning his connection with GE or GE's financial interest in the continued development of the ABM.[7]

The second Republican Party Platform writer was Thomas Gates, a prominent banker with Morgan Guaranty Trust. Morgan Guaranty is an international banking conglomerate long connected with GE; in fact, Morgan is one of GE's largest shareholders, owning several hundred million dollars worth of GE stock.[8] Gates was secretary of the Navy from 1957–1959 and then succeeded McElroy as secretary of defense under President Eisenhower for two years. At the end of his government term, Gates joined GE's board of directors from 1964–1976.[9]

Both Gates and McElroy held the powerful position of secretary of defense in the late 1950s and early 1960s—the precise time period that the new long-range bomber was under intensive research and development. In the position of secretary of defense, both men would have had substantial knowledge of this new strategic bomber. GE already had a financial stake in continuing development of the new bomber. And at this time, GE was attempting to establish itself as one of the main contractors for the new bomber—a position that would lead to billions of dollars in contracts over the next decades.

### The 1968 Republican National Platform

In 1968, Gates and McElroy prepared an official report to the Republican National Committee on America's defense posture. This report strongly criticized Presidents Kennedy and Johnson for what was termed their "appalling" failure to develop enough new weapons to counteract the Soviet "threat." However, Presidents Eisenhower, Kennedy, and Johnson had *all* rejected the need for a new strategic bomber, citing as reasons the reliability of the B-52 bomber and the increasing reliance on cruise missiles, which do not require bombers to fly into Soviet territory.[10]

At the urging of Gates and McElroy, the Republican National Platform of 1968 called for the "speedy development" of the B-1 bomber. *Both Gates and McElroy sat on GE's board of directors at the time they wrote the platform plank*. Thus, GE had a direct financial interest in the outcome of that election.

Richard Nixon ran—and won—on the Republican National Platform in 1968. His election turned Gates' and McElroy's plank position into the military strategy of the land and into production reality for the B-1's major contractors: Rockwell, GE, and Boeing. In June 1970, the Department of Defense (DOD) began awarding contracts for the new B-1 bomber.[11]

### GE's Stake in the 1968 Elections

GE's involvement in the production of the B-1 bomber is extensive; in fact, the B-1 is one of GE's largest military contracts.[12] Only one-and-a-half years into Nixon's term, GE received a $406 million contract to build engines for the B-1 test models.[13] GE now manufactures the F-101 turbofan engine for the B-1B, as well as the engine thrust control subsystem and other engine instruments.[14] GE also produces the B-1 radar and infrared absorbing and jamming devices.[15] Through the years, this has meant billions of dollars in B-1 contracts.

## The On-Again, Off-Again Story of the B-1 Bomber

With the substantial assistance of GE's Gates and McElroy, the B-1 moved from prototype to production, from concept to strategic importance in this country's nuclear arsenal. Yet the B-1 saga continued.

By 1974, the B-1 had fallen far short of military specifications, even though Air Force officials had reduced its performance requirements substantially. A Government Accounting Office (GAO) report showed that the B-1 speed, range, and payload goals had been lowered and that the planes would not fly supersonic at low altitudes. The projected costs of the bomber, already high, were steadily climbing.[16]

### The Marketing Strategy

Rockwell and General Electric stood to lose a great deal of money if they failed to market the B-1 to the military, Congress, the White House, and the American people. As early as 1973, Rockwell began developing a marketing strategy called "Operation Common Sense" to ensure the B-1's popularity and its invulnerability to budget cuts. Most of the expenses associated with Rockwell's public relations campaign were claimed as contract costs by the company and paid for by the taxpayers.[17]

Gene Breckner, Antelope Valley Press.

By 1975, opposition to the B-1 bomber was quite heated, and Rockwell stepped up its marketing strategy to keep the weapon alive. In a special edition of *Rockwell International News*, Rockwell's president asked all employees to contact their congressional representatives to encourage them to vote for the B-1. An estimated 80,000 messages flooded Congress from Rockwell employees, their families, and friends. Rockwell also spent thousands of dollars advertising in trade journals and popular magazines to promote the "need" for the B-1.[18]

### The "Insurance" Strategy

B-1 critics have often charged that there has been little independent evaluation of the bomber or its mission since it was first proposed. This is no accident. An in-depth study of the military-industrial complex conducted by the *Los Angeles Times* in 1983 charged

> Much of the 'outside' analysis of the Soviet weaponry that the B-1 might have to face has been done by direct B-1 contractors or by think tanks, neither of them eager to shoot down a bomber that they or their clients were determined to build.[19]

Similarly, government agencies such as the Defense Science Board and the Air Force Scientific Advisory Board help assess the nature of the Soviet threat and help determine what weapons the U.S. needs in response. For the past 20 years, almost all of the major B-1 subcontractors have held seats on one of these two agencies.[20]

General Electric has been prominently involved in key Defense Department agencies to insure that its financial interests are secured. One example of GE involvement is Daniel Fink, who was first assistant director and then deputy director of the Research and Engineering Department of the DOD from 1963–1967. In 1968, Fink was appointed to the Defense Science Board where he played an active role for nearly 20 years. Concurrently in 1968, Fink became general manager of GE's Aerospace Division, continuing in GE's direct employ into the 1980s.[21]

### The Ultimate Strategy: Jobs Extortion

Perhaps the most brilliant strategy used by the B-1 contractors was one that virtually assured congressional support for the B-1. This strategy was led by Rockwell.

The company determined how it could spread B-1 contracts and subcontracts—and therefore employment—into as many congressional districts as possible. As testament to Rockwell's tremendous success, the B-1 is assembled from 50,000 parts supplied by over 5,200 subcontractors in 48 states, in all but a handful of congressional districts. When faced with possible cuts, the industry's lobbyists can make a good case for the B-1 on Capitol Hill by threatening loss of constituents' jobs.[22]

"At last! A weapons system absolutely impervious to attack: It has components manufactured in all 435 Congressional districts!"

**John Trever**
The Albuquerque Journal
News America Syndicate

## Cancellations...and Reappropriations

Despite GE's interventions and Rockwell's persistent marketing efforts, public opposition against the B-1 grew. The bomber had powerful critics both in the Pentagon and in Congress. In 1977, then Defense Secretary Harold Brown released a Pentagon study showing that the B-1 was an "unnecessary expense."[23] Finally, President Carter cancelled production of the B-1 bomber later that year, citing its exorbitant cost and its obsolescence. Because it had taken so long to develop the B-1, Defense Secretary Brown asserted that Moscow had had ample time to devise air defenses against it.[24]

However, a lucrative weapons system never dies, nor do its contractors ever give up. Three years later, the 1980 Republican Party Platform called for "accelerated development and deployment of a new manned bomber to exploit the $5.5 billion already invested in the B-1."[25] Ronald Reagan was elected on that platform. Shortly thereafter, in 1981, despite opposition from the commander of the Strategic Air Command (SAC), President

Reagan resumed production of 100 B-1 bombers. The bomber was now dubbed the B-1B.[26]

## The Ultimate Revolving Door

President Reagan has presided over the largest peace-time military build-up in this country's history. He significantly increased this country's nuclear arsenal, increasing development and production of two destabilizing first-strike nuclear weapons systems, the B-1 bomber and the Trident submarine. GE garnered major contracts on both of these systems.[27]

Ronald Reagan spent eight years on GE's payroll, as host for and occasional star of the *GE Theater*. He became well known to the public as GE's spokesperson.[28] After 1962, as Reagan launched his own political career, he remained closely connected with powerful GE executives and board members. In his efforts to revive the B-1 bomber in 1981, Reagan relied heavily on Air Force General David C. Jones, at that time Chair of the Joint Chiefs of Staff. Jones strongly supported the B-1 to the Armed Services Committee, arguing that "deploying a new manned penetrator should be top priority."[29] After leaving the Air Force, Jones became a member of GE's board of directors in 1986.

## The Benefits to General Electric

Production of the B-1 has been extremely lucrative for GE. In fiscal year 1981, before Reagan revived the B-1 program, GE received B-1 contracts totaling $3.2 million. The next year, GE received contract awards totaling at least $261 million for the B-1 engines. In 1983, GE's sales rose to $465 million for the engine and other components.[30] At this point, GE was awarded a multi-year contract totaling $1.58 billion to complete the engines for the full B-1B fleet.[31] The B-1 bomber now represents billions of dollars in sales to General Electric.

The lucrative results of GE's influence over government decisions have been noted by the company. In GE's 1982 Annual Report—the year B-1 contracts flowed again under Reagan's orders—the company told its share-owners that "higher defense spending and the transition of advanced research and prototype work into production produced a very strong increase" in 1982 aerospace sales. The report went on to suggest modestly that the government's decisions to go ahead with the B-1B aircraft program "adds to the current healthy GE position in the military market."[32]

## Military Need or Corporate Greed?

One year after Reagan revived the B-1, the bomber was already projected to be obsolete. Defense Secretary Caspar Weinberger announced that the Soviet Union had developed their defenses to the point that the B-1 would only be useful until 1990, two years after estimated completion of the B-1 fleet.[33]

### Exorbitant Costs

The American taxpayer has paid a great deal of money for the B-1 bomber. In 1969, when the B-1's position in the strategic triad had been assured with the able assistance of GE's Gates and McElroy, the Air Force estimated the total cost of each bomber at $35.7 million. In 1977, the year Carter axed the program, the General Accounting Office set the estimates at $112 million per plane—more than tripling the original cost of the program.

In 1981, with Reagan's revival of the B-1, the Pentagon projected the cost of each bomber to be $200 million. And by 1987, in full production, each B-1 is now estimated to cost over $270 million. The costs of the B-1 have increased nearly eight-fold over the original projections.[34]

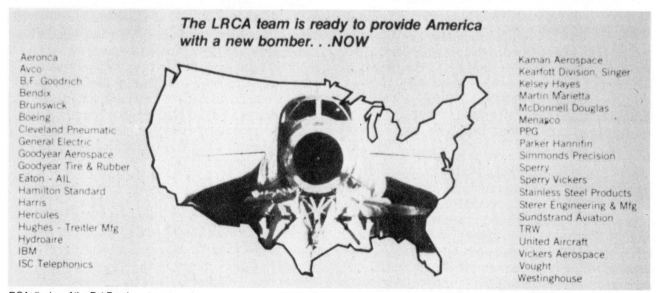

RCA display of the B-1 Bomber at an arms bazaar.                    Source: Center for Defense Information.

## Tying Up the Deal for Years in Advance

The Air Force heavily lobbied Congress to appropriate multi-year funding (rather than funding for one fiscal year at a time, which is the normal procedure) for B-1 production. Congress was threatened that without multi-year funding, B-1 program costs would be likely to rise above the strict limits imposed by a B-1 weary Congress.[35]

General Electric was the prime beneficiary of multi-year contracting. When the 100 B-1's went into full production in 1984, the Air Force deviated from its usual procedures to award GE a $1.58 billion multi-year contract, projected to run for 2½ years. This was the first time the Air Force had granted an associate contractor (as opposed to a prime contractor) a multi-year contract.[36]

When Congress gave the Air Force "carte blanche" by authorizing several years worth of B-1 money at one time, the Air Force agreed in turn to keep the program's cost under $20.5 billion and to deliver the planes on time and in good working condition. It is questionable logic to reward B-1 manufacturers with contracts guaranteed for years in advance, given the ever-present questions of cost-effectiveness, usefulness, and obsolescence. The Air Force has now reneged on most of its agreements, yet most of the money has been paid out to the contractors. When asked why the B-1 program should not be scrapped once again, Air Force officials responded that the contractors would have to be paid extensive cancellation costs, which were built into the contracts.[37]

## Performance in Question

Not only have the military specifications of the bomber been reduced considerably but serious technological flaws have also plagued the bomber. A U.S. House of Representatives report criticizing the B-1 bomber was released in early April 1987. According to a *Boston Globe* article by investigative reporter Fred Kaplan

> Excess weight has shortened the plane's range, preventing it from reaching several targets inside the Soviet Union. The plane's offensive electronics, which help it find the targets for its bombs, and the defensive electronics, which are designed to defeat enemy efforts to shoot the plane down, jam each other. These electronics also send out a radar 'beacon,' attracting the attention of enemy defenses.[38]

General Electric produces four engines for each bomber, the radar, and the infrared absorbing and jamming devices.

In the fall of 1987, during a test flight over Colorado, one of the bombers flew through a flock of birds. The final radio transmission from a crew member said the bomber had "lost engines 3 and 4, with an engine on fire." The bomber crashed, killing three crew members.[39] In early October,

low-level flights were forbidden during the early morning, the early evening, and at night when larger numbers of birds are normally in the air. Such flights were also forbidden along routes known to cross the migratory paths of large birds. Ten days later, the Strategic Air Command suspended *all* low-level B-1 flying.[40]

The B-1 was originally designed to implement a low-level, bomber-penetration military strategy. Yet the bomber was fatally damaged by a flock of birds, which might be expected to be flying at low altitudes.

## And the Saga Continues

From GE board members writing the B-1 into the 1968 Republican Party Platform, to the various strategies used by GE and Rockwell throughout the 1970s to keep the B-1 alive, to former GE employee Ronald Reagan reviving the B-1 in 1981, this nuclear weapon system has survived against formidable odds. More importantly, the B-1 represents billions of dollars in sales—and substantial profits—to the system's main contractors. GE's position in the military-industrial complex, and its vast connections in the worlds of business and high finance, have served the company well.

Yet the B-1 saga—and GE's role in it—does not end here. Even before the 100th B-1 rolls off the production line in mid-1988, the B-1's capabilities have already been surpassed by the newest fighter bomber under development, the Advanced Technology Bomber, more commonly known as the Stealth.[41] For General Electric, the obsolescence of the B-1 is irrelevant. The company has nearly completed its contract work for the B-1 bomber and will continue supplying maintenance and replacement parts for years to come. And, as would be expected, GE is part of the team now proceeding with the research and development on the new Stealth[42]—a bomber whose original price tag is $600 million each.[43]

# Executive Summary:
# How General Electric Shapes
# Nuclear Weapons Policies for Profits

## 2

INFACT's special report brings to light General Electric's role in perpetuating the nuclear weapons build-up. GE has positioned itself at an extraordinary conjunction of business, government, and military power. The company's prominent standing among U.S. transnational corporations, its leadership in the military-industrial complex, and its long history of political influence all combine to ensure that GE can shape government decisions and policies—especially national security issues—to the company's financial advantage.

## Part I: The Issue Is Global Survival

The need to expose—and change—GE's powerful influence is urgent. There are 50,000 nuclear warheads now poised around the globe. Every day the U.S. builds five more nuclear bombs. The human costs of this out-of-control arms build-up are drastic, as resources are diverted to weapons and basic human needs go unmet. Radiation from the nuclear weapons production cycle is silently killing millions of people in the U.S. and around the world.

The majority of Americans believe this country has enough nuclear weapons, yet weapons production continues at a staggering pace. Despite the lobbying, the petitions, the massive demonstrations, the will of the majority has not prevailed.

In large part, there is no reduction in nuclear weapons because the production of these weapons is an extremely lucrative business, reaping billions of dollars in profits for those companies engaged in their manufacture. With all that money at stake, the nuclear weapons industry works very hard to successfully influence government decisions to ensure an unceasing stream of contracts.

The power of the weapons corporations represents an unprecedented threat to democracy. The nuclear weapons industry hides its deadly activities by insisting that the corporations merely do what the government asks of them. INFACT's special report exposes to the light of public scrutiny what the nuclear weapons industry has worked so hard to conceal. With more complete information about how nuclear weapons decisions are *really*

made, the American people can identify and act on rational options for changing this country's reliance on nuclear weapons.

### INFACT Brings GE to Light

This special report focuses on how General Electric shapes fundamental government policy on war and peace. Using the company's extraordinary relationship with the federal government, GE actively secures its lucrative nuclear weapons business. In order to understand GE's activities, this report first examines GE's role as a prominent U.S. business force. Next it looks at GE's powerful role in the military-industrial complex. The careful steps GE has taken over the past 40 years to attain this leadership position are detailed. Then the report documents briefly the concrete results of GE's activities that have netted billions of dollars of profit for the company—at the expense of millions of people around the world. The report concludes with steps every reader can take to help stop nuclear weapons and to hold GE accountable for its role in driving the nuclear arms race.

## Part II: The World of a Giant Corporation

It is helpful to understand the scope and power of GE as an enormous transnational corporation. In terms of market value, GE ranks as this country's third largest corporation. GE's global reach extends into 50 different countries in search of markets, production facilities and raw materials. The company claims, through its advertising and public relations efforts, to bring good things to life. Yet in its quest to become a transnational giant, GE has often harmed its employees, defrauded its consumers, destroyed the environment, and threatened the general public.

### Company Profile

This is GE at a glance.

- GE's products range from airplane engines to appliances, from financial services to high-tech medical equipment.
- In 1986, the company sold $36.7 billion worth of products and services, earning a net profit of nearly $2.5 billion.

- In 1986, GE had 359,000 employees worldwide; approximately 288,000 worked in the U.S. Thirty-three percent of GE's U.S. employees belong to labor unions. Although GE sales and profits have grown steadily over the past five years, GE has cut well over 100,000 jobs since 1981, when John Welch took over as chief executive officer.

- GE has used its enormous funds to grow by directly purchasing other companies. Most notably, GE acquired RCA for $6.4 billion in 1986, strengthening GE's position as a military contractor and putting the national network NBC under its corporate control. GE recently sold its consumer electronics business to a French company in exchange for that company's large medical equipment business.

## Behind GE's Public Relations

This look at GE probes the underside of GE's operations, exposing the reality behind the public relations front.

- GE has a long history of government fraud, price fixing, and violation of anti-trust laws. In 1985, following a sweep of government reforms, GE became the first weapons contractor to be indicted and found guilty of defrauding the government for overcharging on military contracts.

- GE is currently embroiled in several legal battles over its sale of faulty and unsafe nuclear reactors to power companies throughout the country.

- GE is one of the largest environmental polluters. Cited in 1985 for the largest number of toxic waste sites in the country, the number of Superfund sites for which GE is responsible continues to grow.

- GE also has a long and uneasy history of labor relations. The company has engaged in union busting, runaway shops, and moving factories out of the country—all in the name of more profits.

# Part III: GE Shaping Nuclear Weapons Policies for Profits

With careful planning and good implementation, General Electric is actively engaged in the powerful arenas of both business and government. GE's position as a business leader, combined with GE's success on the military contracting scene, means the company is in an extraordinary relationship with the federal government. GE is perfectly positioned to influence national security decisions to its financial advantage.

# GE: High-Powered Player in the World of U.S. Business

## GE Board Connections for Power and Profit

GE has well-established connections with leading financial and industrial institutions in this country. One way these connections are established and nurtured is through a carefully crafted board of directors. GE's current board has representatives from major corporations, financial institutions and government bodies; GE board members are simultaneously members of policy-making and lobbying organizations and prominent social clubs.

For example, GE's board now includes:

**Walter Wriston**, retired CEO and Chair of Citicorp. He served as President Reagan's economic advisor in the 1980 presidential election.

**William French Smith**, former U.S. Attorney General. He became President Reagan's personal attorney and trustee of his private estate.

**David Jones**, retired Air Force General and former Chair of the Joint Chiefs of Staff from 1978 to 1982. Jones was also a member of a Star Wars Advisory Panel.

## The Ultimate Connection: The U.S. Presidency

GE, the company that "pioneered selling whole ways of life," sold the electrical life by building Ronald Reagan an all-electric home. Today, again with the help of Reagan, GE sells the permanent war economy and the nuclear arms build-up.

Ronald Reagan was host and occasional star of *GE Theater* from 1954 through 1962, eventually becoming company spokesperson. Reagan's stridently pro-corporate philosophy was securely established during his GE years.

After Reagan left GE's direct employ in 1962, he took "The Speech" he had developed while at GE with his and GE's point of view into the arena of electoral politics. His political career was on its way.

During Reagan's presidency, GE's nuclear weapons prime contract awards increased threefold—from $2.2 billion in 1980 to $6.8 billion in 1986.

## Business and Policy Groups

GE executives are members of key business groups that are commonly recognized to exert considerable clout over national policy and government decision making. GE's Chair and Chief Executive Officer, John Welch, is active on three of the most prestigious business groups.

**The Business Council** is one of the few corporate organizations that meets regularly with high-ranking government officials. Many of its members are close to recent U.S. presidents. Since 1951, a GE CEO or board member has held the top Council positions of Chair or Vice Chair for two-thirds of the time. John Welch is currently Council Vice Chair.

**The Business Roundtable** was established for the purpose of direct corporate lobbying of Congress on issues of broad public policy. The Roundtable permits only current chief executive officers (CEOs) into its membership. Welch's predecessor as CEO, Reginald Jones, was a key figure in the founding of the Roundtable. He advocated that business executives participate in the formation of public policy. Today, John Welch serves on the Roundtable's influential Policy Committee, where position papers are approved for circulation to government officials.

**The Council on Foreign Relations** sponsors discussion groups and conferences on foreign and domestic issues that have helped to set the direction of US foreign policy. GE has been active in CFR for the past 65 years. GE's CEO John Welch is a CFR member. Along with Welch, current GE board members Walter Wriston, Thornton Bradshaw, and Lewis Preston are also active CFR members.

### Influential Social Ties

Corporate executives and government officials share common interests; they also share personal connections and loyalties that are firmly established through a network of social clubs and activities.

GE is one of the most highly represented companies among members of these clubs: current GE board members have connections to at least 20 exclusive social clubs, including the Bohemian Club, the Links Club, the Economic Club, and the Augusta National Golf Club.

Phillips S. Peter, Vice President for Corporate Government Relations, heads GE's powerful Washington office. Peter belongs to at least 13 social clubs, where he can entertain members of Congress, military brass, and other officials in a relaxed setting.

# GE: Leader in the Military-Industrial Complex
## Research and Development: Bringing New Weapons to Life

GE, through its large research and development unit, develops new ideas for complicated, expensive, and deadly nuclear weapons. In fiscal year 1986, GE received the third largest amount of Pentagon R & D contracts. GE has used this money to develop new technologies with first-strike capabilities.

- GE has played a leading role in researching and developing Trident I and II missile components, Minuteman III missile components, and the Stealth and B-1 bombers.
- GE has developed the Defense Satellite Communications System III (DSCS III), a system of communications satellites that are essential to dangerous and destabilizing strategies that propose the U.S. can fight and win a limited nuclear war.

- Between 1983–1986, GE has received at least $465.9 million in Star Wars contracts, including a contract to conduct a "feasibility study" for Star Wars.

### Creating the Climate

GE helps create the government and public climate that supports increased nuclear weapons production, a climate that will accept the need for more nuclear weapons.

- GE has received contracts to estimate Soviet military expenditures. These estimates fan the public's fears of the Soviet's strength and influence congressional appropriations for this country's military budget.
- GE has close connections with the Committee on the Present Danger. CPD publishes policy statements and conducts public information campaigns on military issues to warn policy makers and the public of the "growing Soviet military strength and the need to match it." Thirty-one members of the CPD have been appointed to the Reagan administration. CPD founders Max Kampelman and Charls E. Walker both held contracts to lobby for General Electric in Washington.
- GE advertises heavily in military trade journals such as *Aviation Week* and the *Air Force Magazine*. The company's target audience is active and retired military personnel, government officials, and weapons industry employees. These magazines often advocate policy positions. For example, Star Wars is featured prominently, always portrayed as vital to U.S. "pre-eminence in space."

### PACs and Honoraria: Paying for Access

GE uses political action committees (PACs) and honoraria to ensure access to key government decision makers in both the legislative and executive branches. GE is one of the leading users of PAC contributions and other creative financial means to gain preferential access.

- GE does not give PAC money primarily to help win elections but to gain access to Congress. In 1983–84, GE gave PAC money to 27 House incumbents who had no general election opponents, to 103 House incumbents who had no serious race, and to every Senator seeking re-election in 1984.
- The company targets its PAC contributions to key legislators who make important military decisions. During 1983–84, GE PAC recipients included 12 out of 18 members of the Senate Armed Services Committee— more than enough votes to pass any bill out of committee.
- For elections from 1980 through 1986, GE contributed to an average of 290 candidates in each election— consistently the highest number among the top 10 military contractors.
- Two effective loopholes to avoid federal limits on PAC contributions are "earmarking" and "bundling." In 1985, five top nuclear weaponmakers funneled $95,727 to candidates using these techniques. GE

earmarked the most money to candidates and political parties, giving 46 percent of the overall total amount bundled from these 5 corporate PACs.

- Honoraria are another creative way to circumvent federal regulations on PAC contributions. In this case, weapons contractors pay legislators for "speaking engagements." From 1981 to 1985, honoraria payments by the top 10 weapons contractors increased ninefold. GE was the top giver in 1985, paying legislators $47,500.

## Formulating Policy:
### Advisory Committees and the Revolving Door

Through advisory committees and the revolving door, GE develops and advocates the necessary military strategy and national policy to support and legitimate new weapons systems under development.

Governmental advisory committees bring together decision makers in government and industry to forge policy on important issues. GE board members and top executives are active on key advisory committees such as the Defense Science Board, the Advisory Panel on New Ballistic Missile Defense Technologies (Star Wars), and the President's National Security Telecommunications Advisory Committee.

The "revolving door" between the Pentagon, the administration, and weaponmakers creates a community of shared assumptions about national security issues.

**William French Smith**, former Attorney General, and **David Jones**, retired Air Force General, illustrate the revolving door swinging between the highest levels of government and the uppermost echelons of GE.

**Thomas Paine**, an executive who held various positions in the company, was appointed to head the National Aeronautics and Space Administration in 1969. He had to leave NASA in the wake of a scandal involving GE contracts. GE then hired him back. In 1987, Paine headed a presidential space commission that strongly recommended that NASA begin work on a space station. In the fall of 1987, GE was given an $800 million contract for work on the station.

**Daniel Fink** combines the influence of both advisory committees and the revolving door. Fink was Deputy Director of Research and Development at the Pentagon. In 1968, GE hired Fink as General Manager of the Aerospace Group. Simultaneously he sat on the powerful Defense Science Board. Later, Fink was promoted to Senior Vice President of Corporate Planning and Development. He remained on the DSB, and in 1974 joined the Defense Intelligence Agency Advisory Committee.

## Marketing Nuclear Weapons:
### GE's Washington Operations

GE secures its business investment through aggressive marketing—selling the company's nuclear weapons as if they were lightbulbs or refrigerators. GE's presence in Washington, DC, is one of the company's most important operations. Its director, Phillips S. Peter, reports directly to GE's chief executive officer.

- GE's DC office employs 150 staff; many gather information and develop strategies for selling nuclear weapons to government officials. Compared to other weapons contractors, only one rivals the size of GE's DC operations. By the standards of non-weaponmakers, GE's Washington office is enormous.
- GE has a greater number of registered lobbyists than any other weapons contractor, all working to develop close relationships with their customer, the U.S. government.
- GE works with Pentagon officials to extend its lobbying efforts, as illustrated by the C-5 Galaxy vote. The Air Force and the C-5's major contractors, including GE, met regularly to plan and implement their lobbying strategy and then sent Pentagon officials to meet with key legislators.
- Membership in trade associations is an important component of GE's Washington operations. Trade association members testify before Congress, meet with Department of Defense officials, and pressure the executive branch. Influence exerted by trade associations is often effective because they appear to be neutral, speaking for no particular company. General Electric is a member of several powerful weapons-related trade associations, including the American Defense Preparedness Association, the Association of Old Crows (also called the Electronic Warfare Association), the Air Force Association, the Aerospace Industries Association, and the National Security Industrial Association.

## Proceeding According to Plan:
### The Permanent War Economy

GE did not attain its present strategic leadership role by accident. The company's leaders have carefully maneuvered themselves and their company into key positions in government since before World War II.

After collaborating with a Nazi war criminal and damaging the U.S. military position before the war, GE relentlessly pursued the development and use of the first nuclear bombs—later putting these bombs into mass production.

Near the end of World War II, GE's President Charles E. Wilson set the machinery in motion to ensure a permanent war economy. Wilson opposed reconversion to peaceful production, in part because GE's financial wartime fortunes had flourished, increasing from $340 million in sales before the war to $1.3 billion after it. As Executive

Vice President of the War Production Board, Wilson was extremely well connected to high government officials and had insider's access to key post-war decisions.

Reginald H. Jones, Chair and Chief Executive Officer from 1972–1980, was very influential among his business peers and believed strongly that corporations should increase their direct involvement in government decision making. Jones's most notable role was founding the Business Roundtable, which was established on the premise that corporate heads should directly lobby the government.

# Part IV: Nuclear Weapons Profits and The Human Toll

GE has successfully shaped U.S. government policies and decisions in order to garner increased sales—and ultimately profits—from the company's nuclear weapons production. The results of GE's intensive work suggest their efforts have paid off. The results of GE's government influence, however, are not so beneficial for the rest of the world.

## GE's Nuclear Weapons Work

- GE makes critical components for more nuclear weapons systems than any other company, including components for virtually every first-strike system, from the MX missile and the Trident submarine to the Stealth and B-1 bombers.
- GE is the developer and sole producer of the neutron generator, the "trigger" for every U.S. hydrogen bomb.
- GE was the number three Star Wars contractor in 1986, with contracts ranging from assessing the feasibility of Star Wars to designing a nuclear reactor for outer space.
- GE has been active in the full range of the nuclear weapons production cycle—from uranium mining and processing plutonium to producing bomb components and testing the nuclear weapons.
- GE grossed at least $11 billion in nuclear warfare systems in fiscal years 1984–86.

## Unrestrained Weapons Spending Ruins the Economy

By devoting the largest share of the U.S. budget to this country's military build-up, the United States has fallen behind many other industrialized countries economically.

- The 1986 budget deficit climbed close to $200 billion, in large part due to unrestrained military spending. The deficit is so severe that several prominent businesspeople have declared the deficit the number one issue facing this country.
- Because of the huge budget deficits, the U.S. has become the largest debtor nation in the world, with over $2 trillion in debt.

- The U.S. now suffers from chronically high unemployment. Money allocated to weapons projects produces fewer jobs per dollar than money spent in the civilian sector.
- Over 70 percent of government funded research and development is devoted to the military (projected, 1987). This diverts research dollars from health care, education, and industrial innovation.

## Basic Human Needs Denied

The nuclear arms build-up, and the money devoted to it, has placed all the world's citizens in jeopardy. The human costs of our world's priority can be seen not only in developing countries but also in the cities, towns, and farm regions across the United States.

- In 1987, 55¢ out of every federal tax dollar went to the military. In contrast, only 2¢ went for food and nutrition, 2¢ for education, and 2¢ for housing.
- The $1.9 trillion spent on the U.S. military since 1980 has not added security to the lives of millions of Americans with high levels of homelessness, infant mortality, and poor nutrition.
- The world's military expenditures are now in excess of $1.7 million per minute. *Every minute of every day, 30 children die from lack of food and inexpensive vaccines.*

## Radiation: The Deadly Legacy

The National Association of Radiation Survivors estimates that at least 1,050,000 Americans have been exposed to damaging levels of radiation. From the beginning to the end of the nuclear weapons production cycle, whenever radioactive materials are involved, the potential exists for radioactive exposure far above levels deemed "acceptable" even by industry and government standards.

**Step One: Mining**. Native American uranium miners, their families, and neighbors are suffering incredibly high incidences of radiation-related cancers and birth defects. GE was involved in uranium mining through ownership of the Pathfinder Mines Corp.

**Step Two: Production**. The Hanford Nuclear Reservation in Washington state has produced much of the plutonium used in the U.S. nuclear arsenal. GE managed and operated that facility from 1946–64. While GE managed the facility, at least a million curies of radioactive materials were released, including at least one planned experiment where radioactive iodine-131 was released into the atmosphere at a level hundreds of times higher than the radioactive release at Three Mile Island.

**Step Three: Testing**. U.S. testing in the Pacific began in 1946, and the Nevada Test Site was established in 1951. GE has consistently secured Department of Energy (DOE) contracts for work at both the Pacific and Nevada test sites.

A bipartisan congressional investigation in 1984 revealed that more than 17,000 military personnel were at high radiation risk because of the Pacific tests. The people of the Pacific Islands are still feeling the long-term effects of radiation exposure. Several independently conducted studies have shown serious radiation poisoning of "downwinders" from the Nevada test site.

**Step Four: Nuclear Wastes**. Thousands of pounds of radioactive wastes are generated through the production of nuclear weapons each year. Plutonium is a deadly substance. Much of this country's nuclear wastes are now stored on the Hanford Reservation. Nuclear wastes began leaking from Hanford containers in the early 1960s, when Hanford was under GE's management. Because of these leaks, the Columbia River is now the world's most radioactively contaminated river.

**Step Five: Limit Corporate Liability In Case of a Nuclear Accident**. The Price-Anderson Act, passed by Congress in 1957, shifts nuclear accident liability to the federal government, and then limits the amount of money the government must pay for damages from an accident. Beginning in 1955, GE lobbied heavily for the federal government to assume this liability, threatening to withdraw from the government's nuclear programs without this blanket protection. Every time the Price-Anderson Act comes up for review, GE lobbies to ensure its provisions remain favorable to GE's interests.

# Part V: You Can Make a Difference: Boycott GE!

Nuclear weapons pose the greatest threat to global survival facing the world today, and the powerful influence of nuclear weaponmakers, like General Electric, is driving the nuclear arms race. GE's capacity to shape and influence government decisions on war and peace is an unprecedented threat to democracy.

The nuclear weapons corporations can and must be held accountable to the people whose lives they endanger—that is all of us.

A grassroots action organization is now challenging this threat to democracy and global survival. INFACT specifically campaigns to hold corporations accountable for their abusive practices that endanger people's health and survival.

A new definition of national security is being forged by the people of this country. INFACT's activists and supporters are actively contributing to this process, educating the public about the role of corporations and encouraging people to speak out against nuclear weapons.

In 1984, INFACT launched the Nuclear Weaponmakers Campaign, alerting the public to the influential but largely hidden role of the nuclear weapons industry in the arms build-up. The next year, INFACT selected one corporation—GE—to focus attention on the entire industry.

On June 12, 1986, the GE Boycott was called—kicking off the first of many economic pressure strategies to be used against this huge nuclear weaponmaker. Just one year later, an independent, nationwide poll revealed that *over 2 million people* (or one in a hundred) in the U.S. are boycotting GE products and services.

- From the millions who are buying another brand of light bulb, to the doctor who cancelled a $.5 million purchase of GE medical equipment and the architect who stopped specifying GE appliances for his apartment complexes, people across the country are sending a strong message to GE.

- Many diverse organizations, local and national, religious and secular, have endorsed the Boycott and are spreading the word through their membership—from the Social Responsibilities Round Table of the Minnesota Library Association to the national Church Women United.

- Many prominent activists and celebrities have also joined the campaign—from anti-nuclear activist Dr. Helen Caldicott to singer/TV personality Gloria Loring to labor organizer Victor Reuther.

INFACT holds firmly to the belief that individuals can make a difference. By joining INFACT's Nuclear Weaponmakers Campaign—and boycotting General Electric—you put the power of hundreds of thousands of concerned people behind your actions. Your participation *will* make a difference. Boycott GE!

# INFACT:
# The Issue Is Global Survival

## 3

INFACT is a grassroots action organization committed to stopping life-threatening abuses of transnational corporations. Established in 1976, INFACT campaigns to hold corporations directly accountable for their practices that endanger the health and survival of people all over the world.

INFACT is perhaps best recognized as the group that organized the Nestle Boycott—one of the most successful international campaigns ever run. After nearly seven years of intense economic pressure on the world's largest food company, Nestle finally negotiated a settlement with INFACT and our allies. Nestle agreed to conform its infant formula marketing practices in developing countries to an international standard of sales behavior adopted by the World Health Organization. Thousands of infants around the world now have a better chance for survival and good health. INFACT monitored Nestle's implementation progress for two years and then helped establish a sister organization to continue the compliance work.

Infant formula abuse is one of many life-threatening and oppressive conditions in this world demanding change—indeed, conditions that must be changed if the world and its people are to survive. Given world conditions desperately demanding change, combined with our deeply held beliefs that change *is* possible, INFACT joins the efforts of others throughout the world to achieve our basic goal—

To ensure global survival and to create a world that *affirms life*;
- a world where people can adequately meet their basic human needs for food, water, shelter, and good health;
- a world where the opportunity exists for all people to reach their full human potential;
- a world where security is based on cooperation and community.

## INFACT's Nuclear Weaponmakers Campaign

Yet in today's world, INFACT's fundamental goal cannot be realized. Nuclear weapons pose the ultimate threat to global survival. The human cost of the spiraling nuclear arms build-up are drastic, as resources are diverted to weapons and basic human needs go unmet.

Nuclear weapons are big business. Transnational corporations like General Electric first promote the nuclear weapons build-up and then produce these weapons of mass destruction at public expense for private profit.

The unwarranted influence of the weaponmakers must be challenged and reduced. In May 1984, INFACT launched the Nuclear Weaponmakers Campaign to focus on the role of the nuclear weapons industry in producing and actively promoting nuclear weapons.

### 6½-Year Boycott of Nestle Is Ended As Firm Adopts Baby-Formula Code

By Philip J. Hilts
Washington Post Staff Writer

A 6½-year boycott against the Nestle Co. that spread from Minnesota to Finland ended yesterday ... comply in vir-

said it had tried to comply with the code in 1981, "but it meant different things to different people." Yesterday's agreement, the company said, is proof that its efforts to comply "have finally been recognized. This controversy is now resolved."

The spokesman, Oswald B of Brazil, later apologized f remark, but Nestle maintain opposition to a code until af WHO passed one in May, 198 118-to-1 vote, with the States casting the sole negati

But as the boycott wore formula fight, which tle began to take positions liance with the code f ... at

### Pact Ending Boycott of Nestle Products De

From Times Wire Services

WASHINGTON—A 6½-year boycott of Nestle's Co. ended symbolically with a bite of a candy bar. Nestle's Niels Christiansen offered the Nestle's Crunch to Infant Formula Action Coalition Chairman Douglas Johnson at a Thursday news conference, as a way "to end this conflict."

But Thursday, INFACT announced it would end the boycott—on which supporters had spent $3.5 million since 1977—because Nestle had agreed to comply in virtually every detail with the World Health Organization's infant formula sales code.

controversy is now reso WHO passed the cc 1981, in response to agg techniques by infant-fo panies. Advocates said sl breast to bottle, especia developed

The long range goals of the Nuclear Weaponmakers Campaign are to

- Stop the production of nuclear weapons.
- Reduce corporate influence over government decisions and policies that promote nuclear weapons.
- Create a climate that no longer supports nuclear weapons production as an acceptable business activity.

## Strategic Focus:
## One Key Nuclear Weapons Corporation

INFACT campaigns to win—that is, to secure concrete changes in corporate behavior. In October 1985, one corporation—General Electric—was selected to focus attention on the nuclear weapons industry.

Since GE's initial participation in the bombings of Hiroshima and Nagasaki, the corporation has been actively involved in nuclear weapons—their research, development, promotion, production, testing, and deployment. As a leader in the industry, GE is a prime example of how weaponmakers have influenced and shaped the development of nuclear weapons policies and strategy for over 40 years.

INFACT calls upon General Electric to take the lead in exercising moral and corporate responsibility within the nuclear weapons industry.

INFACT activists spreading the word on GE.

INFACT issues a public challenge to General Electric and to the nuclear weapons industry to

- Cease production of nuclear weapons.
- Stop interfering in government decision making on war and peace.
- Stop all direct marketing and promotion of nuclear weapons.
- Implement conversion plans developed in consultation with employees, employee representatives, and affected communities.

# General Electric:
# Bringing Good Things to Life?

**4**

*The continuation of the nuclear arms race is not based on military requirements for nuclear weapons, but on the desire of the nuclear weapons industry to sell nuclear weapons. They are accomplishing this by running the most powerful lobby office in Washington.*

*I believe the GE Boycott will be successful because it will make the American public aware of the facts. And that will be the beginning of the end for the nuclear weapons industry.*
–Commander William Withrow (Ret.), 1987

## GE as a Leader in Nuclear Weapons Production

- GE makes critical components to more nuclear weapons systems than any other company.
- GE grossed at least $11,074,175,000 ($11 billion) in nuclear warfare systems in fiscal years 1984–86.
- GE is the developer and sole producer of the neutron generator, the "trigger," for every U.S. hydrogen bomb.
- GE has been active in the full range of the nuclear weapons cycle—from uranium mining and processing plutonium to producing bomb components and testing the nuclear weapons.
- GE produces components for virtually every first-strike weapon, from the MX missile and the Trident submarine to the Stealth and the B-1 bombers.
- GE was the number three Star Wars contractor in fiscal year 1986, with contracts ranging from assessing the feasibility of Star Wars to designing a nuclear reactor for outer space.

## GE as a Leader in Nuclear Weapons Promotion

- GE has one of the most effective lobbying offices in Washington, with a staff of approximately 150 people.
- GE contracts with the CIA to estimate Soviet military strength.
- GE executives sit on influential government advisory committees such as the National Telecommunications Advisory Committee, which deals with Command, Control, Communications, and Intelligence ($C^3I$).

- GE is an industry leader in PAC contributions and honoraria payments to gain access to and influence in Congress.
- GE is in the forefront of developing new ideas for nuclear weapons systems through research and development, from the bombs dropped on Hiroshima and Nagasaki to the concept of multiple independent re-entry vehicles (MIRVs), to a space-based nuclear reactor for Star Wars.
- GE participates in the "revolving door" at the highest levels, with a former U.S. attorney general and a former chair of the Joint Chiefs of Staff on its board of Directors.
- GE is active in influential policy-making and business groups such as the Business Council, the Business Roundtable, and the Council on Foreign Relations.

## GE Can Be a Leader in Peaceful Production

- GE has converted its manufacturing facilities from military to peaceful production in the past.
- Only 11.8 percent of GE's total sales is from nuclear weapons.
- As a major diversified company, GE has the capacity and flexibility to convert from nuclear weapons work to peaceful production.
- GE has long had a reputation for being responsive to its consumers. As GE says, "We're Not Satisfied Until You Are."
- The business community looks to GE for leadership.

# PART II. THE WORLD OF A GIANT CORPORATION

It is helpful to understand the scope and power of GE as an enormous transnational corporation. In terms of market value, GE ranks as this country's third largest corporation. GE's markets span a vast array of goods and services produced in this country—from consumer products and financial services to industrial equipment and high technology. GE aggressively fights to attain number one or number two positions in each market, thus dominating that landscape.

GE is one of this country's preeminent transnational companies—extending its global reach into 50 different countries in search of markets, production facilities and raw materials.

The company claims, through its advertising and public relations efforts, to bring good things to life. Yet in its quest to become a transnational giant, GE has often harmed its employees, defrauded its consumers, destroyed the environment, and threatened the general public.

# The Company Profile

*Profit is GE's most important product.* [1]

General Electric describes itself as "one of the largest and most diversified industrial corporations in the world." This description accurately reflects the quantity and variety of the goods and services produced by GE. In 1986, General Electric

- sold $36.72 billion worth of products and services
- earned a net profit of $2.49 billion
- manufactured products in at least 20 major industrial fields
- provided services in at least 10 major fields
- had 359,000 total employees: industrial, administrative, professional and management
- manufactured its products at more than 320 plants located in 32 U.S. states and 23 foreign countries.

## What GE Does

GE divides its products and services into several segments, which are more or less reflected in the company personnel structure.

**Aerospace**, which includes much of GE's military and nuclear weapons work, covers equipment, electronic control systems, and components for weapons, space, and aviation. The principal customer is the U.S. government. This segment was greatly expanded by the RCA purchase in 1986.

**Aircraft engines** for military and civilian airplanes produce more gross income for GE than any other business segment.

**Consumer products** include the familiar GE lightbulbs as well as a wide variety of other lighting products such as fluorescent, halogen, and incandescent bulbs, specialty lamps, wiring devices, lighting fixtures, and ballasts, quartz products, and rechargeable batteries.

**Financial services** include several large firms with their own identities: *GE Credit Corporation*, which finances purchases by corporate and individual customers; *Kidder, Peabody*, a stock brokerage firm; *Employers Reinsurance Corporation*, offering property and casualty reinsurance;

and *Gelco*, a transportation and storage leasing firm.

**Industrial products**, in GE terminology, are high-technology goods sold to other industrial companies, such as semiconductors, motors, and transportation equipment and electrical construction equipment. Also included in this segment is *GE-Fanuc Automation Corporation*, a new GE joint venture with a Japanese company to produce factory automation systems.

**Major appliances** include such well-known home-use products as refrigerators, stoves, washing machines, microwave ovens, freezers, dishwashers, clothes dryers, and room air conditioners, sold under the "GE" and "Hotpoint" labels. The major customers for these products are both individual consumers at retail outlets and building contractors and architects who specify these products in residential construction projects.

**Materials** cover a wide range of specially produced substances for industrial uses: plastics, silicones, industrial diamonds, ceramics, and so on. The first big project undertaken by GE's CEO John Welch, Jr. as a young engineer was in this area when he oversaw the development of marketing of Noryl plastic.

**National Broadcasting Company (NBC)**, now owned by GE with the purchase of RCA, includes radio as well as television and is listed as a separate group.

**Power systems** cover equipment for producing electricity through turbines, generators, and nuclear reactors.

**Technical products and services** encompass all high-tech products not covered by other business segments. These include some of GE's fastest growing product lines like medical diagnostic equipment and communications satellites as well as information and computer services.

In this business segment, medical systems include magnetic resonance (MR) scanners, computed tomography (CT) scanners, X-ray, nuclear imaging, ultrasound, and other diagnostic equipment and supporting services sold to domestic and foreign hospitals and medical facilities.

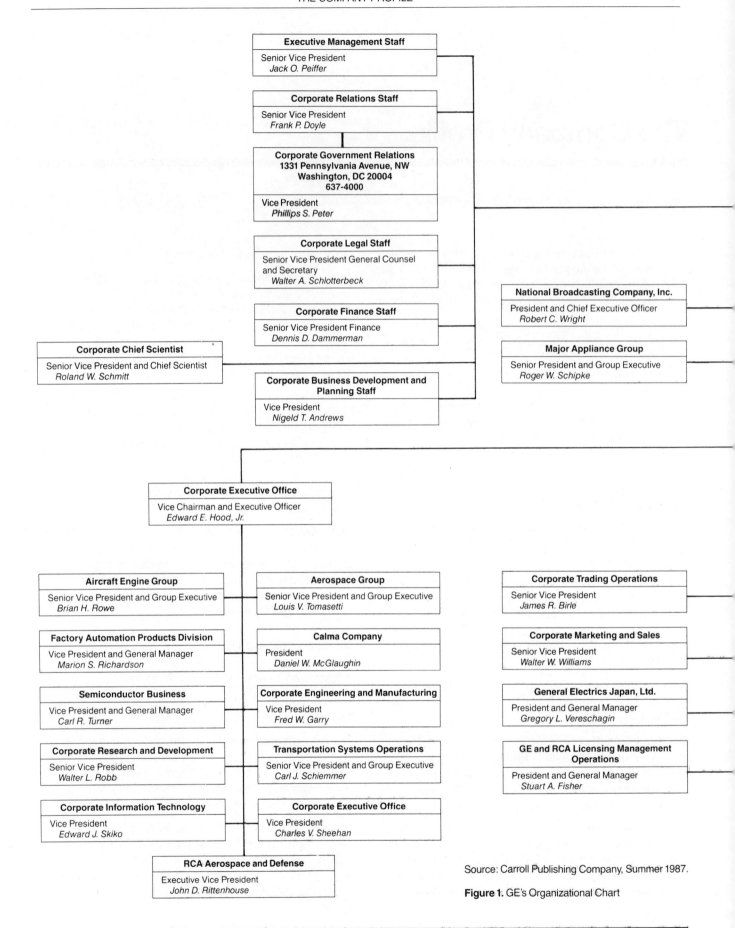

Source: Carroll Publishing Company, Summer 1987.

**Figure 1.** GE's Organizational Chart

**Bringing GE to Light**

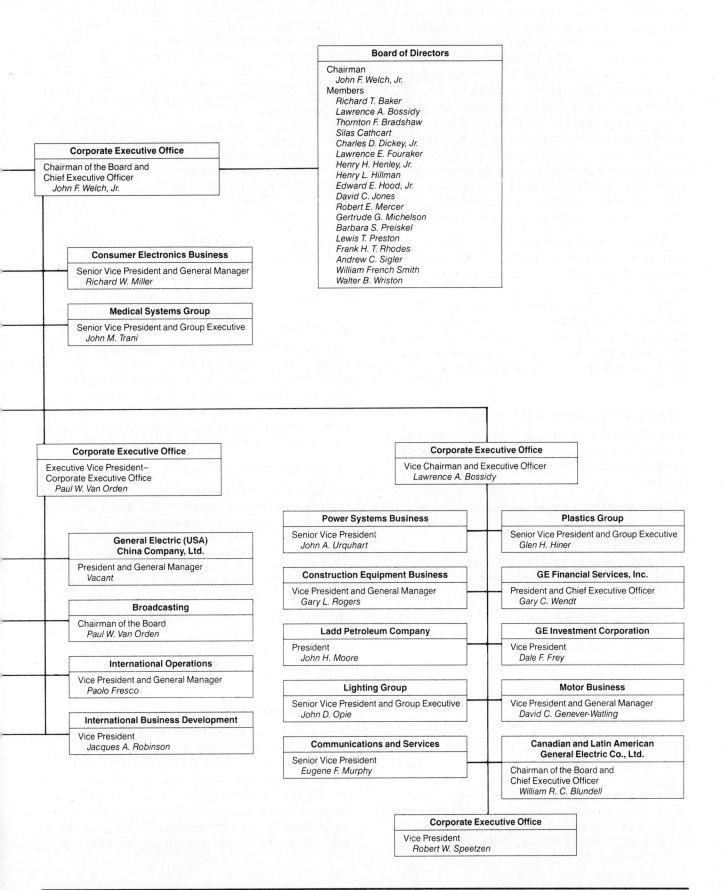

**Board of Directors**

Chairman
   *John F. Welch, Jr.*
Members
   *Richard T. Baker*
   *Lawrence A. Bossidy*
   *Thornton F. Bradshaw*
   *Silas Cathcart*
   *Charles D. Dickey, Jr.*
   *Lawrence E. Fouraker*
   *Henry H. Henley, Jr.*
   *Henry L. Hillman*
   *Edward E. Hood, Jr.*
   *David C. Jones*
   *Robert E. Mercer*
   *Gertrude G. Michelson*
   *Barbara S. Preiskel*
   *Lewis T. Preston*
   *Frank H. T. Rhodes*
   *Andrew C. Sigler*
   *William French Smith*
   *Walter B. Wriston*

**Corporate Executive Office**

Chairman of the Board and
Chief Executive Officer
*John F. Welch, Jr.*

**Consumer Electronics Business**

Senior Vice President and General Manager
*Richard W. Miller*

**Medical Systems Group**

Senior Vice President and Group Executive
*John M. Trani*

**Corporate Executive Office**

Executive Vice President–
Corporate Executive Office
*Paul W. Van Orden*

**Corporate Executive Office**

Vice Chairman and Executive Officer
*Lawrence A. Bossidy*

**General Electric (USA)
China Company, Ltd.**

President and General Manager
*Vacant*

**Power Systems Business**

Senior Vice President
*John A. Urquhart*

**Plastics Group**

Senior Vice President and Group Executive
*Glen H. Hiner*

**Broadcasting**

Chairman of the Board
*Paul W. Van Orden*

**Construction Equipment Business**

Vice President and General Manager
*Gary L. Rogers*

**GE Financial Services, Inc.**

President and Chief Executive Officer
*Gary C. Wendt*

**International Operations**

Vice President and General Manager
*Paolo Fresco*

**Ladd Petroleum Company**

President
*John H. Moore*

**GE Investment Corporation**

Vice President
*Dale F. Frey*

**International Business Development**

Vice President
*Jacques A. Robinson*

**Lighting Group**

Senior Vice President and Group Executive
*John D. Opie*

**Motor Business**

Vice President and General Manager
*David C. Genever-Watling*

**Communications and Services**

Senior Vice President
*Eugene F. Murphy*

**Canadian and Latin American
General Electric Co., Ltd.**

Chairman of the Board and
Chief Executive Officer
*William R. C. Blundell*

**Corporate Executive Office**

Vice President
*Robert W. Speetzen*

**Bringing GE to Light**

Among GE's communications products are cellular phones and hand-carried two-way and one-way radio equipment. GE's information services are provided by *GE Information Services Company*, *GE Consulting Services Corporation*, and the *GE Computer Services* operation. These services include: enhanced computer-based communications services, such as data network services, electronic mail, electronic data interchange, and automated clearinghouse services offered to industrial and commercial customers through a worldwide network; software application packages; custom systems design and programming services; and independent maintenance and rental/leasing services for mini-computers and micro-computers, electronic test instruments, data communications equipment, and interactive graphics systems.

For planning purposes, GE also uses a "strategic" breakdown of its businesses into **Technology Businesses**, **Services Businesses**, **Core Manufacturing Businesses**, and **Support Operations**. "Technology," "Services," and "Core" between them include most of the business segments listed above. "Support Operations" includes business segments not considered to be "key," the manufacturing of products used mainly by other GE divisions, and corporate services like International Operations.

## GE's Market Position: Present (1987)

According to GE's own description of its business segments in the annual report and Form 10-K, the company occupies a leading position in most of its fields of endeavor.[2]

*GE occupies the number one position in*:

Aircraft engines (the F-110 engine for F-16 fighter planes)
Automatic factory controls and drives
Brain/spine/cardiovascular study equipment (Signa MR system)
Communications satellites
Diagnostic X-ray equipment
Electric motors
Industrial diamonds
Major home appliances
Power generation systems
Railcar leasing
Television broadcasting (NBC)
Two-way radio communications

*GE occupies a leading position in*:

Armaments (military weaponry)
Computer leasing (GE Computer Service)
Computer/logistics/engineering services to governments
Corporate mergers/acquisitions (Kidder, Peabody)
Electronic systems for military aircraft
Engineering plastics

Financing (GE Credit Corp)
Industrial laboratories (GE Research and Development Center)
Investment banking (Kidder, Peabody)
Large high-technology military systems
Lighting
Mass transportation drive systems
Medical diagnostic imaging equipment
Nuclear power
Nuclear weapons components
Property/casualty reinsurance (Employers Reinsurance Corp)
Propulsion/guidance systems for missiles
Radio broadcasting (NBC Radio)
Re-entry systems
Semiconductors
Silicones
Surface and undersea radar
Transformers

In overall sales, GE ranked sixth in the 1987 Fortune 500 list. The company ranked *third* in total market value.[3]

## GE's Market Position: Future

In what direction is GE headed? *Business Week*, *Forbes*, and other business publications regularly try to answer this question. *Forbes* recently suggested 10 likely candidates for GE's next acquisition, ranging from the Xerox Corporation to the Merrill Lynch brokerage firm.[4] The article describes GE's gradual purging of the words "general" and "electric" from the corporate name, leaving only "GE."

The article goes on to comment:

> The new GE reflects more than the shift from manufacturing to high technology and finance that is sweeping industrial America. It signals the decision by a great corporation to break, painfully and publicly, with a proud past... Picking up attitudes usually associated with corporate raiders, [GE] is much less tied to its traditional product lines... Nowadays, profit is GE's most important product.[5]

CEO John F. Welch, Jr. has dictated that all GE businesses must be number one or two in their fields—or be sold.[6] He also wants GE to be "the most competitive business enterprise in the world."[7] These aims add up to a formidable goal.

## GE's Workforce

Of GE's 359,000 employees in 1986, approximately 288,000 worked in the United States. Around 95,000—or 33 percent—of GE's U.S. employees belong to labor unions, principally the International Union of Electronic Workers (IUE), the United Electrical, Radio, and Machine Workers of America (UE), and several broadcasting and industrial unions that had contracts with RCA and NBC prior to the RCA purchase. The National Association of

Broadcasting Employees and Technicians (NABET) conducted a bitter strike against GE's subsidiary NBC during the summer and fall of 1987, prompted by, according to NABET, the noticeable hardening of NBC management's attitudes toward its unions after the network's purchase by GE.

GE employees in the U.S. are 27.6 percent women and 11.4 percent racial or ethnic minorities. These percentages drop among professional employees to 16.5 percent for women and 8.5 percent for minorities, and among management employees to 8.5 percent for women and 5.6 percent for minorities.

Finally, the overall number of GE employees has dropped sharply in recent years; well over 100,000 jobs have been lost at GE since 1981, when John Welch took over as CEO. Welch has been nicknamed "Neutron Jack," because of the large staff cuts he has made—the employees disappear but the buildings remain. Unions representing GE's manufacturing workers complain bitterly about the resulting stress on the remaining workers. In a magazine interview, Joseph Egan, chair of the GE unit of IUE, commented "The General Electric Company has a disease—Welch-itis—caused by corporate greed, arrogance, and contempt for its employees."[8]

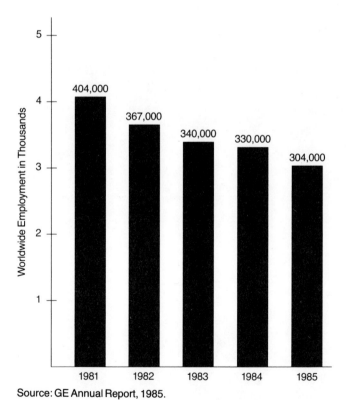

Source: GE Annual Report, 1985.

**Figure 2.** GE Workforce Reductions Since Welch Became CEO

## GE's Financial Position

Welch aims ultimately to make GE worth more than any other company in the United States. The company is already one of the most profitable and valuable in the world.

| | |
|---|---|
| The value of all GE assets at the end of 1986 was | $34.591 billion |
| The largest single component of the assets was "current assets" (cash, marketable securities, money owed by customers, product inventories) | $14.288 billion |
| Other large components were: | |
| Property, plant, and equipment | $ 9.841 billion |
| Investments by GE in other companies and government securities | $ 3.914 billion |
| and other assets | $ 6.548 billion |

Armed with this vast accumulation of resources, GE brings in:

| | |
|---|---|
| 1986 gross income | $36.725 billion |
| 1986 net profit | $ 2.492 billion |
| 1986 total capital invested | $21.462 billion |
| 1986 earnings per share | $5.46 |
| 1986 share owners' equity | $15.109 billion |

GE's business segments contributed to its 1986 gross revenue in the following (descending) order:

1 Aircraft engines
2 Power systems
3 Industrial
4 Consumer products
5 Aerospace
6 Major appliances
7 Technical products and services
8 Materials
9 National Broadcasting Company
10 Financial services

The position of financial services at the end of the list partly reflects the depression in the oil/energy industry, many of whose companies are clients of the GE Credit Corporation.

## Acquisitions and Divestitures

Some of GE's most significant acquisitions and divestitures in the past few years have been:

- the sale of Utah International to the Broken Hill Proprietary Company (Australia) for $2.4 billion in 1984.
- the sale of GE's small household appliance business to the Black and Decker Company for $28 million in 1984.
- the purchase of RCA Corporation for $6.406 billion in 1986.
- an exchange with Thomson S.A. (France) in 1987: GE traded its consumer electronics business for Thomson's $3.5 billion-a-year medical equipment business. GE also received close to $1 billion in cash.[9]

It is widely believed in business circles that GE is constantly on the prowl for other takeover targets.

## GE in the World

GE is a major player in the world economy. In 1986, GE's foreign operations involved:

- 71,000 employees outside the U.S., almost one-fifth of GE's total employment.
- 108 manufacturing plants in 23 countries.
- $4.384 billion in gross income.
- $740 million in net profit.
- $4.090 billion in assets.
- $3.709 billion worth of exports from GE's U.S. operation to customers in Europe, the Pacific and Far East, the Middle East and Africa, and Latin America.

# Behind GE's Public Relations

2

*I don't think they care what hurts who. It's business. — GE employee[1]*

The profile of GE in the preceding section was taken primarily from GE's Annual Report and other GE publications. It is not complete. While GE is the number one and number two leader in many fields, the company is also a leader in pursuing profits over people and in keeping such activities well concealed from the general public. To provide a more complete company profile, this section will take the reader behind GE's image of "bringing good things to life."

Each year, General Electric spends hundreds of millions of dollars on advertising to ensure that the public buys the products GE brings to life. The company promotes its refrigerators, washers and dryers, microwave ovens, and lightbulbs using images of happiness, comfort, and well-being. Hidden behind its advertising slogan, GE also produces faulty nuclear power plants and toxic waste and has a long history of fraud, bribery, and concealment of wrongdoing. This section will touch on just a few examples that show GE in its *true* light.

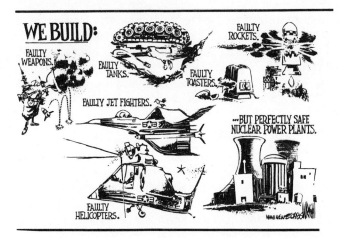

## Dirty Business

GE has a long history of charges that it has defrauded the government, fixed prices, given bribes, and violated anti-trust laws. GE's criminal and civil violations, which include anti-trust violations and defrauding local, state, and federal government, stretch back to 1911. GE was then charged in 1932, 1936, 1937, 1941, 1944, 1947 (twice), 1948 (three times), 1949 (four times), 1952 (twice), 1953, and 1954.[2] A few of GE's more recent and celebrated cases further illuminate its long history of fraud.

**1957–1961**  GE was convicted of price fixing, bid rigging and "unlawful division of the markets" for electrical equipment valued at $1.74 billion a year.[3]

**1981**  GE was found guilty of paying a $1.25 million bribe to a Puerto Rican official to obtain a $92 million contract to build a power plant there.[4]

**1985**  GE and others were investigated for $6.5 million in payments to a South Korean consulting firm controlled by a retired South Korean general. GE had sold gas and turbines to the South Korean Navy and spare engine parts to the South Korean Air Force. While GE maintained that its payments to the South Korean general were legitimate consulting fees, the U. S. government felt the "consultant" may have used his influence to get contracts for GE.[5]

**1986**  In May, officials at a machine-tool company in Lynn, Massachusetts, were charged with giving kickbacks to three former GE purchasing officials to obtain Department of Defense (DOD) subcontracts.[6]

**1987**  In April, it was revealed that GE may have supplied thousands of defective military and commercial airplane engines to its customers. The following engines were discovered to contain cracks in the tubing and brackets: the F-404 used in the F-18 Navy fighter, the T-700 (helicopter engine), and GE's CT-7 for small commuter aircraft.[7]

**Falsifying Time Cards**  A 1984 case reveals the extent of GE's attempt—and apparent success—at defrauding the government. The case began with John Gravitt, a machinist foreman at GE's aircraft engine plant at Evendale, Ohio. The plant employed about 15,000 workers, and one of the engines Gravitt worked on was the engine for the B-1 Bomber.[8]

Gravitt testified that he was instructed to bill the government for time not spent on government projects. Some of the plant's projects for commercial engines were running into cost overruns, so Gravitt was to bill that time to the government on employees' time cards.

When Gravitt refused to falsify the time cards, his supervisors did it. He had expressed his opposition to the fraud, so his supervisors knew his views. In the spring of 1983, Gravitt was "laid off." Though GE later hired thousands of new workers, Gravitt was never called back to work.[9]

Gravitt wrote to an executive vice president of GE, Brian H. Rowe, in late June 1983 about the problems at the Evendale plant, and Rowe assured him that an investigation would follow. GE sent an internal auditor, R. G. Gavigan, to check on Gravitt's claims. Gavigan then told Gravitt in a meeting that *80 percent of Gravitt's allegations were proven true, and the other 20 percent could not be disproven*. Yet Gravitt learned, since his wife still worked for GE, that no disciplinary action was taken and the billing procedure for the time cards was never changed.[10]

In October 1984, Gravitt sued GE under a Civil War law, the False Claims Act, which allows a citizen to sue on behalf of the government and gives the citizen a share of all damages collected.[11]

In response to the suit, GE reviewed a sampling of vouchers and concluded that GE had actually undercharged the government. W. R. Mackey, division counsel for the aircraft engines plant in Evendale, maintained that Gravitt was not fired, denied all his allegations,[12] and said that his suit under the False Claims Act was "like a bounty hunter."[13]

On further examination by the government, however, at least 186 time cards were found to contain false charges. GE agreed to settle out of court. The company paid $2,000 each for 117 falsified time cards, even though 186 had been discovered. *Moreover, the Justice Department examined only 9,100 time cards of the 60,000 involved in the case.*[14] Only a fraction of the falsified time cards were ever found.

## GENERAL ELECTRIC ADMITS FALSIFYING BILLING ON MISSILE

### PLEA CHANGE UNEXPECTED

### $1.04 Million Fine and Refund of $800,000 Set — Former Aide Implicates Others

**By JEFF GERTH**
Special to The New York Times

WASHINGTON, May 13 — The General Electric Company pleaded guilty today to defrauding the Air Force by filing 108 false claims for payment on a missile contract. It was fined $1.04 million, the maximum allowable, and ordered to pay back the $800,000 that was falsely billed.

The company was indicted on March 26 and the trial was to begin today. The plea was unexpected and stemmed from new information provided to Federal prosecutors by Roy Baessler, a former G.E. manager. Not only did he acknowledge his role in the false billings, but he implicated "higher management" in the scheme, according to the Justice Department.

## First Weapons Contractor to Be Indicted by Federal Government for False Billings

In 1985, GE did not fare so well in a case of overcharging at its space division plant in Philadelphia. GE was indicted for fraud in "one of the largest cases involving false billings against a major contractor," according to Justice Department officials.[15] In May, GE plead guilty to all 108 counts of filing false claims after testimony by former GE manager Roy Baessler. Baessler admitted being part of the fraud and implicated "higher management," the Justice Department said.[16] The company was fined $1.04 million plus the $800,000 that was found to be falsely billed on employee time cards.[17]

The fine had little financial impact on GE, as it amounted to only 0.04 percent of the $4.5 billion in government contracts they were awarded in that year.[18]

Nor did the case have much impact on "business as usual" for GE's government contracts. When GE was indicted on March 26, 1985, its government contracts were suspended indefinitely.[19] However, as a security chief at the space division's plant told a member of the Brandywine Peace Community in Philadelphia, " 'Do you know the importance of the systems produced here? Do you really think the Pentagon is going to jeopardize them because of this?'... Besides, we have lots of contracts that extend over years.' "[20]

GE's confidence proved justified. The company won two contracts during the suspension: one for airplane engines and one for the Defense Satellite Communications System (DSCS III) because "nobody else could provide the essential hardware."[21] Other work piled up: the "Peace Shield" air defense package for Saudi Arabia went on hold because GE was to provide huge radars as government-furnished equipment to the prime contractor, Boeing. TRW was unable to contract for a space station research project because GE was the main subcontractor.[22] After a meeting between GE Chief Executive Officer Jack Welch and U.S. Air Force Secretary Orr, the suspension was lifted on April 18, 1985, merely three weeks after the indictment.[23]

## Nuclear Negligence

GE has long been a proponent of nuclear energy. With 39 nuclear power plants in the U.S. and more worldwide, as well as a space-based nuclear reactor under development, GE is a leader in this field. Yet GE's nuclear reactor design, the Mark series, is known by GE to be unsafe. GE memos disclosed in 1987 revealed that GE has known how dangerous its reactors are since the late 1950s, yet it continued to build and sell them and tried to cover up their deadly flaws.

A prime example of GE profiting from a reactor design with deadly flaws is the Zimmer plant near Cincinnati. Cincin-

## A match puts more smoke in the air than a nuclear power plant.

*Nuclear power plants don't burn anything to make electricity. And where there's no fire, there's no smoke. That's why so many people concerned about the environment now favor nuclear power. It's just about the cleanest way there is to make electricity. Safety has always been the first consideration in building nuclear power plants. Take radiation, for example. A typical plant adds an average of less than 5 millirems/year of radiation to the natural radiation of its site. That's less in a year than the extra radiation you'd receive on one round-trip cross-country jet flight.*

## Men helping Man

GENERAL ⓖⓔ ELECTRIC

Source: *General Electric Investor*, Winter 1971.

nati Gas and Electric, which bought the plant design from GE, found such "insurmountable" design flaws in the reactor that it had to convert to a coal-fired plant in 1984 in order to use it—at a cost to the utility of $360 million.[24] The utility filed suit against GE, charging that GE knowingly sold faulty nuclear power plants and that GE had tried to con customers into paying for necessary modifications. In September 1986, GE failed in an attempt to have charges of fraud and racketeering dismissed.[25] During the case, information from some of GE's internal documents, memos known as the Reed Report,[26] were ordered turned over to the utility. After several months of filing Freedom of Information requests and high visibility around the case, the report was finally made public.

The report revealed some frightening facts. During tests of the Mark II reactors in 1958–59, steam discharges in a California test reactor were so violent that the vibrations were recorded by a nearby laboratory as an earthquake. The reactor also showed problems with sudden, uncontrollable surges of water. An October 1964 GE report further revealed that the reactor's steam condensation system was "poorly understood." Through the late 1960s

BUSINESS WEEK

## Top of the News

NUCLEAR POWER ▬▬▬

## A NUCLEAR CLOUD HANGS OVER GE'S REPUTATION

Utilities say it knowingly sold flawed plant designs

The serendipitous discovery of misplaced documents at a federal courthouse in Cincinnati has put General Electric Co. in the hot seat. The highly sensitive papers, which were supposed to be sealed, were left on a table in the court clerk's office, where a Cleve- cause of design flaws and cost overruns. Zimmer's owners charge GE knowingly sold them a flawed design and seek damages that could reach $1 billion. GE wouldn't comment on the suit.

The memos concern an internal study called the Reed Report. Prepared in 1975

and early 1970s, data still showed severe vibrations in Mark II reactors in Illinois, Switzerland, and Sweden. In a West German plant with a GE reactor, violent shudders ripped open the containment system, causing a radioactive water spill.[27]

The Reed Report also reveals design flaws in a new reactor GE was trying to market in the mid-1970s, the Mark III. And while GE told customers about design flaws in its older reactors—after they had been built and had to be redesigned—GE did not tell customers about flaws in the newer reactor.[28]

In November 1987, GE agreed to settle with Zimmer for $78.3 million dollars.[29]

Thirty-nine out of 100 U. S. nuclear power plants are made by GE.[30] Some of these are:

- The Pilgrim plant in Plymouth, Massachusetts, which has one of the worst safety records in the country. The owners of Pilgrim are considering suing GE.[31]
- The Perry I plant near Cleveland, which had to be redesigned at a cost of $800 million. GE is refusing to pay, which may result in the ratepayers absorbing much of the cost.[32]
- The Vallecitos plant in California. This plant started up in 1959 and was shut down in 1977 when the U.S. Geological Survey found *an active earthquake fault near the plant*.[33]
- The Morris, Illinois, plant, which never received an operating license from the Nuclear Regulatory Commission (NRC). This plant was supposed to reprocess used nuclear fuel for the utilities, but GE covered up the problems at the plant. Northeast Utilities and several other utilities filed suit against GE in 1976 for $300 million in damages for breach of contract.[34]

In 1972, GE's reactor design was investigated. A top safety advisor with the Atomic Energy Commission (AEC), Stephen Hanauer, recommended that GE not be allowed to use the Mark II design for its reactors. But another AEC safety advisor, Joseph Hendrie, rejected that recommendation on the grounds that the GE system was "firmly imbedded in the conventional wisdom" and that a reversal "would generally create more turmoil than I can stand thinking about." Joseph Hendrie later became chair of the Nuclear Regulatory Commission.[35]

## Toxics/PCBs

Among the many deadly chemicals with which GE has polluted the environment are PCBs, which were banned in 1976 because they were found to cause cancer.[36] GE moves slowly to remedy its PCB spills, or any of its other chemical spills that continue to endanger thousands of people and foul the environment:

**Lenox, Massachusetts**   When GE used PCBs in its power transforming business in Lenox, about 20 tons of PCBs had leaked or been discharged into the nearby Housatonic River. In 1981, GE agreed to take measures to clean up the PCBs. As of August 1987, a month after some youngsters were seen still swimming in the contaminated river, GE had made no progress or any measures to help clean up the river.[37]

**Waterford, New York**   At the company's silicon products plant there, at least 20 chemical spills were reported between 1983 and 1986, dumping thousands of pounds of hazardous chemicals into the water and air. From the beginning of 1986 until May, there were nine chemical spills at the GE plant. At least five went into the Hudson River.[38] According to the Environmental Protection Agency (EPA), the GE plant in Waterford has regularly violated limitations on toxic chemicals.[39]

**Hudson Falls, New York**   As of 1977, at this electrical plant and one at Fort Edwards, GE had dumped 137 metric tons of PCBs into the Hudson River. GE studies have tried to imply that no cleanup was needed because the PCBs were rapidly breaking down naturally. However, other scientists disputed these findings.[40]

Almost 10 years later, on May 6, 1986, the state of New York banned bass fishing in the Hudson River because the fish were contaminated with PCBs. The ban was estimated to cost the state's economy $10 million a year. *GE was solely responsible for dumping 400,000 pounds of PCBs into the Hudson*, according to a petition filed with the Federal Communications Commission.[41]

## Superfund Sites

The 1985 Superfund list published by *Mother Jones* magazine listed GE at the very top, responsible for 22 toxic waste sites. The EPA had identified a total of 195 sites in the U.S. that were to get Superfund money to clean them up because the government considered them so hazardous.[42]

In April 1986, Representative Thomas Downey (D-NY) released another list of the top 10 contaminators of Superfund sites. Nine were oil or chemical companies—the other was GE. It was number 2 on the list with *26 sites*.[43] By August 1987, GE was listed for *35 sites*.[44] More hazardous sites are being found every year.

## Labor Relations with "Neutron Jack"

GE employees explain their nickname for GE's chair, "Neutron Jack," by saying he's like the neutron bomb—whenever he visits a plant, the buildings are left standing but the people disappear.[45]

Welch's aggressive efforts to cut costs and increase profits have resulted in 100,000 layoffs since he became chair and CEO in 1981.[46] People have often been laid off with only a few months left to go before they qualify for their pensions; jobs have been eliminated or moved to nonunion factories; and work has been shifted to other countries.

Moving factories out of the country has become a common ploy by U.S. corporations as a way to acquire cheap, nonunion labor. In October 1987, GE decided to close two factories: one in Decatur, Indiana, and one in Holland, Michigan. A thousand people lost their jobs. Much of the work those factories did was moved to Juarez, Mexico, where people are paid $1 an hour compared to $11 in the U.S.[47] In 1982, GE closed down an electric iron plant in Ontario, California, costing 1000 people their jobs. GE moved much of this work to Singapore (where workers earn less in a day than Ontario workers make in an hour) and to Brazil.[48]

In June 1987, GE announced that it was moving a gas turbine manufacturing division from Schenectady, New York, to South Carolina. In November of 1987, the company announced plans to close a large motor manufacturing plant, also in Schenectady. By the end of 1987, 3,350 jobs were expected to be gone from that area.[49]

## The Cicero Case

In October 1987, GE announced the closing of a union refrigerator plant in Cicero, Illinois, cutting 1,200 jobs. GE planned to move the work to a nonunion plant in Decatur, Alabama. GE had to sink $160 million into the Decatur plant in order to make the move. The move was worth it because a worker there makes $3,750 less a year than a Cicero worker.[50]

Both the Cicero union and the state of Illinois tried to convince GE to stay in Cicero. The president of the union local said, "We were willing to make concessions, but the company never told us what they wanted." Illinois officials confirm this: "GE never asked for anything from the state. The company just left."[51]

What the company could not ask for in Illinois is the kind of anti-union climate it can have in Decatur, Alabama. The state AFL-CIO says that Decatur is one of Alabama's least organized areas. Says a Decatur GE employee, "I don't think a union has a chance to come in here....When it comes down to it, GE was going to do whatever was best for the company. I don't think they care what hurts who. It's business."[52]

But aside from the issue of who is hurt by such a ruthless policy, is it actually good for the company? Welch seems oblivious to the misery his policy is causing. He contends that it is not dampening employee morale, "I don't sense that. I sense a rapidly escalating appreciation for the world competitive market, and for what we have to do to work smarter together."[53] However, a union leader in Evendale,

# GE, Do You Really Bring Good Things To Life?

On September 28th, General Electric announced plans to move its Hotpoint refrigeration operation. The company has decided to lay off 1250 members of Local #571 of the Sheet Metal Workers' International Association in Cicero, Illinois and move their jobs to a non-union plant in Decatur, Alabama.

Many people have questioned GE's plan because it just doesn't make sense:

- GE has openly admitted that the workforce in Cicero consisting of a large percentage of women, blacks, and hispanics is one of their most productive anywhere.
- The plant in Cicero has been a profitable operation for GE.
- It's not because Alabama won a bidding war by offering a better incentive package than Illinois. Illinois Governor Jim Thompson told GE that the state would at least match any agreement offered by Alabama.

**So Why Is GE Closing the Cicero Plant?**

We believe it is a case of union busting clear and simple. GE believes that it can cut labor costs by cutting out the union. The company wants to turn its back on loyal employees, many of whom have spent their entire working lives making General Electric the nation's third largest corporation.

On October 29, 1987, at their convention, the AFL-CIO joined with the Sheet Metal Workers in its strong opposition to the closing of the GE/Hotpoint plant, and will work closely with the union in its efforts to prevent the unjustified closing of the Cicero, Illinois plant and the resulting loss of jobs and damage to the community.

UNTIL GE "REALLY BRINGS GOOD THINGS TO LIFE," WE URGE YOU NOT TO PURCHASE GE APPLIANCES OR PRODUCTS.

We do not have a dispute with the dealer or store owner. We seek his cooperation as we seek yours.

*A message from the Sheet Metal Workers' International Association.*

Source: Sheet Metal Workers' International Association Local #571.

Ohio, says of employee morale, "The relationship between us and the company is zilch."[54]

GE's penny-pinching has already backfired: in Murfreesboro, Tennessee, workers' wages were cut by $2 an hour beginning in January 1988. When they learned of the cut, the 640 nonunion workers voted to join the International Union of Electronic Workers (IUE)—the first union-organizing victory at GE in 12 years.[55]

## Profits Before People

Workers who have lost their jobs, people who live near rivers polluted with PCBs, people who live near dangerous nuclear facilities, and people who have been victimized by GE's anti-trust violations, pricefixing, and fraud are living with the reality behind GE's "good things" motto.

# PART III. GE SHAPING NUCLEAR WEAPONS POLICIES FOR PROFITS

*This conjunction of an immense military establishment and a large arms industry is new in the American experience. The total influence—economic, political, even spiritual—is felt in every city, every State house, every office of the Federal government....We must guard against the acquisition of unwarranted influence, whether sought or unsought, by the military-industrial complex. The potential for the disastrous rise of misplaced power exists and will persist.*[1]
—President Dwight D. Eisenhower, January 17, 1961

## GE Uses Its Special Relationship with the Federal Government to Profit from Nuclear Weapons Work

General Electric is deeply embedded in what President Dwight D. Eisenhower labeled the "military-industrial complex." Eisenhower, himself a top military officer, saw all too clearly the threat that a strong military-industrial complex poses to our democratic traditions. As he left office in 1961, Eisenhower warned against the "unwarranted influence of the military-industrial complex" in his farewell address to the American people.

When Eisenhower talked about the military-industrial complex, he meant that alliance of a powerful military establishment, congressional supporters, and the weapons industry. He was extremely concerned that this new concentration of power posed a serious threat to "our liberties or democratic processes."[2] Eisenhower's prophecy has endured, and indeed, grown stronger, over the past 27 years.

In 1981, Gordon Adams, a defense analyst with the Council on Economic Priorities, amplified Eisenhower's original warning. Adams analyzed the relationships between the companies that build the weapons, the executive agencies that buy them, and the Congress that appropriates the money to pay for them. He called these relationships "the iron triangle."[3]

Adams concluded that weapons procurement and policy making are dominated by the military-industrial complex and is cause for serious concern. As Fred Kaplan comments in the *Boston Globe*,

> This machinery [referring to the iron triangle], because it has functioned so well for such a long time, makes it harder to choose alternative policies in weapons policy and in national-security policy.[4]

## Lack of Alternatives in Nuclear Weapons Policy Is No Accident

Alternatives have been seriously lacking in this country's nuclear weapons policies. But that is no accident. Since near the end of World War II, General Electric has been shaping U.S. nuclear weapons policies, exerting its influence not to advance this country's national security but to increase its own profits. GE is an immensely powerful transnational corporation. With careful planning and good implementation, the company has cultivated a very special relationship with the U.S. government. This report examines the special relationship that GE has with the government and explores how the company uses this relationship to advance its own financial interests.

By most accepted measures, General Electric is one of this country's preeminent corporations. In 1986, GE ranked number three in market value, number five in net income, and number six in overall sales.[5] In a closed door meeting with analysts in New York in December 1986, GE's Chief Executive Officer John Welch suggested he intends to make GE the nation's largest corporation—overtaking current leaders IBM and Exxon.[6]

Among the nuclear weapons manufacturers, GE is also a leader. In 1986, General Electric ranked as the number 2 Department of Defense contractor[7]; and GE has been in the top 10 for at least the past eight years.[8] GE makes critical components to more nuclear weapons systems than any other company, including the neutron "trigger" for every U.S. hydrogen bomb.[9] The company is key to this country's nuclear weapons apparatus, while remaining largely unrecognized as such by the public.

As a group, the nuclear weapons manufacturers are extremely influential in shaping national security decisions. They are active in those councils of government—both legislative and executive—that participate in deciding key military issues and setting national security policies.[10] None of the weaponmakers, however, is more experienced or more successful than GE.

In summary, GE is a high-powered player in the world of U.S. business and is extremely successful at manipulating the military-industrial complex. Over the past four decades, GE has carefully positioned itself at the powerful conjunction of business, government, and military power. None of the other top Department of Defense weapons contractors come close to GE's business clout;[11] no other U.S. transnational corporation is as successful as GE in the world of military contractors.[12] GE is in the best possible position to influence national security decisions to its own financial advantage.

## GE's World Is Rarely Examined

The company's tremendous influence over decisions of war and peace goes largely undetected by the public. General Electric is part of a tightly knit system of connections and influence; GE operates in a world that is rarely examined and even less well understood.

To make the situation even more confusing for the general public, GE spends millions of dollars every year carefully cultivating its image: "We bring good things to life." Few people know that GE is one of this country's leading producers and promoters of nuclear weapons. To obscure this reality, GE hides its deadly nuclear weapons business behind claims of patriotism and national security—thereby inhibiting most investigation.

It is vitally important to crack open GE's facade to allow for public scrutiny—to examine how GE manages to protect its vital interests, to understand how the company helps create the need for more nuclear weapons.

While scrutinizing GE, however, it must not be forgotten that all of the parts and all of the actors are intimately interrelated—acting and reacting with each other in a relatively closed system. The facade is cracked open to allow for careful examination and to improve understanding. The interrelatedness of the system's parts, however, must always be kept in mind.

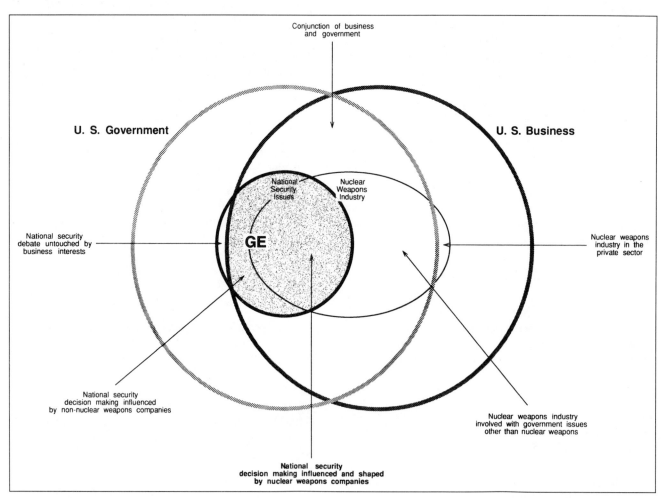

**Figure 3.** GE Spheres of Influence

# GE: High-Powered Player in the World of U.S. Business

1

GE has carefully developed and just as carefully maintains a central position in the powerful sphere of U.S. corporate interests. The company is able to exert considerable clout over a wide array of governmental policy issues, including issues pertaining to national security.

GE has well-established connections with leading financial and industrial institutions in this country, such as Morgan Guaranty Trust, Citicorp Bank, and Champion International. One way these connections are established and nurtured is through a carefully crafted board of directors. People who either run or have run some of the most important U.S. corporations, or have served at the highest levels of government, sit on GE's board.

In addition to its influential board of directors, General Electric executives are members of key business groups—groups that are commonly recognized as exerting considerable clout over national policy and government decision-making. As noted by *Fortune* magazine (March 27, 1978), chief executive officers of America's top corporations "...can and do practice the politics of persuasion on the highest levels of government."

Corporate executives share common business interests; they also share personal connections and loyalties that are firmly established through a network of social clubs and activities. Through these informal connections, policy is discussed, deals are begun, and access to important resources is assured. GE is a masterful player at the game of informal connections.

GE's key position in the business sphere places the company in the top echelon of U.S. business power. This position gives GE the advantage over most other nuclear weaponmakers seeking to influence governmental policy. Of the top 10 nuclear weapons contractors identified by the Department of Defense in 1986, only one—General Motors—is arguably of the same business stature as General Electric. Most of the other large and prominent transnational corporations leading this country's business ranks are not so well placed in the hierarchy of weapons contractors. Thus, GE's business position works to its great advantage in shaping national security decisions.

# GE Board Connections For Power and Profit

**2**

## Introduction

The directors of General Electric reflect and help to create the company's diversity and power. People who run or have run some of the most important U.S. corporations, or have served at the highest levels of government, sit on GE's Board.

Although most of GE's directors are not full-time GE employees, as a group they are crucial to GE's success as an industrial company and as a major weaponmaker. Their important role reflects a general tendency in the corporate world.

The role of directors has changed over the years with increasing legal, social and environmental pressure on corporations. Directors now find themselves legally liable for actions by the corporations on whose boards they sit. In fact, they routinely take out "Corporation Directors Insurance." A 1984 study found that each year directors of large corporations spend an average of 160 hours on board duties, and are paid $24,000 for their services.[1]

GE's board consists of 19 directors. Each of the directors serves on at least one of the seven board committees: Nominating, Operations, Audit, Public Responsibilities, Finance, Management, and Technology and Science.

Three of the board positions are reserved for the GE "Executive Officers," as shown in the following chart:

| GE Position | Board Position | Current Occupant |
|---|---|---|
| Chief Executive Officer | Chair | John F. Welch Jr. |
| Executive Officer | Vice Chair | Lawrence A. Bossidy |
| Executive Officer | Vice Chair | Edward E. Hood Jr. |

One other GE director—Silas Cathcart, previously not a GE employee—was persuaded to come out of retirement to take over GE's brokerage subsidiary, Kidder, Peabody, which had been implicated in an insider trading scandal in 1987. Cathcart had run an industrial company, Illinois Tool Works, but had never run a financial institution. Nevertheless, his close acquaintance with GE's Board, where he had served since 1972, seems to have convinced the board to turn to him rather than an outsider with more Wall Street experience.[2]

Of the 15 GE directors who are not GE employees, three are retired company chiefs, five are company chief executives or high-ranking officers, two are from major financial institutions, two are lawyers in active practice, one is a retired government official, and two are from the academic world. In addition to their full-time occupations, they are exceptionally active and well-connected people; they belong to scores of policy-making private organizations, government advisory boards, and social clubs.

GE's directors enjoy the prestige of being associated with such a major company. Those directors who are not officers of the company earn $27,000 annually as a director's "retainer fee" plus $1,200 for each board or board committee meeting attended, plus travel allowance.[3] Their contacts with other GE directors can be useful for their own business and personal affairs.

The directors also have the chance to shape the policies of a company they admire. Pittsburgh financier Henry Hillman, who has been a GE director since 1972, praised GE's management in a rare magazine interview: "They clearly have this concept of making every part of their business be either number one or number two and a real earner and producer." The same article disclosed that Hillman had reinforced his admiration by quintupling his GE stock holdings to one million shares.[4]

## GE Directors and Their Connections

The GE directors, with an average age of 62 and an average board tenure of 9 years, have had plenty of time to get to know people in their respective fields, and to form a good working team. The acquaintances, contacts, and memberships that the directors bring to the board are at least as valuable to GE as their managerial know-how.

The chart *GE Director Connections* shows the major corporate boards, governmental bodies, policy-making and lobbying organizations, and social clubs to which the GE directors belong, as well the current (or last, if retired) full-time position each occupies. The directors' membership on numerous corporate boards of directors will perhaps be the least surprising part of the chart. Some readers,

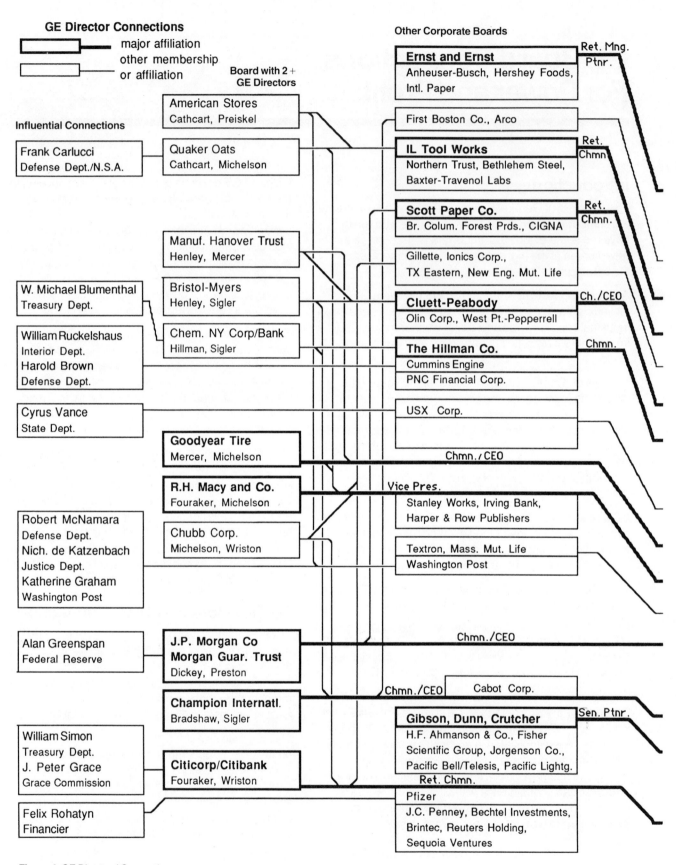

**GE Director Connections**

major affiliation

other membership or affiliation

Board with 2 + GE Directors

**Other Corporate Boards**

**Influential Connections**

Frank Carlucci
Defense Dept./N.S.A.

American Stores
Cathcart, Preiskel

Quaker Oats
Cathcart, Michelson

W. Michael Blumenthal
Treasury Dept.

William Ruckelshaus
Interior Dept.
Harold Brown
Defense Dept.

Cyrus Vance
State Dept.

Manuf. Hanover Trust
Henley, Mercer

Bristol-Myers
Henley, Sigler

Chem. NY Corp/Bank
Hillman, Sigler

Robert McNamara
Defense Dept.
Nich. de Katzenbach
Justice Dept.
Katherine Graham
Washington Post

Goodyear Tire
Mercer, Michelson

R.H. Macy and Co.
Fouraker, Michelson

Chubb Corp.
Michelson, Wriston

Alan Greenspan
Federal Reserve

J.P. Morgan Co
Morgan Guar. Trust
Dickey, Preston

Champion Internatl.
Bradshaw, Sigler

William Simon
Treasury Dept.
J. Peter Grace
Grace Commission

Citicorp/Citibank
Fouraker, Wriston

Felix Rohatyn
Financier

**Ernst and Ernst**
Anheuser-Busch, Hershey Foods, Intl. Paper

First Boston Co., Arco

**IL Tool Works**
Northern Trust, Bethlehem Steel, Baxter-Travenol Labs

**Scott Paper Co.**
Br. Colum. Forest Prds., CIGNA

Gillette, Ionics Corp., TX Eastern, New Eng. Mut. Life

**Cluett-Peabody**
Olin Corp., West Pt.-Pepperrell

**The Hillman Co.**
Cummins Engine
PNC Financial Corp.

USX Corp.

Stanley Works, Irving Bank, Harper & Row Publishers

Textron, Mass. Mut. Life
Washington Post

Cabot Corp.

**Gibson, Dunn, Crutcher**
H.F. Ahmanson & Co., Fisher Scientific Group, Jorgenson Co., Pacific Bell/Telesis, Pacific Lightg.

Pfizer
J.C. Penney, Bechtel Investments, Brintec, Reuters Holding, Sequoia Ventures

Ret. Mng. Ptnr.

Ret. Chmn.

Ret. Chmn.

Ch./CEO

Chmn.

Chmn./CEO

Vice Pres.

Chmn./CEO

Chmn./CEO

Sen. Ptnr.

Ret. Chmn.

**Figure 4.** GE Directors' Connections

**Bringing GE to Light**

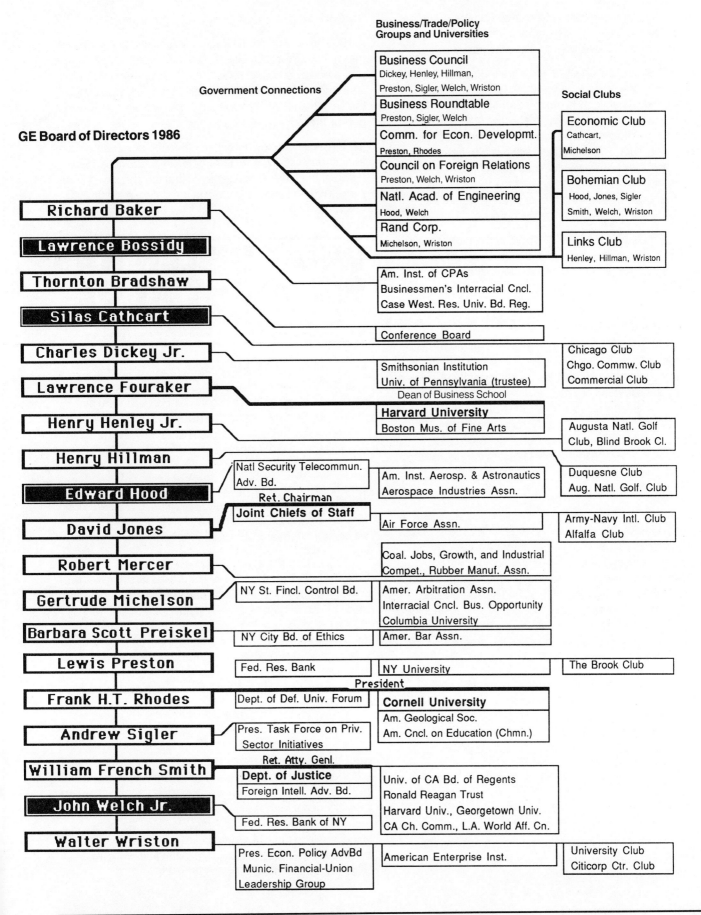

**Business/Trade/Policy Groups and Universities**

**Government Connections**

**Social Clubs**

**GE Board of Directors 1986**

**Business Council**
Dickey, Henley, Hillman, Preston, Sigler, Welch, Wriston

**Business Roundtable**
Preston, Sigler, Welch

**Comm. for Econ. Developmt.**
Preston, Rhodes

**Council on Foreign Relations**
Preston, Welch, Wriston

**Natl. Acad. of Engineering**
Hood, Welch

**Rand Corp.**
Michelson, Wriston

**Economic Club**
Cathcart, Michelson

**Bohemian Club**
Hood, Jones, Sigler Smith, Welch, Wriston

**Links Club**
Henley, Hillman, Wriston

**Richard Baker**

**Lawrence Bossidy**

**Thornton Bradshaw**

Am. Inst. of CPAs
Businessmen's Interracial Cncl.
Case West. Res. Univ. Bd. Reg.

**Silas Cathcart**

Conference Board

**Charles Dickey Jr.**

Chicago Club
Chgo. Commw. Club
Commercial Club

**Lawrence Fouraker**

Smithsonian Institution
Univ. of Pennsylvania (trustee)
Dean of Business School
**Harvard University**
Boston Mus. of Fine Arts

**Henry Henley Jr.**

Augusta Natl. Golf Club, Blind Brook Cl.

**Henry Hillman**

Natl Security Telecommun. Adv. Bd.
Ret. Chairman

Am. Inst. Aerosp. & Astronautics
Aerospace Industries Assn.

Duquesne Club
Aug. Natl. Golf. Club

**Edward Hood**

**Joint Chiefs of Staff**

Air Force Assn.

Army-Navy Intl. Club
Alfalfa Club

**David Jones**

**Robert Mercer**

Coal. Jobs, Growth, and Industrial Compet., Rubber Manuf. Assn.

**Gertrude Michelson**

NY St. Fincl. Control Bd.

Amer. Arbitration Assn.
Interracial Cncl. Bus. Opportunity
Columbia University

**Barbara Scott Preiskel**

NY City Bd. of Ethics

Amer. Bar Assn.

**Lewis Preston**

Fed. Res. Bank

NY University

The Brook Club

**Frank H.T. Rhodes**

President
Dept. of Def. Univ. Forum

**Cornell University**
Am. Geological Soc.
Am. Cncl. on Education (Chmn.)

**Andrew Sigler**

Pres. Task Force on Priv. Sector Initiatives
Ret. Atty. Genl.

**William French Smith**

**Dept. of Justice**
Foreign Intell. Adv. Bd.

Univ. of CA Bd. of Regents
Ronald Reagan Trust
Harvard Univ., Georgetown Univ.
CA Ch. Comm., L.A. World Aff. Cn.

**John Welch Jr.**

Fed. Res. Bank of NY

**Walter Wriston**

Pres. Econ. Policy AdvBd
Munic. Financial-Union
Leadership Group

American Enterprise Inst.

University Club
Citicorp Ctr. Club

**Bringing GE to Light**

however, may be surprised at the large number of high-ranking past or present government officials who rub shoulders with GE directors on these boards.

The right side of the chart, which shows GE directors' affiliations with private and governmental policy-making bodies and social clubs is much less well known. In particular, the two rightmost columns list some of the most powerful private groups that boast one or more GE directors as members. Many political scientists believe that an elite upper class heavily influences the politics and economy of the United States; they point to many of these private groups as the instruments through which the members of this class exercise their power.

The major organizations with which GE directors are affiliated are profiled in the chapters on "Social Ties," "Business Groups," and "Advisory Committees/ Revolving Door."

## Individual GE Directors

A closer look at GE directors reveals their varied areas of influence and expertise. They are presented here grouped according to their major affiliations. Nevertheless, it would be a mistake to think of them in such mutually exclusive clusters as "academics" or "former government officials." The interrelated nature of the U.S. power structure— dubbed the "Military-Industrial Complex" by President Eisenhower—means that these directors can use all their memberships, associations and affiliations for the benefit of General Electric.

**John F. Welch, Jr.** went to work for GE in Pittsfield, Massachusetts in 1960, hired by an engineer who quickly described him as being "on fire."[5] Within two years, he had embarked on his first major achievement at GE—the creation of a new plastic called Noryl, and its aggressive marketing to the auto industry in a campaign that included special ads by comedians aimed at engineers in Detroit[6] and total market saturation in radio, billboards, newspapers, and trade magazines.[7]

Rising quickly in the ranks, he attained the rank of vice president in 1972 and board vice chair in 1979, along with Edward Hood and John Burlingame (since retired). Board chair and CEO Reginald Jones chose Welch as his successor in late 1980, and Welch assumed control in April 1981.

He quickly moved to stamp his identity on the company. First, he reorganized the entire GE structure to reflect his concept of GE's "three circles of business"[8]:

- **Services:** credit, information, construction, nuclear
- **High Technology:** electronics, medical systems, aerospace, aircraft engines
- **Core:** appliances, lighting, equipment, motors

In 1983 he sold off GE's large mining subsidiary, Utah International, for $2.4 billion. With cash gained in that sale, plus a borrowed $5.4 billion,[9] he turned around two years later and made his most dramatic move to date: the purchase of the RCA Corporation for $6.28 billion, the largest non-oil merger in U.S. history.

The RCA purchase catapulted GE to the number two position among U.S. military contractors. As *Business Week* noted at the time, Welch "crowed that the combined companies would have more clout in the defense electronics business."[10]

FORTUNE JULY 7 1986

# WHAT WELCH HAS WROUGHT AT GE

In five years General Electric's perpetual-motion boss has chopped 100,000 jobs, sunk billions of dollars into automated factories, overhauled the corporate culture, and picked up RCA in the costliest non-oil merger ever. He promises still more to come.    ■ *by Peter Petre*

In 1985, Welch's tenure was marked by GE's worst scandal in 25 years: the Space Systems Division was discovered to have overcharged the Air Force in 1980 by $800,000. GE faced more than $2 million in criminal and civil penalties, and was forbidden to bid on government projects for several weeks.

Welch is described by all as aggressive, informal, sharp-tempered—a great contrast to the reserved, formal Reginald Jones. In a relatively short time, he has wrought major changes at GE; his ultimate goal is "to make GE worth more than any other U.S. company."[11]

**Edward E. Hood, Jr.** is the key figure in GE's rise to a pre-eminent place in the weapons and aerospace fields. After receiving an M.S. in electrical engineering and serving in the Air Force, he went to work for GE in 1957. In 1977, during a restructuring under Reginald Jones, he was picked to head the Technical Systems and Materials Sector. He was promoted along with Welch and Burlingame to vice chair in 1979, and stayed in that position until after Welch was named chair.

As an executive officer, Hood currently oversees all weaponmaking and aerospace sectors of GE, including the weapon-related operations acquired in the RCA purchase, and the Pinellas neutron-generator plant in Florida.[12] In 1981 he headed the Aerospace Industries Association (AIA), whose strong Washington lobby makes it one of the most influential military trade associations.[13] As of 1987 Hood is still on the AIA Executive Committee.[14] In 1982 President Reagan appointed him to the National Security Telecommunications Advisory Committee.

**Lawrence A. Bossidy** complements the technical expertise of Welch and Hood with his experience in financial services—a field in which GE sees much of its future. He was hired as a financial management trainee in 1957, and rose through the ranks until he became executive vice president in 1979. He replaced the retiring John Burlingame as board vice chair in 1985. As executive officer, he oversees GE's financial services as well as power systems, lighting, the GE Investment Corporation, and other sectors.[15]

The backgrounds of the above three GE directors cover Welch's "three circles": Welch for **Core Business** and overall coordination, Hood for **High Technology**, and Bossidy for **Services**.

Compared with the other GE directors, these three also stand out for their relative lack of outside associations. None have worked any length of time for any company but GE. Welch, for his part, appears eager to keep GE's top management level as a well-motivated and tightly knit team. On his selection as board chair in 1980, he made it one of his priorities to keep his two top executives, Hood and Burlingame, in the GE fold—"to see, as he puts it, 'that all three of us have a helluva good time.' "[16]

**Walter Wriston** was elected to GE's Board of Directors in 1962. As board chair and CEO of Citicorp and Citibank, he did more than anyone else to change the U.S. banking industry in recent years. First hired at First National City Bank in New York in 1946, he was chosen board chair and CEO in 1970. During his 14 years at the top, he built Citicorp into the nation's largest financial institution,[17] while lending aggressively to Third World nations, and pushing such innovations as the first comprehensive Automatic Teller Machine network[18] and banking by mail.

Described in the *New York Times* as an "apostle of unfettered capitalism,"[19] he made ruthless moves when he thought it necessary: in 1980, he warned New York Governor Hugh Carey that he and other bankers wanted a change in the state "usury laws" limiting credit card interest; when he did not get the hoped-for changes, he moved Citicorp's massive credit card operation to South Dakota.

Wriston brings a wealth of contacts and affiliations to GE's Board, from membership in numerous elite clubs (including the Bohemian Club), to the Business Council (which he chaired from 1981 to 1983), to the Council on Foreign Relations.

He first met Ronald Reagan in the mid-1970s, and served as an economic adviser to Reagan's presidential campaign in 1980. When Reagan was elected, Wriston was proposed as treasury secretary, and was appointed to Reagan's Economic Policy Advisory Board. In 1983 he was proposed as chair of the Federal Reserve Board, and in 1985 as U.S. trade representative. He turned both posts down, but has kept a close relationship with Reagan.[20]

**Lewis T. Preston's** presence on the board since 1976 gives GE an inside connection to another central pillar of the U.S. economy: the Morgan bank and its affiliates. Preston is the chair and CEO of Morgan Guaranty Trust and of the bank's holding company, J.P. Morgan and Company. GE has other tight links with the Morgan bank besides Preston: Morgan owns more GE stock than any other bank—2,310,000 shares in 1980[21]; and GE bonds were issued in notes from Morgan, Stanley and Company.[22]

A century ago, the name J.P. Morgan symbolized ruthless profiteering by big business. In fact, J.P. Morgan started his financial empire by profiting from the Civil War: he bought 5,000 obsolete rifles at $3.50 apiece in New York and sold them, as good, at $22.00 apiece to a Union general in St. Louis.[23]

Now the Morgan bank epitomizes well-run, profitable, ultra-elite banking. Morgan is the only U.S. bank rated AAA by the Standard & Poor and Moody financial evaluation services,[24] and in 1982 earned the highest return on assets of the 15 largest bank holding companies.[25] In Preston's words,[26] "Our client base consists of blue-chip corporations and other better-credit businesses, and we stayed with that...We didn't go searching for loans in South America[27] or risky leveraged buyouts...." Even banking rival Wriston often used Morgan as a model of profitability and good management.[28]

Preston was hired at J.P. Morgan and Company in 1951 and was elected chair in 1980. He contrasts personally with Wriston in ways that parallel the differences between the two men's banks. Preston serves on no non-Morgan board other than GE; rarely does he speak or otherwise appear in the public eye. He forms part of New York City's social aristocracy, as a director of the Council on Foreign Relations, and member of several country clubs. Along with Wriston, he attended Brook Astor's party in 1980 welcoming President-elect Reagan to New York.[29]

**Thornton Bradshaw** joined GE's Board when his company, RCA, was purchased by GE in 1986. He retired from active management at the same time, ending a long and varied career. From 1942 to 1952 he taught at the Harvard University Business School. He then spent four years as a partner in the New York City firm of Cresap, McCormick and Paget.[30] In 1956 he was hired as a vice president at the Atlantic Richfield oil company (later ARCO), attaining the presidency in 1964. Bradshaw was elected a director of the RCA Corporation in 1971.

Called a "superb administrator" by colleagues,[31] Bradshaw was also something of a maverick in the oil industry: a director of the Conservation Foundation, he called the claims of environmentalists "very legitimate,"[32] and defended President Carter's energy policies—including the windfall profits tax,[33] hated by most oilmen.

When RCA was searching in 1983 for a CEO to replace the embattled Edgar Griffith,[34] it turned to Bradshaw, who had recently arranged for his own successor at ARCO. Bradshaw, then 63, signed only a five-year contract with RCA,[35] but he moved quickly to turn around the company's recent poor performance. Starting one day before he officially took control,[36] he installed a new head of RCA's subsidiary NBC, and later vowed to "resist to the utmost" unwelcome takeover attempts.[37]

Before Bradshaw's five-year contract expired, however, an outside purchase offer came along that he did not resist—from General Electric. Using financier Felix Rohatyn as a go-between,[38] John Welch, Jr. initiated a series of informal talks with Bradshaw in a number of New York residences and offices; the talks soon expanded into formal negotiations, with code names for the two companies ("Beam" for GE and "Rock" for RCA).[39] The deal was closed in December 1985 with GE paying $6.28 billion, and Bradshaw reportedly making a $7 million profit on securities and options.[40] Bradshaw then retired.

He continues to be very active in public life: still a director at ARCO, he is on the boards of additional corporations and foundations, and is chair of the conference board.

Source: Center for Defense Information.

BUSINESS WEEK/JANUARY 27, 1986

**The Corporation**

MERGERS

# GE + RCA = A POWERHOUSE DEFENSE CONTRACTOR

THE RESEARCH LABS OF THE TWO GIANTS COULD ACHIEVE THAT ELUSIVE GOAL, SYNERGY—AND BRUISE COMPETITORS

The RCA purchase was a real coup for GE in several ways. It put GE in the front rank of U.S. military contractors, as RCA brought components into the mix which complemented "synergistically" GE's preexisting weapons business.[41] The purchase also brought three RCA directors into the GE fold. Bradshaw was one. The other two, far from being any two ordinary directors, had come from the highest levels of U.S. government: *David Jones* and *William French Smith*.

---

**David Jones**, former chair of the Joint Chiefs of Staff, attended college briefly in North Dakota before quitting in favor of flying school in New Mexico. This led him to his lifelong career in the U.S. Air Force. He was named second lieutenant in 1943, and rose through the ranks, serving as aide to General Curtis LeMay (whom he calls "my mentor"[42]) in 1955. He was promoted to general in 1971 and served as deputy commander of operations in Vietnam, commander-in-chief of the Air Force in Europe, and finally Air Force Chief of Staff in 1974.[43]

President Carter named him chair of the Joint Chiefs in 1978. His job under Carter was occasionally stormy: he and the other Joint Chiefs united to publicly criticize as inadequate the 1980 military budget requested by Carter and Defense Secretary Harold Brown—a very rare occurrence in Pentagon history.[44]

When Ronald Reagan was elected president in 1980, Washington observers felt Jones's position was doomed by his identification with Carter. Nevertheless, Jones was retained as chair, despite some opposition from such right-wing senators as Jesse Helms.[45] Jones had already adapted to the Reagan political climate: in congressional hearings soon after Reagan's election, he stridently urged a rapid military buildup and warned of a Soviet threat.[46] Also in 1981, he sharply contradicted his earlier position and said the B-1 Bomber "should be top priority."[47]

Jones retired from his position as chair of Joint Chiefs in 1982, but has kept active in military circles. He is a national director of the Air Force Association,[48] whose magazine, *Air Force*, often carries prominently placed ads for GE's weapons.[49] The Air Force Association's affiliated group, the Industrial Associates of the A.F.A., boasts as members not only GE itself but also, separately, GE's Aircraft Engine group.[50] Jones is on the board of USX Corporation (formerly U.S. Steel), and belongs to several country clubs.

Jones has, naturally enough, spoken out frequently on defense issues. He has criticized the Nuclear Freeze and "No First Use" (of nuclear weapons) movements.[51] During the Iranian crisis in 1980, Jones and the Joint Chiefs drew up contingency plans for President Carter that included the use of nuclear weapons against the U.S.S.R. Later he said, "When there is the possibility of a major conflict with the Soviet Union, there is always a discussion of nuclear weapons. That is fairly standard."[52] He has called for a stronger Joint Chiefs of Staff,[53] and for a highly-prepared global military posture.[54]

John Welch Jr. praised Jones's leadership qualities at the 1987 annual meeting and sidestepped the issue of his insights and contacts in the Pentagon.[55]

---

**William French Smith** became a GE director in 1986. As Ronald Reagan's friend and personal lawyer, his election consummated the long GE-Reagan connection, begun when Reagan became a GE spokesperson in 1954. Smith served as Reagan's first attorney general—the official who "more than anyone but the President himself...sets the moral tone of an Administration, symbolizing its commitment or lack of commitment to impartial justice."[56]

Originally from New Hampshire, Smith moved to California in 1946 with a law degree from Harvard, and was soon hired as a partner at the law firm Gibson, Dunn and Crutcher. He has been a close friend of Ronald Reagan since at least 1965[57] and helped persuade Reagan to run for California governor in 1966.[58] Smith thereafter became Reagan's personal lawyer and a trustee of his personal estate. Reagan appointed Smith to his first government post in 1968: Regent of the University of California.[59]

As U.S. attorney general Smith became, in the admiring words of the conservative *National Review*, "the point man of the Reagan social counter-revolution."[60] For example, he deemphasized the naming of women and minorities as federal judges, and openly called for more political and party patronage.[61] He reversed the federal government's long commitment to affirmative action,[62] and he sought to weaken anti-trust laws, saying "bigness in business does not necessarily mean badness."[63] He restricted public access to government records under the Freedom of Information Act.[64] Referring to a "groundswell of conservatism," he embarked on a crusade against "activism" by the Supreme Court and other federal courts.[65] And he tried to greatly expand the scope of executive branch privilege in refusing to release documents to Congress.[66]

In 1984, Smith was invited to a submarine christening and launching ceremony at the General Dynamics Corporation Electric Boat Division. General Dynamics was then under investigation by the Justice Department for multi-million-dollar cost overruns. Faced with this conflict of interest, Smith chose to attend the ceremony and excuse himself from the investigation being run by the department he headed.[67] The Senate later cited Smith for contempt-of-Congress when he refused to provide subpoenaed files on the General Dynamics case.[68]

Smith left the attorney general post in 1985, making way for another Reagan associate, Edwin Meese III. He returned to Gibson, Dunn and Crutcher, which since 1980 had become California's largest law firm.[69]

In addition to his ongoing Reagan ties, Smith is extraordinarily well connected in Southern California. He serves on the boards of Pacific Telesis, Pacific Bell and other corporations. He is a proud member of the Bohemian Club—in fact, his spokesperson, asked in 1980 whether Smith would resign from the club because of its men-only policy, said Smith was "not wrestling with it [the issue of whether to resign]. He's not even thinking about it."[70]

With Smith's long ties to Reagan and other Republican powers, he is a valuable asset to GE in its quest for greater government and Defense Department influence. And as the only director with a base in rapidly growing Southern California, or anywhere in the West, he provides a geographic balance to the board.

---

Seven other GE directors either run, or ran until they retired, their own businesses.

**Andrew Sigler** is chair and CEO of Champion International. Champion is a Connecticut-based manufacturer of paper and other forest products. Sigler has worked there since 1957. He has distinguished himself by his harsh criticism of institutional investors and strong opposition to corporate "raiders."[71] As head of the Business Roundtable task force on takeovers, he testified before Congress that "Hostile takeovers initiated by raiders and conducted at a frenzied pace...lead to unacceptable abuses."[72] In 1984, under Sigler's leadership, Champion arranged a friendly takeover of the St. Regis Corporation for $1.7 billion, heading off a hostile raid by the notorious Rupert Murdoch.[73]

Sigler is fairly active in business and government circles. He is director of several corporations, a member of the Business Roundtable, and a member of President Reagan's Task Force on Private Sector Initiatives.[74]

---

THE BOSTON GLOBE    FRIDAY, JUNE 5, 1987

# Kidder pays $25 million to settle insider case

**By Peter Szekely**
**Reuters**

WASHINGTON – Kidder, Peabody and Co. Inc., one of Wall Street's top securities firms, agreed yesterday to pay $25 million to settle government charges that it illegally used insider information to trade stocks and assisted Ivan Boesky in his illegal activities.

---

**Silas Cathcart** was drafted by the GE Board in 1987 to take over GE's Wall Street subsidiary, the Kidder, Peabody

Group.[75] Previously he had headed Illinois Tool Works Inc, a Chicago manufacturer of engineered tools and fasteners. Hired there as a sales trainee fresh from college in 1948, he became chair of the board in 1972. He retired in 1981. He is a director of Quaker Oats, Bethlehem Steel and several other major companies; the only GE director based in Chicago, he is a member of the Chicago Club, the Commercial Club, and the Economic Club, among others.

**Henry Hillman** runs the Hillman Company—a nonpublic company based on the industrial fortune he inherited from his father "Hart" Hillman, one of Pittsburgh's wealthiest men.[76] He keeps a very low profile—in the words of the *Wall Street Journal*, he "is about as invisible as $2 billion can get."[77] His firm specializes in providing venture capital to new enterprises, especially the high technology field. He revealed in 1982 that he had invested $500 million in California's Silicon Valley.[78]

As mentioned above, Hillman is a great proponent of GE's management techniques; he sits on the boards of several other major corporations, is a member of the Business Council, and belongs to numerous clubs, including the Duquesne Club, meeting place of the powers-that-be in Pittsburgh.

**Charles Dickey Jr.**, retired chair and CEO of Scott Paper Company, represents the paper industry, like Andrew Sigler. His father, Charles Dickey Sr., was also a GE director.[79] Formerly an FBI agent, Dickey was hired at Scott in 1946 and was named chair and CEO in 1971. He retired in 1981. Dickey's last years as chair were marked by fierce competition in the paper products field.[80]

He has spoken out at times on issues concerning big corporations. For example, in 1982 he advised Congress to "stop horsing around with the tax laws"[81] when it was considering tightening restrictions on corporate tax-leasing.[82] These corporate tax-leasing laws are critical to GE's financial services sector. Dickey chairs the National Board of Associates of the Smithsonian Institution.

**Henry Henley Jr.** is chair and CEO of Cluett, Peabody and Company, the apparel company that makes the well-known Arrow shirts.[83] This is his second company: in 1939 he went to work for McKesson and Robbins Inc., a pharmaceutical firm. He had made his way up to president there before being hired as president of Cluett Peabody in 1965. He was named CEO in 1970 and chair in 1979.

Henley is a member of the Business Council.[84] He belongs to many golf and country clubs, and is a director of other corporations. His beliefs on business ethics find their way into his talks to Cluett Peabody salespeople, which have

been collected into a booklet titled "Integrity Excites People."[85]

**Robert Mercer**, like several other GE directors, started his career at one company and stayed there: the Goodyear Tire and Rubber Company of Akron, Ohio. He was hired at Goodyear in 1947, named CEO in 1980, and named chair of the board in 1983. In 1986 he announced a major restructuring of Goodyear, including the sale of $2 billion worth of oil, wheel and aerospace components. Prospective purchasers of the aerospace unit included GE, where Mercer was elected a director in 1984.[86]

As an executive in the tire/rubber industry, which has suffered in recent years like so much of U.S. "smokestack" industry, Mercer co-chairs the Coalition for Jobs, Growth and Industrial Competitiveness, a lobbying group. In this role he wrote a newspaper article criticizing the proposed repeal of the investment tax credit and other tax changes.[87] The investment tax credit is one of the reasons GE received *$283 million* in tax refunds from 1981 to 1983 even though it had *$6.5 billion* in profit.[88]

**Richard Baker** went to work in 1940 at the accounting firm of Ernst and Ernst in Cleveland. He was licensed as a C.P.A. in 1942, stayed on with Ernst and Ernst, and finally was named managing partner in 1964. Now retired, he is still a consultant to Ernst and Ernst.

Like several other GE directors, he has been a leading force in the business life of his city. In the early 1960s he helped found the Greater Cleveland Growth Board to fight Northeastern Ohio's industrial decline. The G.C.G.B. later merged with the Chamber of Commerce to become the Greater Cleveland Growth Association. Baker was elected a director and member of the Executive Committee of the Association.[89] He belongs to numerous professional organizations and clubs, and is a trustee of the Cleveland Playhouse, Case Western Reserve University and other local cultural institutions.

The remaining four GE directors come from quite varied backgrounds.

**Gertrude Michelson** is the senior vice president for external affairs at the New York retailer R.H. Macy & Company. She was hired as a management trainee in 1947, was promoted to senior vice president in 1970, and achieved her present position in 1979.

In her career at Macy's she has handled labor, employee and consumer affairs.[90] This background has given her a wide exposure which, along with her contacts in financial circles, undoubtedly helped her in 1980 to be the first woman appointed to the New York State Financial Control Board.[91] In 1982, she and the two other business members of the board[92] sharply criticized New York City's proposed budget as unsound.[93] Active in many circles, Michelson serves on other important boards–the Federal Reserve Bank of New York, the American Arbitration Association, and a city commission to study commercial rents. She is a director of a number of corporations and belongs to the Economic Club and the New York Women's Forum.

**Frank H.T. Rhodes** is president of Cornell University. He was a professor and dean at several universities before he was hired as Cornell's president in 1977. Rhodes has written numerous works in his own field of geology,[94] and in other speeches and writings he has stressed not only the continuing value of the liberal arts[95] but also the need for industrial-academic cooperation to maintain the U.S. technological "edge."[96] He has also criticized "turmoil, disruption and abuse" and "troubling" methods in pursuit of social goals that he respected (the cause at hand was South Africa).[97] Rhodes is a member of several scientific associations.

Large industrial-technological corporations like GE depend on a continuing flow of bright science and engineering graduates into its research-and-development departments, and cultivate good relations with major universities. It is thus appropriate that Rhodes is on the GE Board.

**Barbara Scott Preiskel**, a New York City attorney, is a director of another major nuclear weaponmaker: Textron/Avco. Extremely active in both corporate and civic pursuits, she sits on the boards of several major corporations, the American Civil Liberties Institute, the Ford Foundation, the New York Community Trust (another foundation), and several universities and schools. She has been admitted to the Bar of New York, the District of Columbia and the U.S. Supreme Court.[98]

**Lawrence Fouraker** is the president of the Boston Museum of Fine Arts. A great deal of his career has been spent at Harvard University. After teaching at several universities, he was hired at Harvard Business School (H.B.S.) in 1961, and appointed a full professor at H.B.S. in 1962, finally being named dean of the school in 1970. He has written extensively on bargaining and decision making in business.[99]

Fouraker, like Frank Rhodes, represents a school and university with close ties to GE. Over the past several years, the Harvard Business School has conducted a case study of John Welch, Jr.'s management style. Through written cases, videotapes, and personal appearances by Welch, students have studied his style as a model for managing a major multinational corporation.

## The GE Directors as a Group

In summary, the GE directors come to the board meetings carrying with them valuable resources, representing widely differing sectors of the economy and the business community. On the political side, GE enjoys unique ties to past and present political leaders.

First and foremost are GE's links with President Ronald Reagan himself—starting from Reagan's professional association with the company, which shaped many of his conservative views—and ending with the presence on the board of one of Reagan's closest friends and associates. Overall, the different members of the board place GE in an ideal position to work with the broad spectrum of the U.S. power structure in GE's goal of growth and preeminence in its many businesses.

# The Ultimate Connection: The U.S. Presidency

## 3

GE's nuclear weapons business has grown spectacularly since the company's former spokesperson, Ronald Reagan, became president of the United States in 1981. The Reagan years have been golden years for all the nuclear weaponmakers. In fiscal year 1986, the Pentagon awarded $145.7 billion in prime military contracts, an increase of 90 percent over the $76.8 billion awarded in 1980 before Reagan took office. GE fared even better than most weapons contractors; its prime contracts increased *threefold* during this time, from $2.2 billion in 1980 to $6.8 billion in 1986.[1]

The B-1 Bomber alone has brought GE over $2.3 billion since Reagan revived it in 1982. These planes cost $260 million each. Yet Caspar Weinberger (Secretary of Defense during most of the Reagan Administration) has projected that the B-1 will be obsolete by 1990. GE is part of a team that is already developing the B-1's successor, the Stealth, which will cost $600 million per plane.[2]

Reagan's tenure in office has seen the blossoming of the biggest and most destabilizing pork barrel of the century— Star Wars. Reagan announced the project publicly in 1981. From 1983 to 1986, GE has received over $465 million for research work alone on Star Wars.[3] While touted as a defensive shield against Soviet attack, Star Wars is seen by many scientists as a first-strike system. It could knock out most Soviet missiles and then defend against what would be a very weak counterattack. The effectiveness of Star Wars as a purely defensive system, however, is highly doubtful since some Soviet missiles could easily pass through and inflict unacceptable damage on the U.S. Along with other first-strike systems, SDI serves only to bring the possibility of nuclear war nearer.[4]

The Reagan administration's support for such systems is easier to understand when the administration's underlying assumptions are clear. According to the Reagan administration, the Soviet system is evil and must be abandoned or destroyed. The U.S. must maintain the ability to obliterate the Soviet Union. As Richard Pipes of the Committee on the Present Danger (CPD) puts it, "There is no alternative to war with the Soviet Union if the Russians do not abandon communism."[5] Reagan is on the board of the CPD, an ultraconservative organization that favors increased military spending and has been key in shaping present national security policies.

Reagan himself appears to believe that nuclear war is inevitable. In 1980, he said, "We may be the generation that sees Armageddon."[6]

## The GE Years: Reagan's Political Beginnings

Reagan has long equated "big government" with creeping socialism and considered "big business," along with big military spending, the last defense the U.S. has against communism. The crucial evolution of his beliefs occurred during the years when he was a spokesperson for General Electric. According to Reagan biographer Lou Cannon,

> The audiences on Reagan's GE tours usually were of the service club or corporate variety, and the questions thrown at him often focused on inflation or government regulation. In the process of answering these questions in a manner pleasing to the questioners, Reagan became a defender of corporations and a critic of the government that the corporate leaders thought was strangling them. The process was gradual, but pervasive. Reagan believes in what he says, and he wound up believing what he was saying. *More than anything, it is his GE experience that changed Reagan from an adversary of big business into one of its most ardent spokesmen.*[7] [Emphasis added]

Reagan went to work for GE in 1954 as his movie career was floundering. He began with GE as the host of *General Electric Theater*, a half-hour television anthology series that ran on CBS for eight years. Reagan was the show's continuing host and occasional guest star.[8] Over time, his role with GE grew and he became GE's corporate spokesperson. He spent three months out of the year traveling to GE's 135 plants all across the U.S. and speaking to GE's 250,000 employees.[9] After a time, these tours included speeches not just to the employees but to local business leaders and civic groups as well.

When Reagan spoke on tour, he always delivered what historian Garry Wills refers to as "The Speech"—extolling the virtues of the clean life and free enterprise (especially big business) and warning against big government and creeping socialism. The message, says Wills, was apocalyptic. According to Reagan, "a slow invisible tide of socialism was engulfing America, held back only by a few brave businessmen."[10]

## GE's Gift to Reagan

GE was a "pioneer at selling whole ways of life, at creating a demand before supplying items."[11] To sell the electrical life, GE built Reagan a house with "everything electric except a chair." It included appliances not yet on the market, one of which was a dishwasher with a built-in garbage disposal.[12] As a part of the GE image, it was Reagan's duty to be a conspicuous consumer.

Reagan was always the perfect company loyalist. This was in keeping with the blind loyalty GE demanded of its employees—"Outsiders say that the GE monogram is stamped on the rear ends of its people."[13] Reagan was part of GE's corporate image, as was *GE Theater*. As part of a huge corporation that he saw as one of the last bastions of free enterprise, Reagan willingly accepted GE's censorship of his speech and of GE *Theater*. As Reagan describes one incident,

> Take us, for example—the time we came up with an exciting half-hour play based on the danger to a planeload of passengers lost in the fog with all instruments out of whack. We needed someone to remind us GE made those instruments, sold them to the airlines, and said airlines would consider it tactless if GE told umpteen million potential passengers they might land the hard way.[14]

## Plans to Fire Reagan

Another incident of company censorship involved "The Speech" against big government and its excess. Reagan started citing the Tennessee Valley Authority (TVA), a symbol of New Deal activism, as a horrendous example of government waste and meddling. He was not aware that GE had approximately $50 million in government contracts to supply electrical equipment to the TVA. Even when GE agreed with the politics of Reagan's speeches, the company was not about to endanger its profits, and a plan to fire Reagan was set in motion. When he heard that he was about to be fired, Reagan asked GE President Ralph Cordiner if the TVA reference should be deleted from his speeches. Cordiner naturally agreed, and the reference was quickly dropped. Reagan stayed on with GE until the next controversial incident happened in 1962.[15]

In 1962, *GE Theater* was cancelled, with GE pleading too much competition from *Bonanza*. But a more likely reason is that Reagan was involved in bad publicity around an anti-trust case. Reagan was a client of the Music Corporation of America (MCA), which was indicted in the case.

The Screen Actors Guild was named as a co-conspirator dating from the time when Reagan was its president. Ultimately, Reagan was subpoenaed by President Kennedy's Justice Department to testify before a grand jury. Not daring to keep Reagan on when he was receiving so much attention from the Justice Department, GE dropped Reagan with 24 hours notice.[16]

## Still a Company Man

Reagan's connections to GE did not end with *GE Theater*. He retained the fervent pro-corporation views he had learned so well at GE. In 1964, he delivered "The Speech" from his GE days in support of presidential candidate Barry Goldwater. The speech was a big hit, but not for Goldwater. His campaign failed.[17] Reagan's career, however, had shifted. He was now taking his point of view, and GE's point of view, directly to the arena of electoral politics.

And as Reagan's political career has progressed, a number of his close associates have had ties with GE.

**William French Smith**, who is currently a GE board member, helped convince Reagan in 1966 to run for gov-

Ronald and Nancy Reagan, circa 1954, relax in the living room of their GE all-electric home.

Reagan selling the GE way of life.

ernor of California. Reagan won the election, and during this time period Smith became Reagan's personal lawyer and trustee of his personal estate. When Reagan was elected president in 1980, he appointed Smith as U.S. attorney general. A hallmark of Smith's term was the weakening of the corporate anti-trust laws.[18] This greatly advanced Reagan's and GE's interest in keeping the government from interfering with business.

**Walter Wriston**, a GE board member who has been on GE's board since 1962, has had strong ties with Reagan through the years. He was economic adviser to Reagan's presidential election campaign in 1980. Reagan offered him several government posts after the election, including chair of the Federal Reserve Board and U.S. trade representative. Wriston did not accept these posts but continued as an active member of GE's board.[19]

**Charls Walker**, a prominent GE lobbyist, was a former deputy secretary of the treasury, and chief tax advisor to Reagan.[20] Walker is also a founder of the pro-military Committee on the Present Danger. Currently he sits on the CPD's board along with Reagan. When Reagan became president in 1981, he appointed 31 CPD members to his administration.[21]

GE has reaped many benefits from the pro-military and pro-business climate of the Reagan years. Increased weapons contracts are a prime example. A more subtle benefit is that GE pays less corporate taxes. In 1980, GE paid $330 million in taxes.[22] After the Tax Reform Act of 1981, instead of paying taxes GE received a $283 million refund from the government on profits of $6.5 billion from 1981 to 1983.[23]

GE, the company that "pioneered selling whole ways of life," sold the electrical life by building Reagan an all-electric home. Again with the help of Reagan, GE continues to sell the permanent war economy and the nuclear arms race.

# Business and Policy Groups

## 4

*The CEO can always get a hearing: busy politicians and bureaucrats will juggle their appointment books to see the head of General Motors or of IBM. Today Reginald Jones of GE, Shapiro [of Du Pont], and some of the others can and do practice the politics of persuasion on the highest levels of government. Frequently they meet with the President.*[1]

## Key Business and Policy-Making Organizations

The business community plays an important role in creating the environment in which government decisions are made. GE's influence extends through many channels in the business community, including key business and policy-making organizations. These groups, like the Business Council, the Business Roundtable, and the Council on Foreign Relations, bring together some of the nation's most powerful individuals from both the business and government spheres. The activities of these groups are enhanced by the special weight of the country's corporate leaders and their personal connections with top policy makers, not to mention their huge financial resources. Business groups provide an environment in which discussions between corporate leaders and government leaders can occur away from the public eye, discussions which set the policy-making wheels in motion. By pooling their resources, these corporate heads can change the direction of new legislation through their lobbying efforts.

General Electric's active participation in these business groups provides the company with another important link to government decision making. This chapter outlines three of the most influential groups and discusses GE's role in them.

### The Business Council

Founded: 1933.
Members: 220.
Staff: 3.

Business executives. "Dedicated to service in the national interest, with the primary objective of developing a constructive point of view on matters of public policy affecting the business interests of the country and to provide a medium for a better understanding of government problems by business." Members are former and present presidents or chairs of corporations.[2]

The Business Council is a private group of business executives who advise most departments of the government, including the Department of Defense. It hails back to the 1930s when it was known as the Business Advisory Council (BAC), an official governmental advisory group to the Department of Commerce (although its concerns spread into other areas such as those of the Department of State). The BAC's membership drew heavily from the realm of large corporations, usually company presidents or chairs. The Council met six times a year behind closed doors in a variety of locations, including Pebble Beach, California; Sea Island, Georgia; and Hot Springs, Virginia. Here national policy issues were discussed with high-ranking government officials who had been invited to speak; some sessions covered issues involving confidential government information. The BAC would prepare reports for the Department of Commerce on various public policy issues, including anti-trust policy, foreign trade, and monetary policy. Most of these reports were not made public.[3]

This air of secrecy surrounding its activities made the BAC controversial in the rare instances that public attention was focused on it. In 1961, this secrecy prompted Secretary of Commerce Luther H. Hodges to pressure the BAC to open up its meetings to reporters and to be less exclusive in its membership.[4]

Pressure for reform also came as a result of a 1961 scandal in which General Electric was indicted for price fixing in the electrical industry.[5] At this time, Ralph Cordiner, the CEO of GE, was chair of the Business Advisory Council. The publicity surrounding the scandal helped pass new legislation calling for advisory committees to keep minutes of their meetings and open their meetings to reporters. However, such openness was too much for the Council. In 1961, the BAC severed its official ties with the government, shortened its name to the Business Council, and moved its office out of the Department of Commerce.[6]

## The Business Council Today

"Members meet three times a year to discuss public policy and economic issues with top officials of government...."— *The Business Council*, 1987[7]

The workings of the Business Council have not changed much from its earlier days. It is still a secretive group. Top business leaders continue to dominate its ranks and provide its funding, and the Council still has the same access to government. The Business Council is one of the few corporate organizations that meets regularly with high-ranking government officials, and many of its members are close to recent U.S. presidents. President Reagan has addressed the Council on several occasions.

The climate created by the Business Council for business-government interaction influences our nation's policies. The Business Council has often played a role in supplying people to serve in government positions. Two examples have involved GE executives: former GE director Robert T. Stevens served as Secretary of the Army from 1953 to 1955 directly after chairing the BAC in 1951–1952; and former GE director and BAC Vice Chair Neil McElroy was Secretary of Defense from 1957–1959.[8]

The upper ranks of GE and its board have provided leaders of the Business Council since its founding. Gerard Swope, President of GE from 1922–1940, acted as the *first chair of the Business Council* in 1933. Presently, GE executives John F. Welch and Walter Wriston sit on the Business Council. Listed below are top GE executives who held key positions on the Business Council:[9]

| Executive | Position at GE | Position(s) at Council | Year(s) |
|---|---|---|---|
| Gerard Swope | President | Chair (BAC) | 1933 |
| Robert T. Stevens | Director | Chair (BAC) | 1951–52 |
| Phillip D. Reed | Chair | Vice Chair | 1951–52 |
| Ralph Cordiner | CEO | Chair | 1960 |
| Neil McElroy | Director | Vice Chair | 1965–66 |
| Ralph Lazarus | Director | Vice Chair | 1967–68 |
| Fred Borch | Chair/CEO | Chair | 1969–70 |
| Walter Wriston | Director | Vice Chair | 1973–74 |
| Edmund Littlefield | Director | Chair | 1975–76 |
| Reginald Jones | Chair/CEO | Chair | 1979 |
| John Welch, Jr. | Chair/CEO | Vice Chair | 1987 |

## The Business Roundtable

"Its membership roster reads like a 'Who's Who' of the Fortune 500... If all the members of the Roundtable were to be combined into a separate nation they would have a gross national product second only to that of the United States."[10]

Founded: 1972.
Members: 160.
Staff: 16.

Major U.S. corporations represented by their chief executive officers. An "influential lobbying force" representing the views of American business. Members examine public issues that affect the economy and develop positions that seek to reflect sound economic and social principles. Maintains 11 task forces. Conducts extensive research, often drawing on the staffs of member companies for talent and expertise.[11]

The Business Roundtable, most of whose members also belong to the Business Council, is one of the most powerful lobbying forces in DC. It was formed in 1972 by a merger of three smaller business groups. In contrast to the Business Council, the Business Roundtable lobbies Congress and only allows current chief executive officers into its membership.

The relationship between the Business Council and the Roundtable was summed up by Irving S. Shapiro, chair of the Du Pont Corporation and former chair of the Roundtable: "The Roundtable is only for chief executive officers. Once I'm through with that I am out. There's a counterpart to the Roundtable... that's the Business Council.... It is not an advocacy organization. It simply deals with public issues. The Roundtable was created to have an advocacy organization... (not by) the Business Council, but by the same people. I am a member of the Council and will stay with that. People who are retired stay with it the rest of their lives if they choose to."[12]

The Roundtable presently boasts CEOs of roughly 150 major corporations, each of which pays from $10,000 to $35,000 in annual dues, providing a annual budget of approximately $2 million.[13] The Roundtable was founded on two unique premises: that chief executives would themselves lobby in Washington, and that the group would focus on large public policy matters and not narrow business interests.[14]

As such, the Roundtable enjoys an influence out of proportion to its relatively small size. "By far the most successful lobby in Washington on economic policy these days," says the *New York Times*, "the group backs up its views on Federal policies with the jobs and votes of the country's largest corporations."[15]

Members of the Business Roundtable put a lot of time and energy into working against legislation that they believe threatens their profits. They have been responsible for stopping the Consumer Protection Agency proposed during both the Ford and Carter administrations. They have also fought hard to weaken anti-trust legislation.[16]

Although the Roundtable has hired a number of high-powered lobbyists, most of its clout derives from bringing CEOs directly to Washington. Reginald Jones—John Welch, Jr.'s predecessor as chief executive officer of GE, and a firm believer in getting big business involved in the nation's internal affairs—was a key figure in establishing the Business Roundtable in 1972. To his business colleagues Jones urged

Business executives must participate personally in

the formation of public policy...This is an unavoidable responsibility of business leadership today, for companies large and small.[17]

Reginald Jones is listed in 1987 as an Honorary Member of the Roundtable's Policy Committee. Jones's predecessor as CEO of GE, Fred Borch, served as the Business Roundtable's Chair. Borch, in fact, was one of the founders of the Roundtable. He chaired the March Group, a group of CEOs of major American firms. The March Group under Borch merged with two other big-business advocacy groups to form the Business Roundtable in 1972.[18]

Jack Welch is not only a member of the Business Roundtable but he also sits on its Policy Committee, along with GE board member Andrew Sigler and Welch's predecessor at GE, Reginald Jones. The Policy Committee reviews all activities of the task forces and committees of the Roundtable.[19]

## Council on Foreign Relations (CFR)

"...their deliberations often reach the highest levels of government via the considerable connections of the participants in these sessions." — *New York Times*[20]

Founded: 1921.
Members: 2,376.
Staff: 95.
Local Groups: 38.

Individuals with specialized knowledge of and interest in international affairs. Purpose is to study the international aspects of American political, economic and strategic problems. Research projects are carried out by professional staff advised by study groups of selected statesmen, business leaders and academic experts.[21]

Founded in 1921, the CFR is known as one of the most important foreign-policy groups in the United States. Most of its 2,300 members are executives, lawyers, and financiers who represent the largest banks and corporations in the country. The CFR headquarters has been a gathering place for some of the most influential policy makers in the U.S.: secretaries of state, CIA directors, newspaper editors, and corporate executives. GE is a major funder of the CFR, as is the J.P. Morgan and Co. with its vast GE stockholdings.[22]

The CFR sponsors discussion groups and conferences on foreign and domestic topics, which in the past have set the direction of U.S. foreign policy. For example, in 1957–58 the CFR published *Nuclear Weapons and Foreign Policy*, a report by Henry Kissinger who had been asked to lead a CFR study group. Kissinger's study group included senior officials from the State Department, the CIA, and the three armed forces. It also included two former chairpersons of the Atomic Energy Commission.[23] The report greatly influenced the Kennedy Administration.

Among the criteria for being a CFR member in 1921, besides being male and American, was the ability to abide by a code of "confidentiality": a member could be expelled for publicly disclosing anything said at a Council meeting.[24] This is a curious code, considering the impact exerted on foreign policy by the Council on Foreign Relations:

- The Stimson Committee, which recommended the use of the atomic bomb against Hiroshima and Nagasaki, drew its membership heavily from CFR membership.[25]
- The idea for the World Bank, International Monetary Fund and the United Nations along with much of the post-war planning came from a CFR study project.[26]
- It was the CFR that planned the framework for an integrated world economy revolving around the U.S. And they also first stressed the need to protect U.S. interests overseas — which were often identical to the personal financial interests of CFR members.[27]
- It was also a series of CFR study groups that stressed the need to "defend" Vietnam. The CFR's role in formulating America's disastrous Vietnam policy actually eroded CFR's influence at the time.[28]

However, the CFR's influence is still very much alive today, along with its exclusive membership and its role in supplying officials for government agencies:

- All but one of the secretaries of state since John Foster Dulles have been CFR members, including Dean Rusk, Cyrus Vance, Edmund Muskie, Henry Kissinger, and Alexander Haig.[29]
- Almost all CIA chiefs have been former Council members, including Richard Helms, William Colby, George Bush, and William Casey. Allen W. Dulles, former director of the Council on Foreign Relations, helped establish the CIA and served as its director.
- Many U.S. presidents and vice presidents have been CFR members.[30]

Many of GE's chief executive officers have participated actively in the Council of Foreign Relations ranks: Gerard Swope, Fred J. Borch, Reginald Jones, and John Welch, Jr. Former GE board members who have belonged to the CFR include Neil H. McElroy and Thomas Gates (both ex-secretaries of defense), Ralph Lazarus, and Charls Walker. Walter Wriston, Lewis Preston, and Thornton Bradshaw, present GE board members, were listed as CFR directors in 1986-87. Preston also served as chair of the Executive Committee and chair of the Development Committee, and both Preston and Wriston were on the Finance and Budget Committee.[31] Fred Borch, a founder of the Business Council, entered the CFR in 1967. Former GE President Charles A. Coffin was a founding member of the CFR in 1922.[32]

GE director David C. Jones, the retired chair of the Joint Chiefs of Staff and a CFR member, appeared with former Secretary of Defense Harold Brown as the main speaker at a CFR general meeting in May 1987. The topic of the meeting was "The Effects of Soviet and U.S. Political Situations on Arms Control." Many other CFR events and discussion groups during 1987 have focused on similar topics, such as "Military Force Projection: Its Current and Future Role in U.S. National Security Strategy," "Salt II: Help or Hindrance to American Security?" and "Force Mobility: the Key to Deterrence."[33]

The Council on Foreign Relations is one of the most influential policy-shaping organizations in Washington, and GE has maintained an active membership in the group since its founding.

## Other Policy-Making and Professional Groups

General Electric directors and executives are affiliated with a host of business and policy organizations beyond the three profiled above. These include

- The *Conference Board* and the *Committee for Economic Development*: like the Business Council and Roundtable, these are general-interest business lobbying/research groups.

- The *Rand Corporation* and *American Enterprise Institute*: these "think tanks" or research groups provide more detailed information and analyses to the government and to the active lobbying groups. They are heavily supported financially by large corporations, and GE directors and other corporate officials serve on their boards of trustees. Both are noted, in varying degrees depending on the issue at hand, for a conservative political orientation. GE board member Gertrude Michelson is a trustee of the Rand Corporation.[34]

- *The National Academy of Engineering*: this professional association does not usually show up on lists of important policy bodies, but GE's profits depend heavily on engineering advances, and three top GE officials—John Welch, Edward Hood, and GE Chief Scientist Roland Schmitt—are members of the NAE. Welch, in fact, was elected in 1986 as chair of the NAE's Council, a governing body created in 1982 to provide more input from industrial corporations. The NAE was founded in 1964 as a scientific academy associated with the National Academy of Sciences. Increasingly, it is involving itself in public policy on technological issues. According to *Chemical and Electrical News*, as chair "Welch ... likely [would] provide a powerful boost to NAE's bid to become the focus of technology policy development in the U.S."[35]

What about GE itself? It belongs, as a corporation, to the following groups,[36] which include some of the strongest corporate lobbying forces in Washington.

*General Business Organization*
Chamber of Commerce of the U.S.
National Assn. of Manufacturers
Business Roundtable

*Weapons/Aircraft*
Aerospace Industries Assn.
Air Force Association
American Helicopter Society
American Defense Preparedness Assn.
National Security Industries Assn.
Old Crows (or Electronic Warfare Assn.)

*Nuclear Power*
American Nuclear Energy Council
Atomic Industrial Forum
American Nuclear Society
The U.S. Committee for Energy Awareness

*Electronics*
National Electrical Manufacturer Assn.
Electronic Industries Assn.
American Electronics Assn.

*Exports*
Council of the Americas
The Business Group on the Export Administration Act
The Coalition for Employment through Exports

*Taxes/Finance*
The Carlton Group
American Council for Capital Formation
Tax Foundation
American Financial Services Assn.
American Equipment Leasing Assn.

*Medical Equipment*
Health Industries Manufacturing Assn.

## Conclusion

The business community often creates the climate in which government decisions are made. Actually, it is difficult to draw a clear line between government and business because they are intertwined in so many ways. Many government officials come from the big business community and return to it after office. The close connections that have been fostered between the various branches of government and the business community make it hard to distinguish between business groups' giving advice and helping to direct the nation's policies.

GE's size alone as the nation's third largest corporation gives it great influence with the highest government officials. But by being at the center of the business community and the business power network for over 40 years, GE has that much more power to shape public policy in its own favor.

## 5

# Influential Social Ties

Imagine, if you can, Ronald Reagan, George Shultz, George Bush, and Jack Welch of GE looking on as an assembly of priests, elders, acolytes, and torch bearers burn an effigy before a sculpted owl forty feet tall. Stretching the imagination a little, picture a corporate lawyer dressed in a body stocking and wings, playing the role of a wood nymph.

Well, stretch your imagination no further. Scenes like these occur at the Bohemian Grove encampment in California, an exclusive summer camp that brings together our country's political and corporate leaders for a good bit of carefree fun and hobnobbing. But when Ronald Reagan and his cabinet members are camping out in the woods with Jack Welch or Edward Hood of GE, or the presidents of General Dynamics, United Airlines, Bechtel Corporation, Dart Industries, Westinghouse, and the Morgan Guaranty Trust, it suggests an exclusive gathering of the powers that run the United States.

Such clubs are places where these men (and very rarely women) can spend time together away from public scrutiny, with no regulations or guidelines on what topics are discussed.

This atmosphere is perfect for creating bonds between government and corporate leaders. We can learn a little about how these social bonds are formed by looking at the Bohemian Club and GE's involvement in it.

## Bohemian Club and Grove

As its name implies, the Bohemian Club was founded in 1872 in San Francisco by struggling artists and journalists as a counterweight to the elite men's clubs of the day. Its membership policy actually excluded the wealthy. Ironically, wealthy businessmen soon took the club over because they were the only ones who could afford to run it.[1] The San Francisco headquarters of the club has evolved since then into a typical exclusive businessmen's club.

What really sets the Bohemian Club apart is its annual two-week summer encampment in Bohemian Grove, the Club's wooded 2,700-acre retreat near Santa Rosa in northern California. During the encampment, executives from this country's largest corporations along with politicians such as Ronald Reagan, Henry Kissinger, Caspar Weinberger, and their peers live in small, modest camps scattered in the redwood trees. These 130 or so camps are like small fraternity houses, each bearing a distinctive name like "Moonshiners" or "Toyland," and each distinguished from the others by some trait or ritual.

The encampment is inaugurated in a bizarre ceremony called the "Cremation of Care." In this ceremony, red-robed "priests" burn an effigy of "Dull Care," representing the day-to-day duties of the campers, before a statue of an owl (the Club symbol). This is the ceremony described at the beginning of the section.

The men who attend the encampment are forbidden to bring briefcases or official papers, but they don't give up their roles as leaders. Prominent men give daily "lakeside talks" on current issues. Many historical events are said to have started at the Grove, including the decision to build the atomic bomb in 1942[2] and Richard Nixon's political rehabilitation in 1967[3]. In an article published in January of 1981, William Domhoff, a sociologist who has extensively studied the role of social clubs in American society, correctly predicted that several of Ronald Reagan's friends from the Bohemian Grove—George Shultz and William French Smith—would be appointed to his presidential cabinet.[4]

"Looks like those guys at Bohemian Grove went too far this time with their cremation of dull care."

Government connections are not the only links to be promoted at the Grove. According to a 1970 study done by Domhoff, the directors or officers of 40 of the 50 largest industrial corporations in America were at the Grove as members or guests. Of the top 25 corporations, only two were missing. Twenty of the top 25 commercial banks were also represented.[5] In 1980–81, 326 members of the Bohemian Club were listed in *Who's Who in America*.[6]

GE has been well represented at the Grove. David C. Jones, a GE board member and ex-chair of the Joint Chiefs of Staff, is a member of Dog House camp. GE director William French Smith and former director Edmund W. Littlefield—along with George Shultz, Gerald Ford, and Henry Kissinger—belong to the Mandalay camp.[7] Mandalay's membership is so powerful and exclusive that one member commented, "You don't just walk in there...you are summoned."[8] Jack Welch and his predecessor Reginald Jones have both been guests at Mandalay. Other guests at the Grove have included GE directors Edward Hood, Andrew Sigler, and Walter Wriston.

## The Ultimate Networking

In today's world, you often hear that to get a good job or to get ahead, you need to network. This advice comes from seeing the success men have had in the "old boys' network." These exclusive social clubs are the ultimate method of networking. They provide one of the foundations of the "old boys' network."

The Bohemian is just one club among a network of high-powered social clubs. Most of these clubs are much less conspicuous business or country clubs such as the Links Club, the Augusta National Golf Club, and the Duquesne Club. They each provide their own unique environments, traditions, and events where the members can socialize. William Domhoff, as a result of his study of these social clubs, believes that they serve to strengthen the cohesiveness of an elite class in our country.

The ties of corporate leaders to these clubs were outlined in another study by Domhoff published in the 1970s. He examined the membership lists of clubs listed in *Who's Who in America* for chairs and directors of the 20 largest industrial corporations. Domhoff found that GE was one of the best-represented companies among members of

these clubs. GE's board had 21 connections to eight of the 11 clubs examined.[9] The Links Club, once called "the New York rendezvous of the national corporate establishment," was most heavily represented at GE, which had seven of its directors as members.[10]

Currently, GE continues to be well connected to these exclusive social clubs. In 1987, GE board members had connections to at least 20 business clubs, including three connections to the Links Club and three to the Economic Club. Both of these New York clubs have members from all over the country. Many board members also belong to local clubs such as the Chicago Club and the Duquesne Club in Pittsburgh.[11]

These clubs are a place to have private lunches or dinners. They are a place for introductions to the right people and a place where connections and trust are built. Deals may be begun or policy and strategies discussed. These clubs provide a place to have all of these talks and meetings out of the public eye.

Golf and country clubs are a key type of social club. These are places people go to relax and get away. Yet, there is nothing like spending a few hours on the golf course or a long weekend at the Augusta National Golf Club to get to know people, make critical connections, or find out valuable information all in an informal setting.

Two GE board members, Henry Henley and Henry Hillman, belong to the Augusta National Golf Club, one of the most exclusive in the country. Other well-known golf clubs patronized by GE board members include the Blind Brook Club and the Fox Chapel Golf Club.[12]

In October 1987, while speaking to students at the Harvard Business School, Jack Welch was asked if he still had time for sports since becoming CEO of GE. He replied that yes, he still has time to play golf, and in fact now plays on much better courses—undoubtedly referring to some of the exclusive clubs mentioned here.[13]

Whether politicians and corporate leaders actually plan national policies on the golf course, or whether they just make friends with each other, the club environment strengthens the bonds between government and business in ways that can translate into both policies and contracts later.

# GE: Leader in the Military-Industrial Complex

**6**

Nuclear weapons decision making and policy setting is a complicated and multi-faceted process involving the Pentagon, the administration, the Congress, the American public, and the formerly well-hidden weapons industry. Most people believe that decisions about nuclear weapons are made only by the Pentagon, or by public officials who have some accountability to the people. Only recently is the deeply embedded influence of the nuclear weapons industry coming to the public's attention.

The following chapters examine in detail how it is that the industry, and most particularly General Electric, ensures that more nuclear weapons are built—and that more money flows into their corporate coffers. In simplified form, the role of the corporations in the decision-making system works like this:

- The corporations *develop* the idea for complicated, deadly, and expensive weapons—and also begin to develop the necessary technology.
- Then they help create the "climate" that will accept the need for more nuclear weapons—both among the general public and with the government.

- Simultaneously, the corporations will develop and advocate the necessary military strategy and national policy to support and legitimate the new weapon system—a threat has to be found to justify the system; or some change needs to occur in existing policy to accommodate the new idea.
- While creating the climate and advocating policy changes, the corporations must also ensure access to key government decision makers in both the legislative and executive branches.
- And finally, the corporations secure their business investment through the procurement process—selling nuclear weapons as if they were ordinary household products.

Of course, this system does not necessarily work in a linear fashion. The different parts all interact, shape, and influence each other in a closed system that operates outside of public accountability; a closed system that makes it very difficult to examine and choose alternative national security policies.

# Research and Development: Bringing New Weapons to Life

7

> *We'd like to think that the government first orders what it needs to defend the country and then the companies build it. But all too often it is the dollar that leads us into developing a new weapon and then we just have to look around for a threat to justify it.*
> —Retired Admiral Gene R. La Rocque[1]

As the first and formative stage in nuclear weapons production, the research and development (R & D) of new weapon systems plays a critical role. This stage determines the nature of future weapons and impacts the formulation of nuclear weapons policy. We generally assume that the government sets priorities on research and development projects according to the nation's defense needs. Often, however, it is General Electric and other nuclear weaponmakers that take the initiative for researching and developing new weapon systems. Corporations like GE set the pace in defining new weapons and new weapon strategies long before the general public and most members of Congress are even aware of them.

There are two types of weapons R & D funded by the government:

**1.** R & D contracts are awarded by the Department of Defense (DOD), the National Aeronautics and Space Administration (NASA), and the Department of Energy (DOE) to corporations in order to develop technologies for those government agencies.

**2.** Independent R & D (IR&D):

> One defense program in particular provides contractors with assistance in shaping new weapons systems—independent research and development (IR&D). Through this program, the Pentagon reimburses companies for a portion of the cost of research and development efforts that the companies both initiate and control. The reimbursement is negotiated between each contractor and the Defense Department...IR&D assists companies in pursuing whatever projects they feel are worthy...IR&D reimbursements are not contingent on the government using resulting technologies.[2]

## GE's Research and Development

In fiscal year 1986, GE received the third largest amount of government R & D contracts from the Department of

Defense: $924 million.[3] This figure, a $39 million increase from the year before, does not even include R & D money from the DOE or NASA.[4]

GE has used much of this money to develop technologies with first-strike capabilities, serving to make the global military environment even more unstable. GE has played a leading role in researching and developing Trident I and II missile components, Minuteman III missile components, and the "Stealth" radar-escaping long-range bomber.[5] Since the late 1970s, GE has been developing the Defense Satellite Communications System III (DSCS III), a system of "survivable" communications satellites of the type that are pivotal to strategies for fighting a protracted nuclear war.[6]

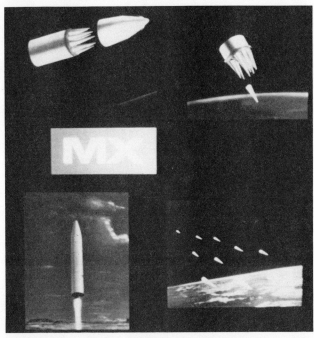

An example of an MIRV on an MX unloading its "passengers," nuclear bombs.
Source: Center for Defense Information.

The ability to destroy Soviet missile silos and command posts before an attack is launched against the U.S. (termed a first-strike capability) came with the technology of re-entry vehicles (RVs) and Multiple Independently targeted Re-entry Vehicles (MIRVs). These are "buses" which carry nuclear warheads through space and drastically increase the numbers, accuracy, and explosive power of warheads per missile.[7] GE developed the first re-entry vehicle, the Mark I. GE's Space Division/Re-entry Systems Operations, located in Philadelphia, Pennsylvania, developed the Mark 12 RVs for Minuteman III missiles.[8]

GE has also increased its R & D contracts in Star Wars. It has established a separate Star Wars division at Valley Forge, Pennsylvania. GE has received at least $465.9 million in Star Wars contracts from 1983 through 1986.[9]

## Corporations Setting the Pace for New Weapons

The day is past when the military requirement for a major weapons system is set up by the military and passed on to industry to build the hardware. Today it is more likely that the military requirement is the result of joint participation of military and industrial personnel, and it is not unusual for industry's contribution to be a key factor. Indeed, there are highly placed military men who sincerely feel that industry currently is setting the pace in the research and development of new weapons systems.

— Peter Schenck of the Raytheon Corporation and former president of the Air Force Association[10]

There is an increasing trend in Pentagon research and development for companies like GE to independently develop weapons in anticipation of government R & D funding. The hope is to make these weapons "desirable" to the buyers for further development. This is what prompts independent research and development. Once development on a weapon has begun, the momentum is created to further develop and produce it. It is easier to show the "need" for a weapon once it is already in existence. So IR&D projects often develop into increased R & D projects funded by the Pentagon. Corporate pace setting through independent research and development is encouraged by the fact that roughly $1 billion of public money is used each year to reimburse companies for their IR&D work as well as to cover expenses companies incur preparing proposals for government contracts.[11]

This Pentagon reimbursement of independent research avoids public notice and is rarely examined by congressional committees. Yet these early IR & D programs can develop into large and expensive weapons programs, such as Star Wars, the Cruise missile, and the Trident programs. The development of these programs has its own implications for our country's military and diplomatic policies. Even when these projects develop into full R & D contracts, it is only the most developed projects that are overseen by the congressional committees responsible for military R & D projects.[12]

It is also traditional for the Pentagon to use GE and other corporations that stand to profit from building a weapons system as the main source for information on the system's feasibility and estimated development costs. This is what happened with the Star Wars program where ten corporations, including GE, were awarded $1 million each to provide reports on the feasibility of a Star Wars system.[13] This information is crucial in influencing decisions on whether or not to further develop and produce a weapon. Corporations that are likely to make billions of dollars on this project are unlikely to provide impartial information on the weapon's potential.

### More R & D = More Defense Dollars

The importance that GE places on R & D can be seen in the fact that in fiscal year 1986 the company spent $3.3 billion for R & D. Of that total, $1.3 billion came from GE's own funds.[14]

Without having to work under the scrutiny of the public and Congress, GE can develop new weapons. If approved for further government R & D or production, this turns into more contracts for GE. Contracts for a new weapons sys-

```
WORK
-------------------------------------------------------
SP-100 Space Nuclear Reactor, Phase II, Technology Flight Readiness
SP-100 Space Nuclear Reactor, Phase II, Technology Flight Readiness
National Aerospace Plane propulsion/scramjet module conceptual des(1of2
GREMLIN (G-Resistant ElectroMagnetic Launched Interceptor)Des&Dev(1of3
Radiation hardened VLSI component technology (1 of 4)
BSTS (Boost Surveillance & Tracking System) requirement def (1 of4)
Exo EML projectile subsystem integration fire control/guidance (1of5)
SMATH II demonstration of components (1 of 2)
Advanced space systems hardness
SBKEW Fire Control Technology Demonstration / Research & Data (1 of 3)
SP-100 Space Reactor - Phase I - Thermo-electric Fast Spectrum
Advanced switch technology (1 of 3)
Hardened MMW antenna window systems for Endo & Exo interceptors
Multimegawatt power system architecture, conventional & nuclear (1of3)
Advanced barrel technology (1 of 3)
Large aperture radar sensor technology study - 5 (1 of 6)
Integrated test system/environment
Multi-shot Electromagnetic Gun Test Fixture (1 of 2)
Generic VHSIC space components (1 of 4)
Electrical performance of the ENNK cooled metallic radome-Phase II
Novel materials for high power switches electronics & optical systems
High Altitude Active/Semiactive Seeker concept definition (1 of 3)
SDI space based power needs and generating systems (1 of 6)
G-Range Electromagnetic launcher & homopolar generator power supply
Integrated Blade Inspection System A
V-Band low noise transistor and
EMA (Electromagnetic Accelerator) end design and utility analysis
X-ray flourescence
Rapid surfacing//CBN/diamond tool science (1 of 7)
NELS II operation and evaluation (1 of 2)
Electrical performance of the ENNK cooled metallic radome Phase I
High power IHP MESFET
HPM hardening development
Effects of laser radiation
Space-based KEW Sensor Suite Definition (1 of 2)
Unspecified SDI funding
Space laser damage assessment methods
Signature measurement radar operation at Kwajalein Missile Range
Trailblazer II hypervelocity launcher experiment (T2E) (1 of 3)
RADC surveillance lab support
Ribbon printer
National Test Bed Concept Definition (1 of 4)
SDI Systems Architecture Phase II (1 of 5)
Theater architecture for European ATBMs - proposal to Army SDC
LEDI - proposes hypervelocity endo-atmospheric guided EMI projectile
SDI Systems Architecture Phase II (1 of 5)
Laser imager component development
Theater architecture for European ATBMs - proposal to Army SDC
New rail coatings and rail insulator materials for EMLs
```

Examples of GE's Star Wars contracts, fiscal years 1983–86.
Source: Council on Economic Priorities.

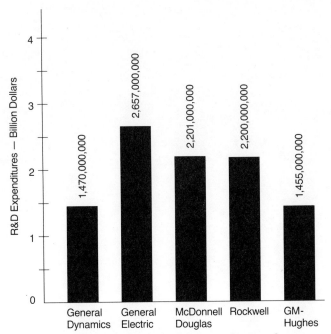

Source: Figures from *Top Guns* by Philip J. Simon, Common Cause, 1987.

**Figure 5.** Top Five Weaponmakers DOD R & D Awards, 1984–1986

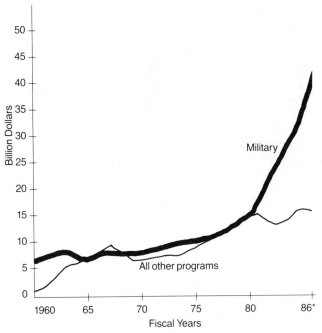

*1986 represents budget authority; preliminary estimates by the National Science Foundation.

Source: *World Military and Social Expenditures 1986* by Ruth Leger Sivard.

**Figure 6.** U.S. Government Spending for Research and Development

tem often go to the corporation that has done the R & D work on it.

It is also interesting to note that in fiscal year 1986, 36 percent of the total dollars awarded by the Pentagon for R & D went to the top 10 military contractors.[15] Aggressive lobbying efforts are helping to keep R & D money and the potential for more weapons contracts in a few select hands.

## R & D for a Better Future?

Increased military R & D also helps redirect our country's economic and scientific resources into the military and away from human needs. U.S. government expenditures for R & D were approximately $5.8 billion in 1987. Seventy-one percent of that was devoted to military R & D, with the lion's share going for weapons. This figure has tripled in the past decade.[16] The other 29 percent of the budget included space research and technology and energy research, both of which have military applications. More and more contracts are also going to universities to do military research.

## Conclusion

The U.S. cannot afford to misdirect scientific and economic resources at a time when the country is quickly dropping behind in the global market for nonmilitary technology. Our world cannot afford this scientific brain drain in a global environment where scientific knowledge sorely needs to be applied to solving problems of human suffering. Despite this human need, the pace is stepped up to develop and build more and more dangerously destabilizing weapons at tremendous human and economic cost.

In order to understand and change the direction our country is taking, we must continue to examine how military research and development sets the pace in weapons development and, as such, impacts the military, social, and economic direction of the nation. That responsibility should not rest in the hands of those who profit in the short term from weapons development.

**Bringing GE to Light**

# Creating the Climate

## 8

*We made up the bomber gap, the missile gap and many other gaps, and by the time Congress found out our figures were phony—that we were actually ahead of the Russians in those areas—it was too late. We already had the new bombers and missiles built.*
— Retired Admiral Gene R. La Rocque[1]

## Whipping Up Hysteria

During the "Bomber Gap" scare of 1958, some members of the Council on Foreign Relations urged President Eisenhower to launch a "preemptive" atomic strike against the Soviet Union. Eisenhower believed that the council members were wildly overestimating the Soviet threat, and he suspected the weapons contractors of deliberately helping to alarm the public.[2]

Unfortunately, this scare tactic by weaponmakers is still used—on the general public and on the government—to justify huge budget allocations for more and more nuclear weapons. Anti-Soviet hysteria is not the only tool weaponmakers use to keep the money coming. Slick advertising enhances the image of the U.S. military, whose effectiveness is tied to the fortunes of the weaponmaking corporations. Weaponmakers also deliberately mislead the public and the government about arms control issues while also encouraging cold war attitudes towards the Soviets.

In February 1987, a *New York Times* article expressed some disbelief at a new report from the Joint Chiefs of Staff. The report concluded that the Soviet Union is "moving significantly ahead" in the technology required to make nuclear warheads, whereas last year, the Joint Chiefs reported the two sides "equal" in that regard.

The article went on to say, "What makes the switch particularly puzzling is that the Russians have not carried out any nuclear tests for more than 18 months, while the United States has conducted 26 tests in the same period."[3]

In fact, the U.S. has often taken the lead in spurring the arms race and developing new and more deadly technology. (See Figure 7.[4]) How, then, can the military-industrial complex make the claims it does about Soviet military strength, and why does the government allow itself and the public to be misled?

## Threat Inflation—Case Histories

**In the 1950s, it was the "Bomber Gap."**
*The fear was that the Russians would have 600–700 long-range bombers by 1960.*

What they actually had by then was 190. Throughout the life of the gap, the US apparently always had a superiority of at least 300 bombers.

**In the 1960s, the "Missile Gap."**
*The USSR was expected to have 500–1,000 intercontinental ballistic missiles by 1961.*

Later it developed that what they actually had then were 10.

**And the "ABM Gap."**
*The USSR was expected to have by the early 1970s 10,000 interceptors in a nationwide anti-ballistic missile (ABM) system.*

The actual count proved to be 64 interceptors and essentially a defense against bombers rather than missiles.

**In the 1970s, the "Hard-Target-Kill Gap."**
*New Soviet missiles, the SS-19 in particular, were judged accurate enough to destroy all US land-based missiles.*

Assessments in the 1980s found this unrealistic for several reasons; among them, the SS-19 was found to be less accurate than originally gauged by more than one-third.

**In the 1980s, the "Spending Gap."**
*An unrestrained growth in Soviet military spending, plus the presumed danger to the ICBMs, had opened a "window of vulnerability" in US defenses.*

A CIA re-assessment in 1983 showed that Soviet procurement had levelled off during 1977–81 and that the increase in overall spending was half earlier projections.

**And the "Laser Gap."**
*The USSR could deploy nuclear-powered X-ray lasers without further testing, while the US, behind in technology, required nuclear tests.*

In response to a congressional inquiry in 1986, the CIA stated that it did not believe the Russians could deploy the weapons without additional tests.

Source: *World Military and Social Expenditures 1986* by Ruth Leger Sivard.

**Figure 7.** Threat Inflation—Case Histories

## Companies Bid to Do Soviet Estimates

A March 1985 article in the *Boston Globe* entitled "Just How Much Do the Soviets Spend?" reveals this startling fact: *the CIA turns, not to its own analysts, but to U.S. weaponmakers to compute the costs of Soviet weapons.*

Companies compete for contracts to estimate the costs of the "Soviet counterparts" to U.S. contractors' weapons projects. For example, GE was awarded a contract to estimate the cost of Soviet aircraft engines—GE is a leading aircraft engine manufacturer for the U.S. Air Force.[5]

Weaponmakers have a vested interest in reporting exaggerated figures because the more money Congress thinks the Soviets are spending on their weapons, the more

money Congress will spend on U.S. weapons. Reports of increased Soviet military spending also influence the general public. If people believe the Soviets are spending more on their military, people's fear of the Soviets grows. This fear of the Soviet threat allows weaponmakers and the Pentagon to push for higher and higher levels of U.S. military spending.

U.S. military contractors, wildly inefficient at controlling their own spending, are dubious candidates for the job of estimating Soviet military spending. The *Globe* cites a

# ACTION   REACTION

## in the Nuclear Competition

The dynamics of the nuclear arms race ensure that development of a new weapons system by one power will in a relatively brief period be followed by a comparable achievement by the other. Both powers have had "firsts." Neither has stayed ahead for long. The US generally has a technological lead of several years, but the futility of the race for short-term advantage is demonstrated by a chronology of developments to date.

**US 1945  atomic bomb  1949 USSR**

The nuclear age began with the explosion of a US A-bomb of 12.5 kilotons (equivalent to 12,500 tons of TNT) over Hiroshima, Japan. The single bomb, which destroyed the city, introduced to the world a concentrated explosive force of unprecedented power. Within four years, the USSR conducted its first atomic test.

**US 1948  intercontinental bomber  1955 USSR**

By 1948, the US had begun to replace the propeller planes of World War II with long-range jets. The first planes developed for strategic (intercontinental) bombing required refueling to reach another continent. In 1955, the US began deployment of the all-jet intercontinental bomber, and the USSR soon followed suit.

**US 1954  hydrogen bomb  1955 USSR**

The H-Bomb multiplied the explosive force of the A-bomb 1,000 times. The first US thermonuclear bomb had a yield equivalent to 15,000,000 tons of TNT; a year later the USSR tested a bomb in the million-ton range.

**USSR 1957  intercontinental ballistic missile (ICBM)  1958 US**

Following intensive development by both nuclear powers, a land-based missile to carry nuclear warheads intercontinental distances was successfully flight-tested by the USSR in 1957, and by the US a year later. By 1962 both nations had ICBMs with a range of 6,000 miles, each missile able to carry a payload equivalent to 5–10,000,000 tons of TNT.

**USSR 1957  man-made satellite in orbit  1958 US**

Sputnik I by the USSR initiated a space race which quickly took on military functions; the first US satellite was launched into orbit the following year. Well over half the superpowers' satellites have been military; for surveillance, targeting communications, etc.

**US 1960  submarine-launched ballistic missile (SLBM)  1968 USSR**

A nuclear-powered submarine that could fire long-range missiles from a submerged position was the third means of strategic delivery. The US produced the nuclear-powered Polaris, with missiles with a range of 1,200 nautical miles. Eight years later the USSR had comparable nuclear subs.

**US 1966  multiple warhead (MRV)  1968 USSR**

Multiheaded missiles increased the number of targets a missile could hit. US MRV'd missiles carried three warheads each with sixteen times the explosive force of the Hiroshima bomb. The USSR had them two years later.

**USSR 1968  anti-ballistic missile (ABM)  1972 US**

The USSR deployed 64 defensive missiles around Moscow. The US began construction of the Safeguard system in 1969 and had one site complete when a treaty restricting ABMs was signed in 1972. Generally judged militarily ineffective, ABMs were restricted to one site in each country in 1974. Subsequently the US site was closed.

**US 1970  multiple independently-targeted warhead (MIRV)  1975 USSR**

Further development of multiple warheads enabled one missile to hit three to ten individually selected targets as far apart as 100 miles. The USSR began to flight-test MIRVs three years after the US put them in service and in 1975 began deployment.

**US 1982  long-range cruise missile  198? USSR**

Adaptable to launching from air, sea, and land, a new generation of missiles with a range up to 1,500 miles is in production. The cruise missile is small, relatively inexpensive, highly accurate, with the unique advantage of very low trajectory. Following the contours of the earth, and flying under radar, it will be able to destroy its target without warning. The US is reportedly 7–8 years in the lead in this technology.

**US 1983  neutron bomb  198? USSR**

This nuclear weapon releases its explosive energy more in the form of an invisible, penetrating bombardment of radiation rather than in heat and blast. The decision to produce and stockpile the enhanced radiation warhead in the US was announced in August 1981. The USSR promptly announced that it has the capability but had deferred a production decision.

**US 199?  anti-satellite weapons  199? USSR**

Because satellites play vital military roles, they have also inspired a search for weapons to destroy them. The USSR began testing interceptor satellites in 1968. Both superpowers are attempting to perfect lasers to destroy enemy satellites and nuclear missiles in the event of war.

Source: *Basic Facts on the Nuclear Age,* New Century Policies.

**Figure 8.** Action/Reaction in the Nuclear Competition

Pentagon cost analysis as an example: "Hughes Aircraft produces some of its missiles and electronics so inefficiently that if it were to make $400 color televisions in the same way, it would charge consumers $100,000 for each set."[6]

## Committee on the Present Danger

"The [CPD] study...is titled, 'Can America Catch Up? The U.S.-Soviet Military Balance.' And the answer to that question is 'Yes, we can catch up, but not at the present and projected rate of increase in the overall defense effort.' "—Max M. Kampelman, CPD founding board member.[7]

Increased military spending is promoted very directly by the Committee on the Present Danger (CPD), one of the most influential organizations affecting policies of the Reagan Administration. The committee, whose membership includes many high-ranking officials in the Reagan administration, publishes policy statements and conducts public information campaigns on military issues to warn policy makers and the public of the "growing Soviet military strength" and the need to match it.[8]

Prominent on the committee since its 1976 inception have been two men whose firms are key to GE's Washington lobbying operation: Max M. Kampelman and Charls E. Walker.

## ALERTING AMERICA

### The Papers of the Committee on THE PRESENT DANGER

Edited by Charles Tyroler, II
Introduction by Max M. Kampelman

PERGAMON·BRASSEY'S

Max Kampelman, whose firm lobbied for GE, promotes the nuclear arms race.

Kampelman served as general counsel on the committee's founding board. It was he who developed the CPD's original articles and bylaws.[9] He also belonged to the law firm of Fried, Frank, Harris, Shriver, and Kampelman—a firm now retained by GE for lobbying purposes.[10] Still on the committee's board of directors, Kampelman is now Reagan's ambassador extraordinary and plenipotentiary for arms reduction negotiations in Geneva.[11]

Charls Walker, deputy treasurer under Nixon and a former member of Reagan's Economic Policy Advisory Board, heads the prestigious lobbying firm of Charls E. Walker Associates. Walker and his firm have lobbied for General Electric since 1973.[12] A founder of the CPD, Walker got the Committee off the ground in 1976 by raising its first operating funds. He continues to serve on the CPD's board of directors,[13] thus doubly promoting GE's interest in an increased arms buildup: both as a lobbyist and through his committee work.

President Reagan, himself on the committee's board, readily acknowledges the influence of the committee: "The work of the CPD has certainly helped to shape the national debate on important problems."[14] Members of his 1987 administration recruited from the CPD included: William Casey, CIA director; Paul Nitze, special representative for arms control and disarmament negotiations; Kenneth Adelman, director of the Arms Control and Disarmament Agency; Fred Charles Ikle, under secretary of defense for policy; John F. Lehman, Jr., secretary of the Navy; and George P. Shultz, secretary of state.[15] This means the Committee can affect U.S. military policy at the very highest levels of government.

Not satisfied to influence the policy makers, the committee also nurtures support for arms spending among the general public. One common CPD technique is the public opinion poll. The CPD often releases these polls to show strong public sentiment against the Soviets, against negotiating with the Soviets, and against U.S. reductions in weapons. The committee's questions are usually "loaded," or meant to provoke a certain answer.

One example is a "national, in-depth poll" entitled "U.S. Public Attitudes Toward Arms Control, INF [intermediate nuclear forces] and the Summit," which the CPD sponsored on the eve of the 1987 U.S.-Soviet Summit meetings. While even the CPD had to admit that there was strong support for an agreement to eliminate medium-range nuclear missiles in Europe (73 percent), the CPD proclaimed that "that support turns to strong opposition when the resulting agreement is seen to leave the Soviets with advantages in other nuclear and conventional forces."[16] Two of the questions that addressed this issue were:

Would you favor or oppose such an agreement if it left

the Soviets with an advantage in other nuclear weapons in Europe?

*and*

Would you favor or oppose such an agreement if it left the Soviets with an advantage in conventional forces in Europe?[17]

Another committee poll was "Public Attitudes Toward the U.S.-Soviet Military Balance, the Strategic Defense Initiative [Star Wars] and Central America," also taken in November 1987 to influence the outcome of the U.S.-Soviet Summit.[18] Playing on people's fear of a Soviet threat is bound to turn many against an agreement. A poll such as this can confuse the issue of whether or not people really do support an INF agreement or a summit, and can help cause the government to misunderstand the attitudes of the American people.

## Weapons Sales Job

> Of course, we do face real threats. But like commercial advertisers of dandruff shampoos or products to remove 'ring around the collar,' the advertisers play on the insecurities we all feel. —Retired Admiral Gene R. La Rocque[19]

The military trade journals target not the public but active and retired military personnel, government officials, and weapons industry management and employees. They are filled with stories of dedication and valor, awards and tributes, the latest in military technology, and more high estimates of Soviet military strength. The weaponmakers associate themselves with a tradition of bravery and dedication beyond duty and equate courage and strength with the newest and most expensive weapons systems the companies can devise. When the government shows any reluctance to commit huge amounts of money and resources to their newest porkbarrel projects, the companies claim that this is a "cavalier attitude" toward the military.

One of the most influential military magazines is *Aviation Week*. Read by many influential policy makers in the government, the military, and the weapons industry, it often acts as the industry's spokesperson to influence policy changes. It even helps shape public opinion through the general media. According to Tom Gervasi of the *Columbia Journalism Review*, "As a primary source of military information for the general press, it is more influential than some reporters will readily admit."[20]

The publisher of *Aviation Week*, James Pierce, says of the advertisements in the military press:

> Advertising is the way—virtually the only way—you can cover all the individuals from top to bottom, with influence on the decision....Advertising can be the *tie-breaker*.

Employees in the government are estimated to change jobs every two or three years. With advertising, you can keep making the same basic selling points to buyers as they play musical chairs.[21]

GE, as a leader in manufacturing aircraft engines for the military, consistently places ads in *Aviation Week* (often prominently displayed on the inside front cover) and in other trade journals.

If
it
flies,
floats,
beeps,
hovers,
orbits,
soars,
tracks
or
attacks...

its progress is
our most important product

GENERAL ⊛ ELECTRIC

Source: *The World of a Giant Corporation.*

An important magazine published by the Air Force Association (AFA), *Air Force Magazine,* also regularly carries GE ads, also often on the inside front cover. The magazine's 40th anniversary tribute to the Air Force carried a feature article, "At Risk in Space," which asserted that "Soviet prowess and a cavalier attitude at home endanger U.S. preeminence in space." Star Wars was featured prominently as vital to U.S. "preeminence in space."[22]

The AFA presents an annual award, the H. H. Arnold Award, for the "most outstanding contributions in the field of aerospace activity." The award is often presented to government officials or members of Congress, and is thus a good way to recognize and encourage the executive branch and Congress to cooperate with the aerospace industry. *The 1981 recipient was David Jones.* In 1983, *Ronald Reagan himself* received the award.[23]

## Not Patriotism—Profits

GE and others help create a public and governmental climate ripe for a nuclear weapons build-up and a permanent war ecomony. The weaponmakers use a convenient enemy, the Soviet Union, to create fear in the public and in the government. When the government buys the exaggerated Soviet threat, it will buy the weapons.

GE has powerful tools to create the fear it needs for its nuclear weapons market. A GE lobbyist sits alongside a U.S. president on a committee that fans the public's fears of the Soviets and writes policy on arms control and U.S.-Soviet relations. GE even helps the CIA estimate Soviet military spending. And as long as people think the Soviet military build-up is increasing, they are more willing to increase our own build-up.

GE sets up itself and its weapons as the bold response needed to counter the Soviet threat. GE's advertising ties the company to a proud military tradition and portrays GE as a guardian of our national security and a faithful servant of the government. Yet all the while, GE is turning its cry for patriotism and freedom into profits.

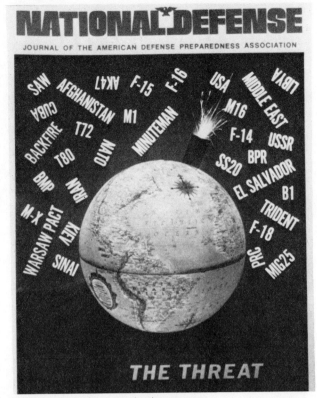

Promoting the threat, promoting the weapons.
Source: Center for Defense Information.

# PACs and Honoraria—
# Paying For Access

## 9

*As far as the general public is concerned, it is no longer 'we the people,' but PACs and the special interests they represent, who set the country's political agenda and control nearly every candidate's position on the important issues of the day.*
— Senator Barry Goldwater (R-AZ) in a 1985 debate on PACs.

*We cannot expect members of Congress to act in the national interest when their election campaigns are being financed more and more by special interests.*
— Senator David Boren (D-OK) in the same debate.[1]

General Electric's political action committee (PAC) is innocuously titled "The Non-Partisan Political Support Committee for General Electric Company Employees."[2] It is part of a growing trend over the past 10 years—a recognition by weaponmakers that they must work closely with Congress to influence legislation and ensure a steady stream of nuclear weapons contracts.

The Federal Election Campaign Act of 1974 set forth the guidelines on political action committees.[3] PACs raise money from individuals and then disburse that money to election campaigns. PACs are allowed to contribute up to $5,000 to any federal candidate in any one election. Generally, PAC dollars are given by special interest groups to gain preferential access and influence in Congress. Fred Wertheimer, president of Common Cause, comments:

> It's not a question of buying votes. It's a question of relationships that get built, obligations and dependencies that get established... [These] put PACs at the head of the line as opposed to the great bulk of a Congressperson's constituents.[4]

Corporations take the role of PAC contributions seriously. In 1976, soon after it became legal for corporations to form PACs, one-third of a representative's campaign spending, on average, was covered by PAC contributions. By 1978, that amount had risen to 38 percent, and by 1980, 45 percent of representatives' campaign spending was covered by PAC money. The percentage remained the same until 1984 when it rose sharply: *In 1984, PAC dollars constituted 59 percent of representatives' campaign spending.*[5]

The increase continued into the 1986 congressional elections when the top 10 Pentagon contractors, including GE, contributed a record $2.9 million to the candidates. The total PAC money in 1980 for those contractors was only

one-third that or $949,779.[6] In 1986, the top recipient of large contributions ($2,000 or more) of PAC money in the House was William Dickinson (R-AL), the minority leader of the House Armed Services Committee.[7]

In an era of growing military budgets, the top 10 weapons contractors contribute heavily to incumbents. In the 1986 congressional elections, these contractors gave 87 percent of their PAC money to incumbents running for re-election, compared with 70 percent of PAC dollars to incumbents from PACs overall. Weapons contractors target

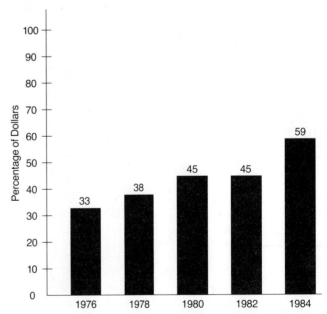

Source: Figures from *Top Guns* by Philip J. Simon, Common Cause, 1987.

**Figure 9.** Percentage of Campaign Spending Covered by PACs, 1976–1984

their contributions at incumbents who sit on key military-related committees and incumbents from districts or states with a large weapons-contractor presence. For example, in 1985–86, Boeing gave $31,525 in contributions to senators and representatives from Washington State, where most of Boeing's factories are located.[8]

The PAC's true role in influencing Congress is not in actually helping people get elected to Congress. While many members claim their votes are not for sale, PAC contributions gain special access for corporate lobbyists. Similar access is not available to peace, environmental, and other public interest lobbies that represent the less affluent general public.[9]

## GE's PAC Record

GE is one of the leading users of PAC contributions and other creative financial means to gain preferential access to Congress. To ensure access to Congress, in 1983–84 GE gave PAC money to 27 House incumbents who had no general election opponents and to 103 House incumbents who had no serious race (they won 70 percent or more of the vote). GE also contributed to every senator seeking re-election in 1984.[10]

Since GE was not trying to help its friends win election, what was the company's aim in making these contributions? Consider that close to two-thirds — 12 out of 18 — members of the Senate Armed Services Committee have received PAC money from GE.[11] Two-thirds of the members voting for a military spending bill is more than enough to get that bill passed out of committee.

GE's PAC contributions in 1979–80 were $133,875. In 1985-86, GE's contributions jumped to $243,100 — an increase of 82 percent.

For elections from 1980 through 1986, GE contributed to an average of 290 candidates in each election — consistently the highest number among the top 10 military contractors. From 1981 to 1986, no lawmaker was given more GE PAC money than Charles Wilson (D-TX), who received $5,500. Wilson was a key member of the House Defense Appropriations Subcommittee.

In 1985–86, GE gave 24 percent of its $213,350 in contributions to incumbent members who sit on the military authorizations or appropriations committees.[12]

### Fiasco at NBC

In 1986, the company tried to form another PAC by coercing employees at a major television network.

GE acquired NBC with its purchase of RCA in 1986. Later that year, GE appointed Robert C. Wright as president of NBC. Wright had been president and CEO of GE's financial services and the GE Credit Corporation. One of Wright's first major moves was to issue a memorandum to Corydon B. Dunham, NBC's executive vice president and general counsel, and other network officials, saying that NBC should form a political action committee. In this memo, he implied that NBC employees who refused to contribute to the PAC were disloyal—in Wright's words, "[They] should question their own dedication to the company...." Wright went on to emphasize the need for employees to ensure "that [NBC's] important issues are clearly placed before Congress."

Wright continued, in flawless Orwellian Doublespeak:

> The point is simply to reinforce our support for the men and women of Congress who must continually face the continuing and time-consuming task of re-election. By showing our tangible support for the process, the office and the officeholders, we are in a better position to have our views intelligently and fairly viewed by Congress.[13]

The question of whether or not a TV news network should have a PAC raises important issues: What are the implications of a major nuclear weaponmaker owning a television news network? How will GE's ownership of NBC affect what we see—or don't see—on the news or in the programming? Already in GE's first year of ownership, NBC aired a program on how well the French nuclear power industry works.[14]

Many NBC employees criticized Wright's interest in the PAC as a conflict of interest rather than as a concern for

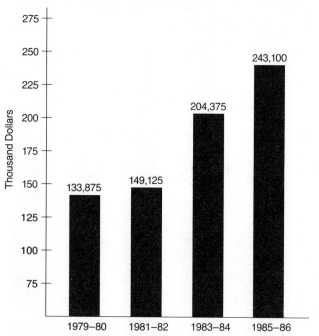

Source: Figures from *Top Guns* by Philip J. Simon, Common Cause, 1987.

**Figure 10.** GE PAC Contributions, 1979–1986

**Bringing GE to Light**

democracy. Lawrence K. Grossman, president of NBC News, said there was "no ambiguity" about his own opposition to the news division's participation in the PAC. He added, "The news division's policies would preclude anybody from NBC news from participating in anything like that." George F. Schweitzer, vice president of communications for the CBS Broadcast Group, said CBS did not have a PAC because "we operate a large, worldwide news organization and we feel that would be in conflict with the basic operation of that news organization."[15] The idea for an NBC PAC drew so much fire that it had to be abandoned.[16]

## GE Evades Laws Governing PACs

Two effective ways to avoid federal limits on PAC contributions are "bundling" and "earmarking." These two techniques are now becoming more widespread. Bundling occurs when groups gather numerous individual checks made out to a candidate's campaign and then present them together to the candidate. With earmarking, the contributor writes a check out to the PAC and notes that the money is for one or more specific candidates. The PAC then writes a check to the candidate(s) to pass along the contribution. Under 1986 Federal Election Commission (FEC) regulations, the bundled or earmarked money does not count against the PAC's contribution limits.[17]

General Dynamics, Hughes Aircraft, Rockwell, United Technologies, and GE together bundled or earmarked $95,727 in contributions to candidates during 1985. Among those PAC contributors, *GE earmarked the most money, giving more than $44,000 in such contributions to candidates and political parties that year—close to half the overall bundled/earmarked total.*[18]

## Paying Lawmakers to Talk— and to Listen

Another creative way of circumventing FEC regulations on PAC contributions is through honoraria, whereby weaponmakers pay legislators hefty sums for speaking engagements. Besides the speaker's fee, congresspersons are often reimbursed for travel, lodging, and meals.[19] These speaking engagements often take place at warm-weather resorts and hotels.[20]

Honoraria are not only a way to heavily finance a candidate but are also, in the words of waste management lobbyist Frank Moore, "... an excellent means to provide a two-way exchange between members [of Congress] and our executives." Honoraria provide an excellent way to buttonhole a candidate and argue the company's point of view as well.[21]

According to an article in the *Wall Street Journal* in June 1986, "honoraria have an odd legal status."[22] The House

and Senate both forbid their members from taking any gifts valued at $100 or more from lobbying groups.[23] Yet lawmakers can accept as much as $2,000 for a single "speaking" engagement. Members of Congress may also make more than one paid appearance in a day, and not all appearances involve speeches—by the legislator, at least.

Denis O'Toole, a lobbyist for the American Bankers Association, admits to being "somewhat amazed" at the practices of weapons contractors, "who often pay $2,000 for a lawmaker to stroll through a weapons plant and chat with local managers."[24]

From 1981 to 1985, honoraria payments by the top 10 weapons contractors of 1986 rose ninefold, from a total of $26,100 in 1981 to $236,163 in 1985. *The top giver in 1985 was General Electric, which paid legislators $47,500— almost twice the entire 1981 total for all 10.*[25]

In 1985, 77 percent of the honoraria from the top 10 weapons contractors went to legislators who sat either on the Armed Services Committees or Defense Appropriations Subcommittees. *General Electric gave honoraria to 27 Members of Congress: 20 of those were members of the Senate and House Armed Services Committees or Defense Appropriations Subcommittees.*[26]

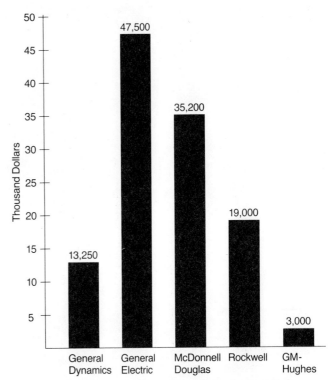

Source: Figures from *Top Guns* by Philip J. Simon, Common Cause, 1987.

**Figure 11.** Honoraria Payments by Top Five Weaponmakers in 1985

| Year | Total | Total Defense-Related Dollars | Percentage |
|------|-------|-------------------------------|------------|
| 1981 | $ 5,600 | $ 0 | — |
| 1982 | 26,000 | 18,000 | 69% |
| 1983 | 41,500 | 23,500 | 57% |
| 1984 | 38,656 | 22,500 | 58% |
| 1985 | 47,500 | 36,500 | 77% |

Source: Figures from *Top Guns* by Philip J. Simon, Common Cause.

**Figure 12.** GE Honoraria Payments, 1981–1985

# Conclusion

While GE and other weaponmakers have many ways of ensuring that the government pursues their interests, they turn increasingly to political action committees to keep the doors of congresspersons open. Even though the government has established regulations designed to limit such access, the weaponmakers, GE most notably, have found ways to evade the rules through bundling, earmarking, and honoraria.

Congresswoman Patricia Schroeder (D-CO), a member of the House Armed Services Committee, has remarked that corporate donations have become an active part of congressional deliberations. She said, "I've had people on my committee ask how many tickets a company bought to a fund-raiser, while we're trying to decide on what planes to buy."[27]

PAC money and honoraria are being used successfully by GE and others to ensure that Congress favors their deadly interests over those of its constituents, the American people.

**Bringing GE to Light**

# Formulating Policy: Advisory Committees and The Revolving Door

10

Weaponmakers would have people believe that they participate in politics because it is their patriotic duty and that they merely compete for the lowest bids to do government work. However, long before the lobbying begins and the bids are submitted, the weaponmakers are influencing the government. They are formulating policy, developing new systems through research and development, gathering valuable information and solidifying contacts that ensure huge contract awards and very few questions asked. Two key avenues for gaining the information, the contacts, and the influence weaponmakers have are governmental advisory committees and the migration of personnel back and forth between weaponmakers and the government, known as the revolving door.

## Advisory Committees

A crucial element to the hand-in-glove operations of nuclear weaponmakers and the government is the position of industry employees on key governmental advisory committees. These committees bring together decision makers in the government and industry to help forge policy on important issues in nearly every area of national policy.[1]

Advisory committees have a history dating back to World War I. However, it was during World War II that the problems of mobilizing for the war effort led the U.S. government to depend heavily on the expertise and support of private industry. The advisory committees, employing men from the industries considered essential to the World War II effort, began in June 1941. There was some question as to whether the committees violated anti-trust laws. However, the attorney general ruled that they did not. He stipulated, though, that each committee had to be "generally representative of the entire industry"; it had to meet in Washington and be chaired by a government officer; and *it was to be advisory only*.[2]

By the beginning of 1942, Washington had become inundated with committee members. No order affecting industry could be issued by the War Production Board until it had been submitted to the committees. According to Donald M. Nelson, who had been vice president of Sears, Roebuck prior to working with the war management agencies, this process resulted in an "almost perfect meshing of the industrial and governmental gears in war production."[3]

The committees met before programs had crystallized and their help was obtained in basic planning. As a result the government received the advice and recommendations of industry on all matters—including the review of orders. Industry received an opportunity to express itself continually and thus assisted in formulating government policy.[4]

Another means of enlisting the help of business was to have leading business executives work for the committees temporarily. The government salary was not what these men were used to, however, and the government decided they could continue to be paid by their peacetime employers while working with the committees. These men were called WOCs (for "without compensation") or "dollar-a-year" men. The practice of company executives taking "leaves of absence" from private business to work for the government also began at this time.

The government tried to avoid placing WOC executives in posts where they would be dealing directly with their own private companies. However, the government worried that the WOCs could not use their expertise most fully, so some exceptions were made to this rule.

These exceptions soon drew criticism, most notably from the committee headed by Senator Harry S. Truman. The committee believed that the inside information gained by the WOCs was used for their private companies' advantage. The committee also charged that the men from large companies discriminated against small business. The committee concluded, "In a very real sense the dollar-a-year men can be termed 'lobbyists.' "

The assumption that war was an aberration in the normal flow of life did not last long after the final victory in Europe. The advisory committees were dismantled along with the rest of the war machinery. But in 1947, the Voluntary

Agreements Act established a whole new network of governmental advisory committees, which continue to influence government policy to this day.[5]

## Committees Formulate Policy

Getting on the inside track, weaponmakers meet and work directly with government officials. They learn what the newest regulations look like and what the new programs are likely to be. The information also flows from corporations to the government—assuring that government officials know both the present and future plans of the companies so that when the need arises, the government knows which companies are there to fulfill it.

Not only do the companies get to make their pitch for a weapon system or make their bid for a contract; the advisory committees, on which the nuclear weapons industry is heavily represented, *actually formulate policy*.

According to defense analyst Gordon Adams, "Outsiders holding advisory positions within bureaucracy have been at the center of some of the most celebrated policy disputes that have arisen within the national government since World War II."[6] The membership of the committees tends to be a tight circle; the industry representatives and the government personnel come together with many shared assumptions and have an interest in preserving their "symbiotic relationship."[7] Alternative or public perspectives are usually absent, and only a limited range of technical disagreement survives.[8]

The Federal Advisory Committees Act of 1972 attempted to improve the situation by stipulating several requirements:

1. All committees had to file the minutes of their meetings with the Library of Congress, making them available for public access;

2. Open meetings had to be held when certain questions were under discussion;

3. Committees were required to strive for "balanced" representation, to seek out alternative viewpoints; and

4. Committee members were also prohibited from participating in studies in which, to their knowledge, they, their spouses, minor children, organizations, or employers had a financial interest.

How well have the advisory committees been complying?

1. Many committees claim exemptions on the requirement to file their minutes for public access. What reports are filed are often "thin and misleading" and are not filed regularly.

2. Half the meetings of the committees are still closed-door, for such reasons as matters of "national security" or "trade secrets."

3. Committees often interpret "balanced representation" to mean including more women, minorities, or people

from different geographic locations—not alternative viewpoints on national security.

4. Although all the committees contain substantial industry representation, few require full disclosure of affiliation. Only the initial annual report filed with the Library of Congress provides a listing of place of employment. No subsequent committee reports indicate the extent of a firm's interest and/or contract involvement with the agency or the weapons systems on which the committee is advising the government.[9]

## Defense Science Boards:
## "The Military-Industrial Complex at its Worst"[10]

The Defense Science Board (DSB) is a particularly blatant example of a biased committee membership serving its own interests. It is also a particularly influential committee.

The Defense Science Board "advises the Secretary of Defense and the Director of Defense Research and Engineering on overall scientific and technical research and engineering and provides long-range guidance in these areas." The DSB also advises its counterparts in each branch of the service—the Army Science Board, Naval Research Advisory Committee, and Air Force Scientific

An MX missile—cold launch test.
Source: Department of Defense.

Advisory Board. Its task forces have studied such questions as "MX missile basing, anti-submarine warfare, international arms agreements, and DOD computer policy."[11] GE managers have been active on this committee.

The Committee on Government Operations approved and adopted a report entitled "Defense Science Boards: A Question of Integrity" on November 15, 1983. A section of the report called "Defense Science Board: The Military-Industrial Complex At Its Worst" detailed instances of non-compliance with the Federal Advisory Committee Act, and apparent conflicts of interest and bias, seriously questioning whether the situation could improve.

The Federal Advisory Committee Act provides that:

1. The committees and panels should have procedures for announcing and preparing minutes for meetings;
2. Panel advice and recommendations should not be inappropriately influenced by the appointing authority; and
3. Panel membership should be fairly balanced in terms of representative points of view and functions to be performed.[12]

In a review of the board's 33 task forces established between January 1977 and September 1982, the inspector general found that:

- Of 198 meetings held during that period, minutes were available for just 32 and only 158 had been announced in advance.
- Committee members were usually selected from the chair's personal acquaintances or through the "old boy" network within the military-industrial complex.[13]

In one case in early 1981, the DOD planned to implement a policy on computer systems although the policy had been rejected by the General Accounting Office (GAO). However, based on a recommendation by a Defense Science Board Task Force composed mainly of industry representatives, the DOD decided to go ahead anyway. Furthermore, the GAO found that 7 of the task force's 11 members had financial interests in one or more of the firms then holding contracts for pilot projects under the proposed new policy. The comptroller general testified:

> It should be understood that the stakes underlying the policy alternatives are high... Given the tilt of task force membership toward interests that support the proposed policy, it is our view that the conclusions of the

task force cannot reasonably be looked upon as having been objectively reached.[14]

The defense inspector general reported that of six DSB task forces examined in detail, five involved advice that could be advantageous to the firms with which their members were affiliated.

Another glaring example of conflict of interest presented involved the studies of two DSB panels concerned with high energy lasers and DOD space-based laser weapons research, both a part of Star Wars. The two committees were chaired by Dr. John Foster, a vice president of TRW (a nuclear weapons contractor) and former DOD director of research and engineering. The panel was established to determine the viability of those weapons in Star Wars.

Dr. Foster's forwarding memorandum for the final committee report, however, admits that the panel was biased in one direction and had no intention of developing an objective evaluation of this issue. In the memorandum, Dr. Foster said:

> I should point out that this group was not one which set out to find fault. In fact, every member of this panel has been a strong supporter of the U.S. laser weapons program, most of us since its inception. We remain strong supporters, convinced that this program is healthy and promising, as evidenced by the fact that we recommend an increase of $50 million/year.[15]

The GAO was also asked to review the operations of the DOD senior scientific advisory committees of each branch of the services—the Army, Air Force, and the Navy. In a section of the report on the DSB entitled "Services' Senior Scientific Advisory Committees: More of the Same," the GAO found that among a sampling of 18 panels reviewed, 11 had members who were either employed by or had financial interests in organizations with contracts in areas that could be affected by their recommendations. One Army panel studying ballistic missile defense was composed of eight members, five of whom had apparent conflicts of interest.[16]

One of the members of the Defense Science Board was GE's William A. Anders, Vice President and General Manager of GE's Aircraft Equipment Division.[17] Also on the DSB at the time of the investigations was Daniel Fink, General Manager of GE's Aerospace Division from 1968

through the mid-1970s. Fink then moved to vice president of corporate planning in the 1980s.[18]

Sitting on the Advisory Panel on New Ballistic Missile Defense Technologies—again, Star Wars—in 1985 were Daniel Fink and GE's newest board member, retired Air Force General David Jones.[19]

Walter Wriston, currently on GE's board, was active on the Industry Advisory Council (IAC), which advised the Department of Defense from 1962 to 1972. In October 1970, Wriston, then with First National City Bank, suggested that changes be made to make weapons contracting more profitable. If weapons contracting became more profitable, he reasoned, then private financing for the weapons business would increase.

The IAC established a subcommittee to recommend changes in procurement practices to increase private financing—mainly bank loans. Indications are that as a result of these changes, originally suggested by prominent banker Wriston, U.S. banks received $700 million in new loans. This committee is no longer in existence.

The IAC was involved in broad policy discussions as early as 1962, when then Secretary of Defense Robert McNamara formed the organization to rally business support for his controversial changes in military procurement and management.[20]

GE's strategy over the years has been to place some of their key managers on key advisory committees, such as the Defense Science Board, or to have one person sit on multiple committees, as Daniel Fink does. This gives the company access to information about future programs of the government and assures that GE and other weaponmakers get their programs on the government's agenda. GE can affect decisions on research and development and help to shape policies discussed by these advisory committees—policies communicated directly to the Department of Defense or other branches of the government—within a closed circle that excludes the general public and, at times, even the elected decision makers.

### Advisory Committee Involvements of Top GE Executives[21]

| Name | GE Position | Committee | Dates |
|---|---|---|---|
| Daniel J. Fink, President of D.J. Fink Associates, Inc. | Former General Manager of Aerospace Division (1968 to mid 1970s) | Defense Science Board (DOD) | 1968–present |
| | | Defense Intelligence Agency Advisory Committee | 1974–83 |
| | Former Vice President of Corporate Planning and Development (1979–82) | USAF Scientific Advisory Board; Chair—advanced air vehicle surveillance and warning study | 1984–85 |
| | | Advisory Panel on New Ballistic Missile Defense Technologies | 1986–present |
| Edward E. Hood, Jr. | Vice-Chair of the Board and Executive Officer—oversight of GE Aerospace and other weapons systems (1979–present) | President's National Security Telecommunications Advisory Committee (DOD) | 1982–present |
| David C. Jones | Board of Directors (1986–present) | Advisory Panel on New Ballistic Missile Defense Technologies | 1985 |
| Thomas Paine | Former Manager, TEMPO Division (1963–68) Former Vice President and Group Executive, Power Generation Group (1970–74) | National Commission on Space (NASA) | 1985–present |
| Frank H. T. Rhodes, President, Cornell University | Board of Directors (1984–present) | Department of Defense (DOD) University Forum[a] | 1985–present |
| Brian H. Rowe | Senior Vice President and Group Executive, Aircraft Engine Group (1979–present) | Defense Policy Advisory Committee for Trade Policy Matters (DOD)[b] | 1982–present |
| Laddie Stahl, Manager of Special Programs and Project Development Operations | Corporate Research and Development (present) | Army Science Board (DOD)[c] | 1985–present |
| Walter Wriston | Board of Directors (1962–present) | Industry Advisory Council (DOD) | 1970–72 |

a. The DOD University Forum "was established to enable the Department of Defense and the universities to address together the range of mutual concerns and opportunities that will shape future research and education of importance to defense."

b. The Defense Policy Advisory Committee for Trade Policy Matters "provides the Secretary of Defense and the U.S. Trade Representatives with policy advice and information regarding defense trade policy issues and domestic base uses."

c. The Army Science Board "advises the Secretary of the Army, the Chief of Staff, the Assistant Secretary of the Army (RDA), the Deputy Chiefs of Staff, and many Army Commanders on scientific, technological and acquisition matters of interest to the Department of the Army."

## Revolving Door

A practice that provides many of the same advantages to the weaponmakers as positions on key advisory committees is known as the "revolving door." This means that a weaponmaking company hires former government personnel. And, when the door swings the other way, employees of weapons contractors are hired by the government. This term is most often used to explain the transfer of personnel between the Pentagon and the weaponmakers.

The revolving door creates a community of shared assumptions about policy issues. Government personnel who take jobs with weaponmakers help the companies with knowledge of the ways of government and procurement strategies. The revolving door also helps the weaponmakers during the contracting process and proves beneficial to governmental personnel who hope for lucrative jobs with weaponmakers upon leaving the government.

If the DOD employee pursues policies the weaponmakers see as unfavorable to the companies, they will probably not offer that employee a job in the future. One of the greatest dangers in this arrangement may be when DOD personnel are still in their government or military jobs. According to the New York Bar, the risk is in "the dampening of aggressive administration of government policies."[22]

Thomas S. Amlie, a civilian official with the Air Force, has written a "stinging critique" of the revolving door. He contends that "the big spenders are promoted and rewarded with cushy jobs after leaving the Government." He continues that, when an officer approaches retirement after 20 years of service, "this nice man then comes around and offers him a job at $50,000-$75,000 per year." If the officer "stands up and makes a fuss about high cost and low quality, no nice man will come to see him when he retires."[23]

## Attempts to Close the Door

Congress has tried to pass measures that would close the revolving door since 1959. That year, it was revealed that

more than 700 retired Pentagon employees had accepted employment in the defense industry. Representative Alfred E. Santangelo (D-NY) introduced an amendment to the Defense Appropriations Bill that would have denied contracts to any company that employed a former general or admiral who had seen active duty within the preceding five years. His amendment was narrowly defeated.[24]

In 1969, Senator William Proxmire stated that the top 100 Department of Defense contractors had employed over 2,000 former military personnel. He pushed for a bill requiring employees shifting from military contractors to the DOD, and from the DOD to military contractors, to file an annual report with the DOD for three years after the switch.[25]

The first systematic review of this new procedure, conducted by the Council on Economic Priorities in 1975, found that *1,400 former DOD civilian and military employees had been hired by the top 100 defense contractors between 1969 and 1973.* Compliance with the procedure by the weaponmakers and the DOD was so poor, however, that the CEP could not even tell the full extent of the problem: over a 3-year period, *at least 1,500 of the required reports were not filed.*[26]

New regulations were approved in 1986. These prohibited Pentagon officials from taking jobs with weapons companies for two years after they leave the DOD.[27] The regulations went into effect April 16, 1987. This caused a flurry of hasty departures from the government, so DOD employees could avoid the restrictions before they took effect. Some of those who beat the deadline were the Assistant Secretary of the Air Force for Research, Development, and Logistics, Thomas E. Cooper; Deputy Assistant Secretary of Defense for Spares Program Management, Maurice N. Shriber; and Deputy Under Secretary of Defense for Planning and Resources, Dov S. Zakheim. Cooper declined to reveal his plans; Shriber and Zakheim planned to join a consulting firm, where they could well be advising weaponmakers on how to sell to the Pentagon.[28]

Two men on GE's board of directors have passed through the revolving door moving between the highest levels of government and the uppermost echelons of a top nuclear weaponmaker: William French Smith and Retired General David Jones. Their careers are elaborated more fully in the chapter on GE's board of directors.

**William French Smith**, Attorney General from 1980 until 1985, was elected to GE's board in 1986. Smith was Ronald Reagan's personal lawyer and good friend. As attorney general he weakened anti-trust laws and restricted public access to government records under the Freedom of Information Act. Smith also attempted to expand the bounds of executive privilege, allowing the president to refuse to release documents to Congress.

Smith's ties to Reagan and his administration as well as his extensive connections in California are key assets to GE.

**Retired General David Jones** (elected to GE's board in 1986) is the former Chair of the Joint Chiefs of Staff. This is a body made up of the heads of all the branches of the armed forces. Under President Carter, he fought for a higher military budget. Under Reagan, he became a vocal advocate of a rapid military build-up and warned of the Soviet threat. Also under Reagan, Jones reversed his opposition to the B-1 bomber and said it "should be top priority."[29] Jones has also spoken out against the Nuclear Freeze and the "No First Use" movements.

Jones retired from the Air Force in 1982 but is still a member of the Air Force Association, whose trade journal *Air Force* often prominently features GE ads.

Another notable "revolving door" connection between GE and the government is **Thomas O. Paine**. Paine joined GE in 1949 as a research associate.[30] In 1956, GE formed its own "think tank," the Technical Military Planning Operation (TEMPO), which Paine headed in the 1960s. He described TEMPO as "a community that serves largely as a go-between for the military community and the industrial community."[31] What TEMPO did, in return for several million dollars a year in contracts from the DOD and other agencies, was to "study and propose solutions to military problems," including weapons research.[32]

In 1968, he was appointed Deputy Administrator of NASA and became Administrator in 1969.[33] During his tenure there, NASA did a multi-million dollar annual business with GE.[34] He resigned from NASA in July 1970, in the wake of

a *New York Times* story in which the Fairchild-Hiller Corporation revealed that NASA, under Paine, had rigged bidding on a $50 million satellite contract to GE.[35]

GE then rehired Paine as vice president and group executive of the Power Generation Group. This group promoted increased use of electric power, with nuclear generation as the primary source.[36]

In November 1987, Paine headed a presidential space commission, which strongly recommended that NASA begin work on a $20 billion space station. Paine views the space station as a "critical element in future space efforts"; other scientists see it as a boondoggle.[37] In early December 1987, *GE's Astro-Space Division was awarded an $800 million contract for work on the station*.[38]

Yet another GE revolving-door figure deserving of mention is **Daniel Fink**. Fink was an aerospace scientist with several large contractors in the 1950s. Through the mid-1960s he was the assistant director, then deputy director of research and development at the Pentagon. In 1968, he was named general manager of GE's Aerospace Group, where he remained through the mid-1970s.[39] While with GE he also was a consultant to a governmental advisory body, the Defense Science Board.[40] As noted earlier, the DSB was then embroiled in a scandal—several members were discovered on task forces and panels, advising the government on projects in which their companies had financial interests.

## Other Door Revolvers

Two former GE board members and a former GE lawyer have been U.S. secretaries of defense:

> Neil H. McElroy, under Eisenhower, 1957–59;
> Thomas S. Gates, Jr., under Eisenhower, 1959–61; and
> Clark M. Clifford, under Johnson, 1968–69.

**Neil McElroy**, also president of Procter and Gamble, was a GE director from 1950-57. After his term as secretary of defense, he went back to GE's board in 1959.

**Thomas Gates**, a banker, was undersecretary, the secretary of the Navy, 1953–59. After his term as secretary of defense, he joined GE's board in 1964.[41]

**Clark Clifford** was special counsel to President Truman, chair of the CIA's Foreign Intelligence Advisory Board, personal advisor to President Johnson, and advisor to presidential candidate Kennedy. He became Johnson's secretary of defense in 1968. In 1964, Clifford was GE's lawyer in an enormous price-fixing scandal. When GE and others were found guilty of "the biggest monopolistic conspiracy in U.S. history," Clifford convinced the Internal Revenue Service (IRS) to rule that the damages GE had to pay for its crime were tax-deductible as a business expense. GE reportedly paid Clifford $2 million for his work.[42]

**Figure 13.** Thomas Paine's Movements Through the Revolving Door

1949 GE Research Associate

1960s GE Think Tank Formed Technical Military Planning Operation (TEMPO) Director

NASA Deputy Administrator • 1968

1969 NASA Administrator [Director]

GE Vice President & Group Executive, Power Generation • 1970

• 1987 Presidential Space Commission Director

Other GE revolving-door figures include some of the most powerful men in government and in the company:

**Charles E. Wilson**   GE president, 1939–50. Vice chair, U.S. War Production Board, World War II. Director, Office of Defense Mobilization, Korean War (from 1950). "One of the most powerful men of the Truman administration."

**Robert Stevens**   GE director, 1946–53. Secretary of the Army, 1953–55. GE director, 1956–70.

**Ralph Cordiner**   GE president, 1950–58, GE chair, 1958–63. Director, War Production Board, World War II.

**Stephen Enke**   Deputy assistant secretary of defense for economics, 1965–66. Appointed head of economics section, GE TEMPO, 1967.

**Frederick Dent**   GE director, 1966–72. Appointed secretary of commerce in 1973. He was a strong advocate of multi-national corporations. [43]

## One For All

New regulations have tried to limit abuse of the revolving door; but as Congress passes new rules, weaponmakers and government personnel have found ways around the rules.

An excellent way to beat regulations is not to take a job with any one military contractor, but instead to start a consulting firm. A fine example of this type of maneuver is Lieutenant General Kelly Burke. In 1982, he was the Air Force's top procurement officer, making decisions on bil-

The F-15 Eagle: One of the weapons Lieutenant General Burke helped to procure.
Source: *Nuclear Weapons Databook*, Volume I.

lions of dollars in business with major contractors. In 1983, Burke became a paid adviser to some of those same weaponmakers, including GE. [44] As head of the Air Force's research, development, and procurement apparatus, Burke helped decide whether to buy such weapons as the F-15 Eagle, the F-16 Falcon, the C-5 Galaxy cargo plane, and the B-1B bomber. All use GE engines.

In 1980, Richard Ichord (D-MO) was a member of the House Armed Services Committee. He chaired the subcommittee on research and development, which authorized billions of dollars for weaponmakers. When he left Congress in 1981 after 20 years, he started a consulting firm with former Representative Bob Wilson (R-CA). Their clients have included GE and 10 of the 13 largest military contractors. [45]

Critics of the revolving door, such as Senator William Proxmire (D-WI) say it "perpetuates a cozy, almost incestuous relationship between the people who buy weapons and those who sell them." [46] Moreover, even though restrictions on the revolving door exist, nothing in the law prevents Burke and Ichord from advising their clients on how to sell to the Pentagon. [47]

Congress has been powerless to stop abuse of the revolving door—particularly because some members of Congress benefit from it. For them, the interchange between government and the weapons industry, in the form of advisory committees and the revolving door, offers lucrative post-government employment. For the corporations, it offers an inside track in the race to win allocations from Congress and contract awards from the Pentagon.

Governmental advisory committees and the revolving door are two key ways weaponmakers can influence government. Attempts by the government to prevent people from sitting on committees whose decisions can benefit them financially have failed because the DOD and the weaponmakers refuse to cooperate. Weaponmakers and those in government who look to them for lucrative jobs have also found ways around the regulations, such as starting consulting firms.

From GE President Charles E. Wilson, who left GE to become the Director of Defense Mobilization, to GE's newest board member, Retired Air Force General David Jones, GE continues to keep the machinery of Wilson's permanent war economy in motion.

# Marketing Nuclear Weapons: GE's Washington Operations

*11*

*Visibility is the last thing I need.*
— GE lobbyist George Troutman[1]

GE's presence in Washington, DC, is one of the company's most important operations. The GE Washington office is referred to as Corporate Government Relations and is the major component of the "Corporate Relations Staff" that reports directly to CEO John Welch, Jr.[2] The Corporate Government Relations division has approximately 150 people working out of offices that GE rents for at least $1.3 million a year.[3]

The high standing in the GE structure chart of this office parallels the situation at other large firms and reflects the increased importance of government contracts to large corporations. A pioneer study of defense-contractor lobbying, *The Iron Triangle,* states, "As politics has become critical to management decision-making, planning the Government relations effort has been more closely tied into the overall corporate strategy. This development is reflected in the corporate structure. Once the head of the Washington office was merely an assistant to the CEO or a member of the public affairs staff. Today he or she is a company vice president with formal standing in the hierarchy."[4]

Of all the weapons contractors, GE's Washington operation is the largest. It is enormous by the standards of corporations outside the weapons industry. For example, Exxon, a corporation even larger than GE,[5] employs only 13 people in its Washington office.[6]

What GE does in this office is similar to the rest of its marketing and advertising strategies; that is, calculating what its potential customers want and then convincing those customers to try out and buy GE products.

Using a small army of corporate specialists, the office is designed to mesh a private sector conglomerate with the public sector conglomerate — the U.S. government. The goal is to sell the Washington market much as one would sell a consumer market... the key customers are no longer the couple shopping for toasters in a suburban shopping mall. They are the Secretaries of the Navy and Air Force shopping for jet engines for the F14, the F15, the F16, the B1 (bomber) and the Stealth bomber....[7]

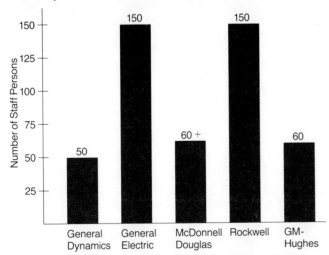

Source: Figures from *Top Guns* by Philip J. Simon, Common Cause, 1987.

**Figure 14.** Staff Size of Washington Office — Top Five Weaponmakers

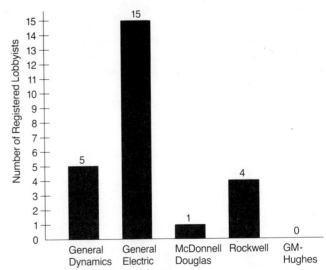

Source: Figures from *Top Guns* by Philip J. Simon, Common Cause, 1987.

**Figure 15.** Top Five Weaponmakers, **Registered** Lobbyists

GE's tremendous success in the weapons market is largely due to the diligence of this Washington office. GE did $6.8 billion in military business in fiscal year 1986, up from $2.95 billion in fiscal year 1981. This rate of increase is even higher than the rate of increase in overall military spending.[8]

## Who's Who in Washington

**Phillips S. Peter**, the Vice President for Corporate Government Relations, directs GE's Washington office. As such, he must coordinate the overall operation of the office and its employees, see to it that the information gathered on the front lines is analyzed and transmitted to GE management, and decide which areas need special attention and pressure at the moment.

Peter has worked for GE since 1963, was named a vice president in 1973, and assumed his present position in 1980.[9] He has served as a director of the National Bank of Washington, as a member of the editorial board of the Virginia Law Review, and as a trustee of Howard University. All in all a fairly typical background for someone of his standing.

### Well-traveled Circles

What is striking about Peter is the large number of club memberships he holds. His golf, country, city, and yacht clubs include the Wee Burn and Episcopalian clubs in Darien, Connecticut; the Landmark club in Stamford, Connecticut; the Farmington Country Club in Connecticut; the Ponte Vedra club in Jacksonville, Florida; the John's Island Club in Vero Beach, Florida (where you must own a house in order to belong); the Racquet Club near Miami Beach, Florida; the Coral Beach and Tennis Club in Bermuda; and the Eastern Yacht Club in Marblehead, Massachusetts. His biggest concentration of club memberships, of course, is in the Washington DC-Maryland area: the Chevy Chase Club, Pisces Club, and F Street Club in Washington and the Congressional Country Club in Bethesda, Maryland.[10] The Chevy Chase Club is said to be "the club" to belong to in Washington, and all of the Washington-area clubs, as well as selected clubs in other areas like the Coral Beach Club and the Racquet Club, are well-known places to entertain members of Congress, military brass, and other officials and to make new government contacts in a relaxed setting.

Within the Washington operation, Peter is part of the "company-wide" unit that represents GE as a whole when dealing with the government, trade associations, and other companies. Some representatives of this company-wide unit are said to specialize in Republicans or Democrats.[11] In this, as in its PAC contributions—which have frequently been fairly evenly divided between the two major parties—GE tries to cover all the bases.

Besides the company-wide unit, the Washington office houses special units to promote the company's aircraft engines; aerospace, radar, electronic, flight simulation, and weapons systems; nuclear power plants; the Export-Import Bank; and medical technology.[12]

How Many Defense Contractors Does It Take To Screw Up The American Taxpayer?

Schorr
Los Angeles Herald

### The Lobbyists

The representatives subject to the greatest legal scrutiny and regulations are the registered lobbyists themselves who deal with the legislative branch of government. GE has more registered lobbyists than any other defense contractor.[13] Phillips Peter is a registered lobbyist, as are 14 other GE employees in the Washington office.[14]

Each lobbyist—which can be either an individual or a firm—is assigned an identification number and each must file a quarterly report listing:

- what company or group he, she, or they represent; in the case of individuals or firms that represent more than one company, this means multiple reports.
- what legislation the lobbyist is concerned with; the reports by many of GE's lobbyists state that they are concerned with any legislation directly or indirectly affecting GE or its components.
- what publications, if any, the lobbyist distributes.
- what money was received from what sources.
- what money was spent and for what purposes.[15]

The full extent of information included in these reports is questionable. For example, in a quarterly report filed in October 1987 by Phillips Peter, he claimed that he had spent only $200.00 during that period for a total of only $300.00 through that year.[16] Surely GE pays its lobbyists for more than taking one person out to lunch or sending a few letters. But this is about all that could have been done for the amount reported.

The following is a list of those GE employees who are registered lobbyists and deal with GE's weapons work:[17]

**Zack Shelly**   a former congressional lobbyist for the U.S. Air Force.

**Robert Barrie**   manager of federal legislation regulations, a former Senate and House staff member, who also ran Hubert Humphrey's 1960 presidential campaign.

**Clifford LaPlante**   a retired Air Force Colonel, who manages congressional and executive branch relations for GE's Aircraft Engine business.

**Tina Beach**   a representative for congressional and industry relations.

**William Patterson**   manager of congressional and executive branch relations for GE's Aerospace business.

**Harry Levine Jr.**   Washington, DC, general manager of the Aircraft Engine Group. Levine was one of the two key lobbyists in GE's fight against Pratt and Whitney for engine contracts for the F-15, F-16, and F-14 fighter planes. GE won almost $10 billion in contracts.[18]

Harry Levine and George Troutman lobbied for GE to get contracts for the F-16 engines.
Source: *Nuclear Weapons Databook,* Volume I.

**Mary Ann Freeman**   a representative of the Aircraft Engine Group.

In addition to the above GE employees, three outside lobbyists currently report that they represent GE:

**J. D. Williams**   of the Williams and Jensen firm, who lobbies on tax issues.

**Fried, Frank, Harris, Shriver & Jacobson**   a major lobbying firm representing around 40 companies and organizations that represents GE on nuclear power. Max Kampelman, who is now one of Reagan's chief arms negotiators with the USSR, was a partner in this firm. Kampelman also helped found the Committee on the Present Danger, an influential and ultra-conservative foreign policy group.

**Heron, Burchette, Ruckert & Rothwell**   a law firm hired by GE in 1986 to lobby for satellite funds. In the fall of 1987 GE won an $800 million contract for the space station.[19]

Important lobbyists who have represented GE in the past, but are not registered currently for GE, include:

**Thomas P. Safford**, **Kelly H. Burke**, and **Guy L. Hecker** a partnership of three former Air Force generals.

**The Washington Industrial Team**   a firm that includes on its lobbying staff the former chair of the House Armed Services Committee Research and Development Subcommittee and the former ranking Republican member of the full committee.

**George G. Troutman**   the lobbyist quoted at the start of this chapter. Troutman was the other key lobbyist involved in the Pratt and Whitney engine fight.

**Charls E. Walker**   of Charls E. Walker Associates, a firm with an enormous client base (31 active clients in 1987, 117 inactive). Walker, referred to in 1973 as "an emerging Republican superlobbyist,"[20] was also a founder of the Committee on the Present Danger.

What about the remainder of the 150 people in GE's Washington office? Many are in fact lobbyists in all but name and legal status. The 1946 law regulating lobbyists does not require any registration of weapons contractor employees who lobby the Defense Department or other executive branch agencies.

## What the Washington Staff Does

In a 1975 report to the Defense Contract Audit Agency, Boeing, a major weapons contractor, gave a remarkable portrait of how a corporation's Washington, DC, representatives typically influence the legislative branch of government.[21] The list below, based on Boeing's report, refers only to legislative branch work, which is subject to greater legal scrutiny than corporate activity directed at the executive branch. According to Boeing, a company's governmental relations office:

- helps prepare bills or amendments, finds congressional sponsors for this legislation, and prepares material to support the legislation;
- follows the course of legislation and decides when company representatives should testify either in person or in writing at congressional hearings;
- recommends which legislators should be visited by company executives and helps prepare background material for such visits;
- attends House and Senate hearings and sessions to report back to the company;
- studies senators and representatives seeking re-election and recommends whether the company political action committee (PAC) should support them;
- encourages legislators and congressional aides to visit company manufacturing facilities;
- prepares and distributes fact sheets to members of

Congress on legislation that would affect the company;

- prepares information on legislation for use by the company's management.

## The Information Exchange

The chief value to GE and other weapons contractors of their Washington offices can be briefly stated in two words: *information* and *pressure*. Information flows two ways.

**To the company**   the Washington office provides raw data and final analysis of what is happening in the Capitol, often in the form of regular reports or a "Washington Newsletter." Another key study of military contractors, *Top Guns*, states that the Washington staff serves as "the eyes and ears of the company's headquarters at the Pentagon. It is axiomatic that information means power in Washington. For defense contractors, information—about next year's budget, the status of the newest weapons systems, or personnel changes at the Pentagon—can be parlayed into contracts. Since the Pentagon is the major market for most of these contractors, they track every nuance of the defense debate."[22]

This is often the most important single function of the Washington office. A study by the Conference Board found that "Asked to cite the most important activity they perform, the largest group of Government relations executives talk about their role in communicating political and governmental information to management: an internally directed activity rather than an externally directed one."[23]

The Washington lobbyists gather this information by regularly visiting key contacts in Congress and in the executive branch, participating in government advisory committee meetings, going to trade association shows and meetings, and attending congressional hearings. They take great pains to build and maintain their contacts. For this reason, longevity in Washington is highly valued and "past experience with the Government is a shining asset."[24]

Maintenance of friendly contacts often includes regular social activity, such as meeting for lunch every few weeks. This aspect of lobbying—the "expense account lunches" and "hunting lodge weekends"—has received much unfavorable publicity in recent years,[25] generating new laws to curtail such activity. According to one lobbyist, "we still take people to lunch, of course, but what congressmen and their staffers need from us is...solid information about our products...We try to put the best face on [them]...."[26]

Sometimes the company representatives also take advantage of their friendly contacts; for example, by looking at a classified document during a meeting with a friend at the Pentagon and then reporting its contents back to company headquarters.

However they do it, the Washington staffers get to be extremely skillful at finding out information—often better than anyone else in town. According to *Top Guns*, "contractors are so effective in obtaining budget and weapons system data that they often know the Pentagon's secret plans. Robert Segal, a former Pentagon investigator, has told Congress that 'classified documents which are prohibited from ever leaving the DOD are regularly trafficked among private consultants [and] companies in the procurement industry.' He said some companies even run 'espionage units' to obtain documents to secure a competitive advantage."[27]

Sometimes the company representatives serve as a medium of communication between the legislative and executive branches of government. One Pentagon official commented that "the best thing about corporate lobbyists is that they pass on to us a lot of stuff that they've learned on Capitol Hill."[28]

**To the government**   the Washington office provides information to the Pentagon and friendly or undecided legislators to help them make decisions or defend decisions already made. This information can take the form of straightforward data or of highly biased arguments and propaganda.

A good example of information to defend a position was a joint effort by contractors producing the F-18 fighter plane to save it from the congressional axe. GE builds the engines for the F-18. A member of Congress in favor of continuing the F-18, James Lloyd (D-CA), recalled that "Troutman [George Troutman, the GE lobbyist mentioned above] made me look smart in front of my colleagues. He kept feeding me information on the performance and cost advantages of the F-18—sometimes practically on the House floor—so I could sound off during the debate."[29]

Besides information transmitted during private meetings in congressional offices or at the Pentagon—or, as in the case quoted above, "practically on the House floor"—the company representatives provide oral and written information in public forums. On the legislative side, these forums are congressional hearings. On the executive side, these forums come during meetings of advisory committees. (See Chapter 10 for more information on advisory committees.)

## Congressional Hearings

Among the most important forums are congressional committee hearings. The Washington staff makes it a practice to attend as many hearings as possible that relate to the Defense Department, weapons spending, or any subject affecting the company. When it comes to actually giving testimony at these hearings, however, it is generally not the Washington staff or lobbyists who appear but company experts and officials from outside Washington.

GE is an active participant in congressional committee hearings relating to defense spending, trade, nuclear power, industrial policy, and other subjects. GE officials have appeared frequently at these hearings in recent years.[30]

## Nuclear Power in Space

To exemplify the tone of these appearances by GE officials, consider the case of the SP-100 project, a program to build a nuclear reactor for outer space. This program is under the joint authority of the Department of Energy (DOE), the National Aeronautics and Space Administration (NASA), and the Defense Advanced Research Projects Agency (DARPA).[31] The SP-100 is considered a part of Star Wars research and development.

Subcommittees of the House Committee on Science and Technology[32] held two sets of hearings on this project, in May 1983 and October 1985. GE had done work on such a program in the 1960s under the Atomic Energy Commission, forerunner of the Department of Energy, and had begun some preliminary work on the SP-100 project itself starting in 1981. GE hoped to capture a continuing large portion of the contracts for this nuclear reactor in space.

Appearing for GE at the 1983 hearings were Alan J. Rosenberg, Vice President and General Manager of the Space Systems Division, and Dr. Bertram Wolfe, Vice President and General Manager of the Nuclear Fuel and Special Projects Division. Appearing at the 1985 hearings was Giles C. Sinkewitz, General Manager of Space-craft Operations at GE's facility in King of Prussia, Pennsylvania.

Following a common pattern for such events, Rosenberg, Wolfe, and Sinkewitz, after being introduced by the legislator chairing the hearing, made statements. They then deposited into the record their detailed written statements, complete with diagrams and even—in the case of Rosen-

berg and Wolfe—their professional biographies, including a photo of Rosenberg.

Their statements reviewed the history of the nuclear reactor project and the problems involved. The major point they wanted to make, not so much by directly stating it but by trying to dazzle the legislators with well-thought-out technical analyses and projections for future development, was that GE was uniquely qualified to carry out the SP-100 project.

Rosenberg's statement included three color charts proposing a timetable for space reactor development through the year 2000, progressing from system studies through technology development and ground demonstrations and flight prototype to final production. Wolfe's statement dealt largely with GE's experience with nuclear reactors, beginning in the 1940s at the Knolls laboratory. Sinkewitz's conclusion alluded to the need for shaping public opinion:

> It is important that there be continuity of support for nuclear power systems...Your [congressional] support for development of space nuclear power systems is essential, and such support must be continuous in order to retain the cadre of skilled personnel and needed facilities...Government and industry must work together to help create a positive public awareness and acceptance of space nuclear power systems which are mandated by the needs of both civilian scientific missions and defense applications.

> GE is strongly committed to the development of advanced nuclear space power systems ... our corporate expertise will be applied to assure the achievement of the safety, performance, reliability and cost effectiveness goals of space nuclear power systems like the SP-100. We are pleased to be a part of this exciting program.

Even though Wolfe talked about GE's experience and Sinkewitz stressed safety performance and cost assurances, during the 1970s GE engineers had prepared a report detailing the many design flaws in GE nuclear reactors. This report, known as the Reed Report, was concealed from the public until 1987. The report leaked out when a reporter was researching a court case in which a utility had sued GE for cost overruns.

The tone of public and on-the-record statements such as these is one of helpful, informed concern for the program and its benefit to the nation as a whole. The direct pressure comes behind the scenes and outside of Washington. In this case, the tone set in the hearings has been successful for GE: the company received $177 million worth of SP-100 contracts between fiscal years 1983 and 1986, out of a grand total of $465.9 million in GE Star Wars-related contracts.[33]

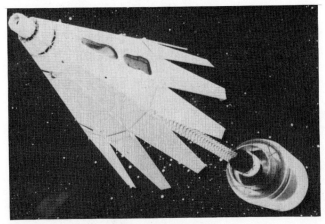

Illustration of SP-100 nuclear reactor for space.
Source: Office of Technology Assessment.

## Planning the Pressure Strategy

Besides gathering information, the Washington staff provides one more key link in the chain. This link is the transformation of the information into *pressure*—applied at the right times, in the right places, to the right people.

It is the job of the Washington office to decide where this pressure needs to be applied. Usually, and especially in the case of Congress, this means the "grassroots." "A few years ago we [contractors] began to understand that while Government policies are executed in Washington, their impetus lies elsewhere, at the grassroots. Since then, we have involved more and more plant managers in letter and telegram writing, personal visits and telephone calls on Governmental policies because their views are more important than those of the Washington lobbyist."[34]

Pressure is planned in Washington based on information gathered there, but it is primarily executed in home districts of representatives and senators. Part of this occurs through the mobilization of company personnel in those districts. GE, with 288,000 U.S. employees working at 225 plants in 32 states, is particularly well positioned for such mobilization.

## A Case Study: GE vs. United Technologies[35]

GE was extremely aggressive. They hide their claws. They've got claws. I don't think there's anything they wouldn't have done to win this.
—Congressional aide, referring to GE's fourteen-year fight to win several key Pentagon contracts for jet fighter airplane engines away from United Technologies.[36]

An excellent example of GE's government relations operation in action was seen in 1984, when GE won the lion's share of production contracts for a series of jet engines used by the Navy and Air Force.

In 1970, the Pratt & Whitney division of United Technologies (UT) beat GE for the contract to build the F-100 jet engine (and the related TF30) to be used in a series of Navy and Air Force fighter airplanes: the F-16, F-15, and F-14. Technical problems soon developed with the UT-produced engines, and the Pentagon felt that UT, secure under the "sole source" system, was not taking its complaints seriously. These grievances, naturally, found their way to the ears of GE representatives.

GE had a fierce determination to win away part of the contract. GE had felt for some time that it was better qualified than UT to provide an engine in the F-100 class, but GE had not been able to convince the Pentagon. It now assigned the case to two of its lobbyists: George Troutman and Harry Levine.

Next GE took the unusual step of building a prototype engine on its own, the F101X, with no Defense Depart-ment funding. GE invited the Navy to look at the F101X. The Navy still showed no interest in switching contractors.

At this point, GE moved into high gear by meeting with legislators and paying special attention to those in whose districts GE had large workforces. One of the latter group was Congressperson Sam Stratton (D-NY), chair of the Armed Services Subcommittee. GE lobbyists suggested witnesses for him to call in subcommittee hearings and questions for him to ask those witnesses.

In 1976, Congress voted $15 million to the Navy for developing the GE prototype engine. The Navy did not spend the money. In 1977, Congress voted $26 million for the same purpose, *and a GE lobbyist managed to insert a clause directing that the money be spent*. Still no action by the Navy. In 1979, at Air Force urging, Congress voted a re-competition for the engine, awarding $305 in research and development funds to GE and $163 million to UT.

GE's congressional partisans—urged on by company lobbyists—fought it out with UT's supporters for several years in committee meetings and hearings.

Neither side shrank from aggressive tactics. For example, GE lobbyists once secured some notes by an important congressperson concerning an upcoming bill-writing session and called their allies and warned them what to expect in the session.

In the end, UT lost. After a private meeting with a few top-level military men familiar with the competing engines, an undecided member of the House Defense Appropriations Subcommittee came down on GE's side in a key vote.

With Congress now officially requiring the re-competition, the Air Force awarded a dual contract for the new supply of jet engines, with $9.8 billion going to GE and $4.2 billion to UT. The Navy followed in the Air Force's footsteps soon after, awarding a $1.75 billion contract for jet engines *entirely to GE*.

A senator later commented on the case, "You didn't have to be a genius to figure out the Air Force wanted to buy some GE engines...." The fact that the Air Force turned out to be GE's chief ally is an interesting footnote. GE's relations with the Air Force have long been very good—and are probably even better now, thanks to GE's new board member David C. Jones, retired Air Force general and former Chair of the Joint Chiefs of Staff.

## GE and Weaponmakers Lobby with the Air Force

One of the planes for which GE builds the engines is the C-5B Galaxy cargo plane, which the company builds on a contract from the Air Force. From fiscal year 1982 through fiscal year 1985, GE received $22.1 million dollars for the C-5 Galaxy engines.[37]

How the C-5 Galaxy plane came to be built is a case study in lobbying by the Pentagon and the contractors. In April 1983, the *St. Louis Post-Dispatch* reported that GE, Lockheed, General Dynamics (GD), and AVCO planned strategy with the Air Force to push the Galaxy through the House of Representatives. This example shows details of how the weaponmakers worked with the Pentagon to lobby Congress.

On May 13, 1982, when the Senate voted against the C-5 Galaxy, the contractors and the Pentagon joined forces. During the rest of May, the Air Force's legislative liaison, Major General Guy L. Hecker, Jr., and GE, Lockheed, GD, and AVCO met for strategy meetings almost every day, sometimes for an hour-and-a-half at a time. Lockheed drafted a letter for the Pentagon to send. Printouts on lobbying strategy contained notes such as: "Get non-defense Committee Chair support (like on B-1)" and "AF [Air Force] draft 'soft sell' Dear Colleague letter."[38] Air Force officials later testified that such strategy meetings had taken place on the B-1 bomber in 1981.[39]

An Air Force memo dated May 24, 1982, said that the Air Force should "energize AFA (Air Force Association) and ROA (Reserve Officers' Association)" to get the C-5 through the House. Another memo, dated May 26, read "Energize all military associations and obtain leadership and 'back home' support."[40]

Strategy meetings continued until the House reversed the Senate and voted for the Galaxy.[41] But the General

The Pershing Missile Launcher is an example of the C-5 Galaxy's cargo.
Source: *Nuclear Weapons Databook*, Volume I.

Accounting Office conducted an investigation and ruled in September 1982 that the Pentagon officials had violated federal anti-lobbying statutes. The GAO said, "The purpose was to do things the Air Force was restricted from doing... by bringing pressure to bear on members of the Congress."[42]

Dina Rasor of the Project on Military Procurement said the corporations used the Pentagon as an arm of their lobbying effort. She added

> When you see a guy from Lockheed coming into your congressional office, you know exactly where he's coming from. You know he's pushing his own product. But when the Air Force comes in, you expect them to be objective. They're supposed to be the experts on national security. You don't expect them to use their stars and medals for the sake of profit and pork barrel.[43]

The collaboration of GE and the other C-5 contractors with the Air Force may have raised questions at the time but the C-5 brought $22.1 million to GE from 1982 through 1985, long after the heat had died down. GE also received another benefit from the C-5 Galaxy affair. General Hecker left the Air Force and subsequently formed a consulting partnership with two other former Air Force generals. GE retained the firm for lobbying purposes.

### Conclusion

GE's government lobbying clearly pays. The examples of the SP-100 and the C-5 Galaxy show how GE helps determine funding for the development of weapons technology and systems and how the company secures lucrative contracts for these systems. GE's lobbyists sell Congress the company's products and in turn provide GE with information to plan its marketing strategy. GE's Washington operations continue to reap huge profits for the company by selling its product—nuclear weapons—to the government.

These examples show how capably GE and other weapons contractors engage in direct lobbying on Capitol Hill. In addition, the weaponmakers have banded together for a second, less direct but very effective form of lobbying.

## Trade Associations

Since trade associations represent an entire industry rather than a single company, they appear more disinterested and are less visible. Yet they are vital to all the companies they represent because they affect policies that can benefit an entire industry. According to defense analyst Gordon Adams

> Trade associations constitute a critical link between industry and Federal officials. Their views appear neutral, since they speak for no company. Sometimes an association in coordination with agency officials can become a *de-facto* policy-maker. This specialized, reg-

ular access increases the influence of the corporations they represent, while it effectively excludes non-specialists and proponents of policy alternatives.[44]

Even this has not been enough to satisfy the associations, however, and many now hire lobbyists to directly lobby Congress (and the executive branch). Some also have set up political action committees.[45] According to trade associations expert Donald Hall, weaponmakers have made the most of cooperation for their common purpose:

Contractors—and their industry associations—are divided by economic self-interest in acquiring the largest possible slice of the defense dollar, but the same contractors are unified in common motivation to influence defense procurement and policy.

Among the common interests of weaponmakers are a need for a regular flow of information, especially on forthcoming research and development; general maintenance of the level of military and space spending; a regular distribution of military dollars among different types of weapons systems; access to DOD and NASA officials in social settings; and an influence over military policy issues in DOD, the White House, and the Congress.[46]

While many of the associations do not have registered lobbyists, members often testify before Congress, meet with DOD officials, and pressure the executive branch. For example, according to *National Defense Magazine*, nearly 170 representatives of weapons-related trade associations and other organizations met in February 1987 for a briefing on the Reagan Administration's proposed 1988 budget.[47]

GE is a member of several powerful weapons-related trade associations. Five of these are presented below.

## The American Defense Preparedness Association

The American Defense Preparedness Association (ADPA) was formerly named the Army Ordnance Associa-

Magazines and annual reports of associations GE is involved with.

tion, which was formed in 1919. The ADPA's purpose, according to its fact sheet, is "to preserve a reservoir of armament know-how, to be an industry-military liaison in technical areas, and to inform the public on matters of national defense preparedness." Its membership includes representatives of government, the military, and the weapons industry. Its publications include *National Defense*, which reports on the research, production, and testing of new weapons systems; *The Common Defense*, a monthly newsletter of commentary on defense developments and policy; *Technical Bulletin*, which lists all ADPA meetings; and the *Annual Report*, which presents a "summary of the past year's accomplishments and highlights milestones."[48]

In 1981, the ADPA claimed 33,000 individual members and 400 corporate members. In the ADPA's own words: "The Association freely admits that it supports the so-called military-industrial complex." In 1981, 48 of the 60 largest weaponmakers were members of the ADPA.[49]

Local chapter activities include such excellent lobbying opportunities as "luncheon and dinner meetings with top level guest speakers, panel discussions and seminars, and visits to defense facilities," as well as "public awareness" education.

Any U.S. citizen may join, but special provision is made for corporate membership. "Membership is extended to key [corporate] personnel... The number of nominees and dues are determined by company size."[50] The bigger the company, the bigger its influence will be.

GE's membership for 1988 is one of the largest of any company, and exceeds even General Dynamics in number of members with the Washington chapter. Three of GE's registered lobbyists are members. The list of GE members follows:

John J. Dillon, General Manager
Phillip J. Martin, Vice President, Washington Aero Operations
Gordon Meriweather, Air Force Programs Manager
E. John Mohler, Army Programs Manager, C³I Programs
Frank Creaser, C³I Programs Manager
Joseph A. W. Wells, Tactical OSD Programs Manager
Lee Doggett, Strategic OSD Programs, Manager
Dave Wilkinson, Civil Space Programs, Manager
Roger S. Busch, Navy Program Manager
Rudolph A. Trefny, Technical & Information Systems Manager

*Aircraft Engine Group*
Harry LeVine, Jr., Program General Manager, Registered Lobbyist
Joel T. Wareing, Air Force Program Manager
Ron E. Krape, Army & DOT Engine Program Manager
Harold G. Franzen, Navy Engine Program Manager
T. Norman Labash, International, Program Manager
Clifford C. LaPlante, Congressional & Executive Office Relations Manager, Registered Lobbyist

**Bringing GE to Light**

General Electric lobbyist Mary Ann Freeman sits on the Washington chapter's board of directors.[51] Another GE official sits on the ADPA's Strategic Defense Division on the executive board—Chris Raber, of the Valley Forge Space Center in Philadelphia.[52] Much of GE's Star Wars work is done at the Valley Forge Space Center.

Two 1987 ADPA members included Louis V. Tomasetti, Senior Vice President and Group Executive, GE Aerospace; and Brian H. Rowe, Senior Vice President and Group Executive, GE Aircraft Engines. Two RCA members involved with aerospace and the military include John D. Rittenhouse, Executive Vice President; and F. H. Stelter, Vice President of Business and Market Development.[53]

Promotional trinkets from a weapons trade show.
Source: Center for Defense Information.

## The National Security Industrial Association

Founded in 1944, the NSIA "provides industrial counsel and guidance to the Department of Defense, the Armed Forces, and other national security-related agencies of the federal government. Enables business leaders to keep abreast of defense developments, requirements, and policies through conferences, briefing sessions, and visits to military installations. Fosters study by industrial authorities of proposed revisions to Armed Forces and federal procurement regulations to assure business acceptance of defense policies affecting contractors."[54]

The NSIA also presents an award each year to "an outstanding American in the area of industry-government cooperation in the interest of national security."[55] Individual chapters of the NSIA also give awards.

These awards often go to members of Congress. In 1986, the Washington, DC, chapter gave awards to Senator John Warner and Congressperson Les Aspin. Warner was a member of the Senate Armed Services Committee; Aspin was Chair of the House Armed Services Committee.[56]

The 1985 winner of the NSIA's highest award, the Forrestal

Memorial, was Senator Sam Nunn. When the award was presented in March 1986, Nunn was Ranking Democrat on the Armed Services Committee.[57]

The 1986 Annual Report of the NSIA lists several GE members in various chapters around the country. The secretary of the Dayton chapter is GE official R. J. Scoles. GE official J. M. Malloy is on that chapter's executive committee.

The Greater Hampton Roads chapter boasts GE official Gilbert W. Snow on its board of directors.

The New England chapter's board of directors includes John J. Morris of RCA Automated Systems.

The executive committee of the Philadelphia chapter includes Francis H. Stelter of RCA's Aerospace and Defense division. The chapter's membership chair is Joseph G. Mullen, also of RCA Aerospace and Defense.

The board of directors of the San Diego area chapter includes Robert Schimmel of GE.

The Washington, DC, chapter's board of directors includes P. J. Martin of RCA. A past president of the NSIA and a member of its board is R. A. Losey, also of RCA.

The secretary of the western region chapter is Paul Fishman of GE. Edward J. Specht of GE is listed on the board of directors.

GE and RCA are also corporate members.

The NSIA's principal vehicle in working with government is its committee program. The committees conduct studies, gather data for the government, and make recommendations on policies, programs, regulations, procedures, and problems. According to the NSIA's Annual Report for 1986, "NSIA committees have become an institution in American defense-industry relationships," and they maintain close ties to the government. GE is listed on the following committees:

Anti-Air Warfare Committee
    Executive Committee: William G. Goodwin, RCA
    Electronic Warfare Ad Hoc Committee: John C. May, GE

Anti-Submarine Warfare Committee
    Executive Committee: Francis M. DeBritz, GE
    Communication, Command, and Control Subcommittee: Ronald Madsen, GE

Automatic Testing Committee
    Army Liaison: Claude (Buz) Presutti, RCA

Command, Control, Communications, and Intelligence Committee
    Executive Committee: Charles E. Barron, GE
    Standing Subcommittee: Air Force Command, Control, Communications, and Intelligence Subcommittee: Chair, Dr. Harold J. Lyness, GE

Manpower and Training Committee
    Training Operations Subcommittee: Franklin A. Hart, GE

Quality and Reliability Assurance Committee
  Army Liaison: Chair, G. S. Hall, GE

Space Committee
  Cost Subcommittee: Chair, G. S. Hall, GE

Members of NSIA's Board of Trustees for 1985–86 (with terms expiring in 1988):

John J. Dillon, General Manager, Aerospace Marketing, GE
J. D. Rittenhouse, Executive Vice President, Aerospace and Defense, RCA

GE members of the NSIA listed in the 1986 Annual Report are

Aerospace Group, Valley Forge, PA
  George B. Farnsworth, Vice President and Group Executive

Aerospace Group Marketing Operation, Washington, DC
  John J. Dillon, General Manager

Avionic and Electronic Systems, Dewitt, NY
  Russell Noll, Jr., Vice President and General Manager

Defense Systems Division, Valley Forge, PA
  Ladislaus W. Wazecha, Vice President and General Manager

Ordnance Systems, Pittsfield, MA
  Nicholas Boraski, Vice President and Gen. Manager

Space Systems Division, Valley Forge, PA
  Allen J. Rosenberg, Vice President and General Manager

Strategic Defense Initiative [Star Wars] Program, Valley Forge
  Christopher L. Raber, Manager

Aircraft Engine Business Group, Evendale, OH
  Brian H. Rowe, Senior Vice President and Group Executive

Evendale Aircraft Engine Production Operation, Evendale, OH
  Harry C. Stonecipher, Vice President and General Manager

Lynn Aircraft Engine Production Operation, Lynn, MA
  Robert C. Hawkins, Vice President and General Manager

Advanced Technological Operations, Evendale, OH
  Robert C. Turnbull, General Manager

Aircraft Engine Business Group, Washington, DC
  Harry LeVine, Jr., Program General Manager

Marine and Defense Facilities Sales Operation, Washington, DC
  T. Tom Balfour, Manager[58]

## The Association of Old Crows

Also known as the Electronic Defense Association,[59] the Association of Old Crows (AOC) was founded in 1964 by what the *Wall Street Journal* called "a small band of World War II intelligence and electronics officers eager to share some drinks and recount their days of battlefield glory." The name comes from the code word "Crow," which was used to identify Allied aircraft that jammed German radar signals during bombing raids.

From this humble beginning, the AOC has grown to 24,000 members and a budget of $2 million. It has 81 chapters, or "roosts" as they call them, all over the world.[60] According to the Encyclopedia of Associations for 1988, the AOC "works for the advancement of electronic warfare with the full cooperation of the U.S. Department of

Department of Defense sponsors meeting of industry and government.

Defense." The AOC also publishes a trade journal, *The Journal of Electronic Defense*.[61]

The AOC, like other military trade associations, helps to create the climate for more weapons. One member of the AOC was given an award at the AOC's 15th Annual Meeting in 1978 for creating "a climate favorable for innovation and new applications for Electronic Warfare throughout the Department of Defense."[62]

Another AOC affair that year was the meeting of the Patriots' Roost in New England. The February 16 meeting was held at RCA Automated Systems Division, with opening remarks by Harry J. Woll, a Vice President and General Manager of RCA.[63] RCA was acquired by GE in 1986.

### Where They Roost

GE has representatives in the Old Crows roosting from Sylmar, California to Syracuse, New York. The following AOC members are listed as "Key People" in the January 1988 *Journal of Electronic Defense*.[64]

Verdugo Roost, Sylmar, California
  RCA/GE Representative Art Freed

Independence Chapter, Willow Grove, Pennsylvania
  GE representatives: Jack Abassi (GE) and Jim Hamlin (RCA)

Empire Club, Syracuse, New York
  GE representatives: Zen Zennor (Syracuse) and James Grant (Utica)

## The Old Crows:
## Where They Roost and Where They Play

**PATRIOT'S ROOST**      **New Hampshire/Massachusetts**

The Patriot's Roost provides an active program for its 1000 members in the greater Boston area. Represented are government organizations at Fort Devens, Hanscom AFB, MITRE and industrial firms such as Digital, GE/RCA, GTE, Honeywell, ITT, Norden, Raytheon and Sanders. Activities include monthly meetings, an educational program and golf outings.

**CAPITOL CLUB**      **Washington, DC/Virginia**

The Capitol Club this year is focusing on membership growth in terms of quantity make-up with particular emphasis on more across the board DOD participation. Our programs will feature a variety, including high level DOD speakers, spring golf outing, Christmas social and a town meeting.

**ARMADILLO JAMMING CHAPTER**      **Texas**

The Armadillo Chapter is the home of the B-1B CCTS and first operational B-1B bomb squadron. The goal of the chapter is to promote electronic warfare awareness among all crew members and the local community. Bringing the USAF's newest and most sophisticated weapon system on line during the last year has proven to be both challenging and exciting.

Source: 1988 AOC Annual Directors, *Journal of Electronic Defense*, Official Publication of the Association of Old Crows, January 1988, Vol. II, No. 1.

**Figure 16.** The Old Crows: Examples of 1988 Chapter Activities

The AOC motto says, "The Old Crow didn't get old by being the fastest of the birds, or the strongest, or the bravest. He got old by being wily." The AOC lives up to its motto by "quietly advising military leaders on complex technical issues, while the Pentagon routinely sponsors and provides space for the group's annual convention and also approves the presentation of classified papers there," says the *Wall Street Journal*.[65]

However, the "full cooperation of the U.S. Department of Defense" is not always enough for the Old Crows. In March 1985, the Wall Street Journal revealed a federal investigation of a prominent Old Crow, Bernie Zettl. Zettl retired from the Air Force in the early 1960s. A founder and former president of the AOC, he was also a consultant to some of the country's largest weaponmakers, including TRW, Northrop, and GTE. In 1985, Zettl was investigated for supplying certain weaponmakers with classified budget and planning documents the Pentagon did not want released. Many of the documents were clearly marked "secret." They contained internal spending projections for many future Air Force and Navy weapons and electronic intelligence-gathering systems.[66]

### The Air Force Association

This trade association is open to "U.S. citizens, both civilian and military, interested in the association's objectives."[67] However, the association also has many "industrial associates," who support the AFA's objectives for "the responsible use of aerospace technology for the betterment of society, and the maintenance of adequate aerospace power as a requisite of national security and international amity." A 1983 list of industrial associates of the AFA includes GE, GE's Aircraft Engine Group, and RCA, along with over 200 other companies.[68]

The AFA produces a monthly publication, *Air Force*. This publication is filled with ads from weapons corporations promoting nuclear weapon systems. GE ads are often prominently placed on the inside front cover.[69]

GE's newest board member, and former member of the Joint Chiefs of Staff, is a member of the AFA—General David Jones. He has been an AFA national director at least since 1983,[70] and he joined GE's board of directors in 1986. Jones received the AFA's highest award, for "outstanding contributions in the field of aerospace activity." Ronald Reagan received the same award in 1983.[71]

### The Aerospace Industries Association

Founded in 1919, this association has 50 companies as members.[72] According to the AIA's 1986 Annual Report, the AIA represents "U.S. companies engaged in research, development, and manufacture of such aerospace systems as aircraft, missiles, spacecraft and space launch vehicles, and propulsion, guidance, control, and accessory systems for the flight vehicles." In other words, it represents companies that make nuclear weapon systems. It "serves as a medium for presenting—to the U.S. government, the public and to international forums—the consensus views and positions of member companies on non-competitive matters related to their business operations and prospects."[73] In other words the AIA promotes policies to the government and the public that benefit their corporate members. Its publications include *Aerospace* and *Aerospace Facts and Figures*.[74]

The report continues, "The industry AIA represents is one of the nation's largest. Its sales in 1986 amounted to $103.5 billion." GE Vice President Edward E. Hood, Jr., is on AIA's board of governors *and* its executive committee.

Richard A. Lauzon of GE was chair of manpower, personnel and training committee for the Aerospace Operations Service of the AIA in 1986.

GE and RCA were also corporate members.[75]

### Business Associations

General Electric, with its diverse product lines, belongs as well to a wide range of trade associations not directly related to the military. Two of the most powerful associations in Washington, with GE among their members, are the U.S. Chamber of Commerce and the National Association of Manufacturers.

The chamber includes chambers of commerce, trade associations, and private companies. The sweeping range of its concerns includes "national issues and problems affecting the economy and the future of the country." It has registered lobbyists, a staff of 1400, and a 1987 budget of $62 million.[76]

The National Association of Manufacturers "represents industry's views on national and international problems to government." It has a staff of 200 and a 1987 budget of $10.5 million.[77]

Some of the other industry associations GE belongs to are listed below:

*Nuclear Power*
Atomic Industrial Forum
The U.S. Committee for Energy Awareness

*Taxes/Finance*
American Council for Capital Formation
Tax Foundation
American Financial Services Association

*Medical Equipment*
Health Industries Manufacturers Association

*Electronics*
National Electrical Manufacturers Association
Electronic Industries Association
American Electronics Association[78]

## Conclusion

Trade associations, with their own lobbyists (official and unofficial), and sometimes their own political action committees, make sure that policies that benefit the weaponmakers industry are acted on by Congress and the executive branch. Setting aside the competitive attitude that prevails in bidding on particular contracts, the weaponmakers band together to ensure plenty of contracts for all. Not only can they influence policy but they can do so while appearing disinterested and concerned for the common good since the associations lobby for the industry overall and not just one company.

Trade associations testify before Congress, meet with key government personnel, host banquets with top-level speakers, present awards to their friends in Congress, hold conventions and exhibits, and publish trade magazines, in addition to lobbying and donating PAC money, to keep the industry's contracts coming. Though they fight among themselves over contracts, the weaponmakers stand together to make the overall pool as large as possible.

# Proceeding According to Plan: The Permanent War Economy

## 12

GE did not reach its present commanding position in business, government, and the military overnight. GE and its corporate "parents" have been carving out the company's place at the top for more than 100 years—since 1878, when the Edison Electric Light Company was organized to finance Thomas Edison's development of the light bulb. The General Electric Company itself came into being in 1892, as the result of a merger between Edison Electric and the American Light Company (also known as Thomson-Houston). The combination gave the new company patent rights over every phase of electric lamp production.[1]

Charles Coffin was GE's first president, and under his direction the company grew quickly. GE's geographic shape was formed by the establishment of major facilities in the northeastern U.S.—in Lynn and Pittsfield, Massachusetts; Schenectady, New York; and Cleveland, Ohio. GE has maintained its manufacturing presence in those cities, though substantial cutbacks have been made in recent years. Schenectady was the site of GE's first industrial research center.[2]

## GE: Backed by Morgan Financing

Company promotional literature describes Coffin as the founder of GE. The literature fails to mention, however, the other main player in GE's formation: *J. P. Morgan*. It was the power of the Morgan banking house that fueled the growth of General Electric.[3] At that time, the name Morgan symbolized ruthless profiteering by big business. In fact, Morgan started his financial empire by profiting from the Civil War. He bought 5,000 obsolete rifles at $3.50 apiece in New York and sold them, as good, at $22.00 apiece to a Union general in St. Louis. The rifles were defective, tending to blow the thumbs off of the soldiers attempting to fire them. Morgan had realized his first profit of nearly $100,000.[4]

Morgan's war profiteering continued into World War I, where J. P. Morgan & Co.'s activities were a major focus of the Senate's Special Committee to Investigate the Munitions Industry. The committee found that many of the Morgan bank's armament exports served to "increase the sales of Morgan connected armaments companies in the U.S., including U.S. Steel and General Electric."[5] To this day, GE's interests remain closely intertwined with the Morgan empire.

By World War I, GE was entrenched as a military supplier—foreshadowing its massive war involvement to come. At the urging of the government, GE joined with its main competitor in 1919 to form the Radio Corporation of America (RCA). GE owned 60 percent of RCA but was finally forced to sell it off in 1930 due to antitrust regulations. However, 55 years later, during the Reagan era of lax antitrust enforcement, GE once again acquired RCA.[6]

## GE: Founder of Influential Business Groups

In 1922, Gerard Swope became GE's president, and Owen Young became chair of the board. Swope's international and governmental clout helped him gain the GE presidency. During World War I he joined the general staff of the U.S. Army. As assistant director of purchase, storage and traffic, *he planned the army procurement program*. After leaving government service in 1919, Swope became the first president of International General Electric, formed at that time to take over all GE's international operations. He so successfully increased GE's exports to foreign countries that he was promoted to president of General Electric just three years later.[7]

Also in 1922, board chair Owen Young and former President Coffin became founding members of the Committee on Foreign Relations (CFR); they were joined in 1923 by Swope. Coffin stayed on the CFR only until 1926, but Young stayed on through 1940, and Swope left in 1951.[8]

Swope continued to play the role befitting the head of a large and growing company. In 1926, Swope became the first president of the National Electrical Manufacturers' Association and a member of its governing board—reflecting GE's growing prominence in key trade associations. In 1933, Swope *served as the first Chair of the Business Advisory Council* (parent of the current Business Council) and sat on the boards of several U.S. and European corporations.

Swope continued to intensify GE's growing connections with the federal government. Also while president of GE, Swope was a member of the National Recovery Act's Industrial Advisory Board in 1933, chair of the Coal Arbitration Board in 1933, member of the President's Advisory Council on Economic Security in 1934, chair of the National Mobilization for Human Needs in 1935-36, and member of the Advisory Council on Social Security in 1937-38. In 1942, after leaving GE, Swope became assistant U.S. secretary of the treasury, and served at the same time on the executive committee of the National War Fund. He was also chair of the National War Fund budget committee.[9]

## GE: Conspiring with Nazi War Criminals

While GE's president was involved in key governmental advisory committees and held official governmental positions, GE's international business ties included cooperation with Nazi Germany. U.S. industrial and financial interests were involved in the revitalization of post-World War I Germany. America's official plan to reduce German war reparations was drafted in 1929 by Owen Young, Chair of General Electric, and J. P. Morgan, Jr.[10]

During the period from 1928 to 1940, GE conspired with German industrialist and munitions maker Alfred Krupp to "control trade and commerce, to fix prices, to eliminate competition, pool patents to restrict production, maintain a monopoly, and to impose restraints, limitations, and restrictions upon trade and commerce in hard metals."[11] These hard metals had crucial military applications.[12]

Zay Jeffries, a GE vice president, was chair of the board of Carboloy Co., the GE subsidiary that manufactured the hard metals.[13] GE and Krupp concluded a secret agreement to sell certain hard metals on which they held international patents at very high prices on the world market. Before the Krupp-GE agreement, the price of one hard-metal compound was $48 a pound. *After the agreement, the price sky-rocketed to $453 a pound.* Yet the metal cost only $8 a pound to produce. A GE engineer had even suggested a price of $50 a pound for a "satisfactory profit."[14]

The conspiracy agreement continued until August 29, 1940, the day before GE was brought to trial by the Anti-trust Division of the Justice Department for these practices. GE's collaboration with Krupp definitely helped the Nazi war effort. John Henry Lewin, Assistant to the Attorney General in the Anti-trust Division, said GE's agreement with Krupp was "directly responsible for the disadvantage at which this country [the U.S.] finds itself in comparison with its enemies" in the use and production of hard metals.[15]

Krupp was later convicted of using slave labor in his Nazi

armaments factories. For its collaboration with Nazi war criminal Krupp, GE was found guilty of price fixing with the Nazis during World War II. For this crime, GE, its two subsidiaries, and three company officers were fined a mere $36,000.[16]

## GE: Putting the Pieces in Place

Charles E. Wilson succeeded to the post of president in 1940. In numerous ways "Electric Charlie"[17] Wilson was the crucial bridge between the old GE and the new. "GE entered World War II doing $340 million of business a year and emerged doing $1.3 billion."[18]

This extra business came from the war itself. GE hired 200,000 new employees during the war to produce vast quantities of weaponry: propulsion units for three-quarters of the Navy's warships, radar and radio equipment, search lights, naval gun directors, bazookas, and jet engines.[19] GE's Schenectady, New York headquarters has been described as "the nerve center of one of the world's biggest and most complex war machines."[20]

### The War Production Board

Even before the U.S. entry into the war, in early 1941, Wilson was asked to chair the Regional Advisory Commission for Industrial Morale.[21] In September 1942, he resigned his position as GE president to become vice chair of the War Production Board (WPB), which had full authority over all war production.

General Electric equipment at Oak Ridge producing uranium 235 for the bomb, 1945.
Source: U.S. Atomic Energy Commission.

**Bringing GE to Light**

Wilson and the head of the WPB, Donald Nelson of Sears-Roebuck, coordinated the efforts of 500 business executives involved in industrial production for the war effort. These executives were known as "dollar-a-year men" because they continued drawing their corporate salaries while accepting nominal government salaries.[22]

Political infighting within the War Production Board eventually caused Nelson to promote Wilson to executive vice chair, with broad authority over the full range of WPB operations. Wilson's powerful position undoubtedly helped GE capture such a large portion of war production contracts.

## The Manhattan Project

Another GE development was even more significant than GE's massive war-time production. In 1940, two scientists at the GE Research Laboratory in upstate New York were among the first to demonstrate the possibility of uranium-235 fission.[23]

As the Manhattan Project secretly worked on the atomic bomb between 1942 and 1945, GE's role in the development and ultimate use of the bomb was substantial. GE became an important supplier of process equipment and power supply apparatus. GE also provided the principal electrical apparatus for the Hanford Engineer Works in Washington State,[24] which produced plutonium for the bomb dropped on Nagasaki.

Charles Wilson, in his position on the War Production Board, helped ensure that materials were allocated for the Manhattan Project.[25] Arthur Compton, a physicist and a GE consultant for 17 years, provided another influential GE connection to the atomic bomb. Compton convinced General Leslie Groves, head of the Manhattan Project, to award more of the project's contracts to GE.[26]

Compton served on an interim committee formed by Secretary of War Henry Stimson in March 1945 to advise on whether and how to use the atomic bomb against Japan. Many of the scientists who had developed the bomb vigorously opposed using it on population centers. Compton discredited the scientists' appeals and convinced the committee to recommend dropping the bomb on Japanese cities.[27] Newly inaugurated President Truman followed the committee's recommendation and ordered two bombs dropped on Hiroshima and Nagasaki.

## The Permanent War Economy

Even as early as January 1942, in the first years of U.S. involvement in the war, GE's President Wilson expressed concern about post-war reconversion, that is, what would happen after the war to industries that had converted to war-time production. One of Wilson's concerns was that peace would bring a post-war recession that could threaten the U.S. economic system.

The issue of peace-time conversion surfaced again a few years later, and Wilson participated on the winning side in the debate that has shaped the U.S. economy ever since. The debate focused on the extent to which the industry should convert back to civilian production after the war was over.

Within the WPB, Wilson—and the large manufacturers he represented—opposed a New Deal program to begin reconversion to peacetime production when defense spending dropped as the war wound down. Wilson and the large corporations feared that such a program would let the smaller companies get the jump on the peace-time market before the bigger companies.[28]

Fundamentally, Wilson opposed total peace-time reconversion on ideological grounds. In a significant speech to the Army Ordnance Association in January 1944,[29] Wilson called for a permanent war economy. Many authorities point to this speech and the concepts Wilson advocated as the beginning of today's unprecedented permanent military economy.[30]

In his speech, Wilson proposed a post-war program in which American resources and energy were ready to be thrown into war production at a moment's notice. Wilson characterized disarmament as a "thoroughly discredited doctrine," and argued that the U.S. "... should henceforth mount a national policy upon the solid fact of an industrial capacity for war, and a research capacity for war...."[31]

GE consultant Arthur Compton, a member of the Stimson Committee. Source: *Atomic Quest: A Personal Narrative* by Arthur Holly Compton.

Wilson well understood the importance of timing to the success of his proposals. He said in his speech:

> ...the revulsion against war not too long hence will be an almost insuperable obstacle for us to overcome in establishing a preparedness program, and for that reason I am convinced that we must begin now to set the machinery in motion... [32]

The Army Ordnance Association—the body before which Wilson made his argument for a permanent war economy—is known today as the American Defense Preparedness Association (ADPA). Using advertising, public speaking, and lobbying, the ADPA continues to fan the public's fears of the Soviet "threat." GE is a prominent ADPA member; in fact, one of GE's weapons lobbyists is on the board of directors of ADPA's DC chapter. The ADPA's current priority project is promoting Star Wars—the industry's dream of perpetuating the permanent war economy into the twenty-first century. [33]

## Post-War Mass Production of Nuclear Weapons

In 1944, members of the scientific team working on the atomic bomb were worried about their job status after the war. Arthur Compton, GE consultant and prominent Manhattan Project physicist, recruited a GE executive to help on the post-war planning of nuclear research. Compton selected none other than Zay Jeffries, the GE vice president involved in the Krupp price-fixing conspiracy. Compton wanted Jeffries's help to win approval for pushing ahead with the Manhattan Project and the mass production of the bomb. [34]

Jeffries headed a committee that produced the "Prospectus on Nucleonics"—Jeffries's term for the new nuclear industry. The prospectus proposed the same relationship with the federal government that GE President Charles Wilson, in his Army Ordnance speech, had advocated a few months earlier. The committee concluded that it was "vitally important" for the U.S. to "keep the lead in nuclear research and its industrial applications. They hoped for a future marked by happy collaboration between the universities, the Government, and an independent nucleonics industry." [35]

Compton, however, was having difficulty with his plan. He encountered "near rebellion" among his scientific staff when he suggested that private industry be given the job of building and operating production plants for bomb-grade plutonium. According to *The New World*, a history of the Atomic Energy Commission, Compton believed the scientists objected because

> ...the fallacy of many scientists [was] in assuming that the objective was to build just one bomb which would provide an overwhelming psychological victory in the war....[but] a weapon was no more important than a

nation's continuing ability to use it. *The job was to produce not just one weapon but weapons in quantity in assembly-line fashion* [36] (emphasis added).

This was the beginning of the more than *30,000 nuclear bombs* that have since rolled off the weaponmakers' assembly lines.

Around the same time, in August 1944, Wilson resigned his post at the War Production Board and returned to GE. It was during Wilson's second term at GE's helm that he laid the groundwork for the company's present nuclear energy and nuclear weapons programs.

GE Vice President Harry Winne at a Board of Consultants meeting advising the government on the future of atomic energy.
Source: U.S. Atomic Energy Commission.

With Japan's surrender, many felt that the atomic program should come under civilian control. And soon government interest broadened to include civilian uses of atomic power. The U.S. held a near monopoly on nuclear technology then, and opinion was sharply divided on whether to share it with other countries—in particular the USSR.

In January 1946, a board of consultants was named to advise the government on the future of the new energy source released with the splitting of the atom. The board included GE Vice President Harry Winne. In August, President Truman formally created the U.S. Atomic Energy Commission (AEC), the predecessor of today's Department of Energy (DOE). [37]

Nuclear weapons development, however, remained a top priority; and GE, by this point a favored government contractor, enjoyed the benefits of its earlier work. The Hanford Facility in Washington State, which produced plutonium for the first atomic bombs, had been run during the war by Du Pont. However, Du Pont did not want to continue. Because General Electric had been so closely involved with the Manhattan Project, GE took over management of the plant in September 1946. [38]

The GE-designed N-Reactor at Hanford, Washington, produces plutonium for nuclear weapons.
Source: *Nuclear Weapons Databook*, Volume III.
Natural Resources Defense Council.

Although the initial government contract awarded GE a nominal $1 fee (in addition to operating costs), the government sweetened the deal by contracting with GE for an additional $20 million atomic research center on land owned by the company at the Knolls, near Schenectady, New York.[39]

GE's economic interest in the ongoing development of both nuclear weapons and nuclear power was now established. To direct the company's affairs in the growing atomic arena, GE created a nuclear advisory board of three GE vice presidents, including Harry Winne and Zay Jeffries. GE's contracts with the Atomic Energy Commission eventually totaled *4.2 billion dollars between 1946 and 1975.*[40]

## GE: Consolidating Power in Cold War Times

In December 1950, Charles Wilson returned to government work in the Office of Defense Mobilization. Once again in a high government position, he continued his theme of war preparedness, updated for the new Cold War context. In a speech to the Newspaper Publishers' Association, he urged the media to keep the American public convinced:

> ...that the free world is in mortal danger...If the people were not convinced of that, it would be impossible for Congress to vote the vast sums now being spent to avert that danger...With the support of public opinion, as marshalled by the press, we are off to a good start. But the mobilization job cannot be completed unless such support is continuous...It is our job—yours and mine—to keep our people convinced that the only way to keep disaster away from our shores is to build America's might.[41]

When Charles Wilson returned to government, Ralph J. Cordiner became GE's president. The choice of Cordiner was no surprise. Cordiner had previously served as vice chair under Wilson at the U.S. government's War Production Board. In 1958, Cordiner became GE's chair of the board and chief executive officer.

Cordiner began to implement the expansion and decentralization plans that Wilson had formulated. These plans led GE to establish plants and facilities in many areas far from its traditional base in the northeastern United States—which after the war grew less attractive to employers as it grew more unionized. The South in particular became a favored locale. In June 1953, Cordiner announced that the South would soon be a major center of GE's operations.[42]

The spread of GE manufacturing centers became increasingly important over the years as the company consolidated its political power. Today, many critics of the nuclear weapons industry say that contractors play on the more parochial congressional interests to win support for their weapons programs. "Members of Congress know that their political careers may depend on their success in bringing weapons work home. Contractors know that their presence in certain congressional districts could be the key to a major contract."[43]

With manufacturing and retail facilities in 32 states, employing approximately 288,000 people in the U.S., GE is extremely well positioned to exert this kind of influence. And GE does. Referring to competition with GE to produce aircraft jet engines in the late 1970s and early 1980s, a representative from United Technologies complained that "we're only big in maybe 20 congressional districts; General Electric is big in 200 congressional districts. That's what we're up against."[44]

### Military Planning Operations

In 1956, during Cordiner's presidency, GE's "think tank" TEMPO was formed. TEMPO—which stands for TEchnical Military Planning Operation—was headed for several years by Dr. Thomas O. Paine. (See chapter on the Revolving Door for the scandal surrounding Paine's tenure as head of NASA.) Paine described TEMPO as "a community that serves largely as a go-between for the military community and the industrial community."[45]

In return for several millions of dollars each year in contracts from the DOD and other government agencies, TEMPO experts studied and proposed solutions to military problems. TEMPO's studies usually concerned weapons system analysis, and covered plans to shore up economies of governments to which the U.S. supplies weapons. By 1975, TEMPO began undertaking more ambitious studies, such as social sciences and "humanities," to better understand and control less developed countries. Since much of TEMPO's work was secret, it is not possible to know exactly what weapons or what national security policies GE developed in its military planning office.[46]

## Electrical Price-Fixing Scandal

In addition to shaping this country's national security positions, GE's illegal corporate practices continued under Cordiner. His presidency was rocked by the price-fixing scandal in 1961, probably the worst ever to hit GE. This scandal involved a conspiracy between managers from GE and other electrical-equipment manufacturers to raise prices in unison on products ranging from $2 insulators to multimillion-dollar turbine generators. The Justice Department indicted 29 corporations and 45 individuals.

GE eventually had to pay the largest fine of any of the companies indicted—$437,000—plus more than $57 million in settlements with the U.S. government and other customers. In addition, three GE officials were jailed briefly, and others were forced to resign.[47]

GE hired one of Washington's most influential lobbyists, Clark Clifford, to argue its case. Clifford was a long-time advisor to Presidents Truman, Kennedy, and Johnson and served as Johnson's Secretary of Defense in 1968. Clifford convinced the IRS that GE's damages should be tax-deductible. *GE was able to deduct about half of its initial outlay in damages, $95 million, from its taxes.*[48]

Cordiner, following in the tradition of his predecessors, had many connections to both business and social groups. He was president of the Business Advisory Council from 1959 to 1961, after being on the council since 1952. From 1956 to 1958 he was chair of the Defense Advisory Committee on Professional and Technical Compensation in the Armed Forces. He was also a member of the National Association of Manufacturers and the National Electrical Manufacturers Association. His membership in social clubs included the Links Club and the Economic and University clubs of New York City, the Mohawk Club in Schenectady, the Cotton Bay Club in the Bahamas, and the Blind Brook Club of Port Chester, New York.[49]

## The Vietnam War Years

Fred J. Borch was GE's president from 1964 to 1972. During this time period (1964–74), GE received more than $12 billion in military contracts—*over $3 million each day*.[50] This figure reflects in large part GE's military production for the Vietnam War. GE stepped up production of special weapons for "electronic war" or "automated war," a new strategy for U.S. intervention in civil wars in less developed countries.

This strategy was politically important because it was warfare based on highly sophisticated electronic machinery,

not ground troops. The strategy was developed specifically for use in Vietnam because President Johnson's policy of sending hundreds of thousands of troops to Indochina made the war extremely unpopular. When Nixon succeeded Johnson as president in 1968, he used these automated weapons—many of them developed and produced by GE—to extend the war. Although Nixon dropped more bombs on Indochina than Johnson had, Nixon was able to run for and win the presidency in 1972 as the "peace candidate"![51]

Corporate involvement in the war went far beyond the supply of weapons. The top 100 military contractors contributed $5.4 million to Nixon's 1972 campaign chest.[52] Business leaders also used their clout to influence public opinion. On September 9, 1965, several executives took out an advertisement in the *New York Times* supporting President Johnson's Vietnam policy:

> The United States has no territorial ambitions, no desire for bases, no intention of seeking special privileges or creating spheres of influence anywhere in Southeast Asia. We are presently engaged in a military effort... made necessary by the presence in South Vietnam of thousands of trained men, sent and directed by North Vietnam in an attempt to overcome the South by terror....

Thomas Gates was one of the business executives who signed this advertisement.[53] Gates, a high-ranking executive with Morgan Guaranty Trust Co., was also a GE board member at the time.

From planning military strategy in its TEMPO operations, to wartime production of electronic warfare systems, to influencing public opinion through advertising, GE helped shape the Vietnam years. Borch, like his predecessors, also operated comfortably in the more subtle arenas of business influence. He chaired the Business Council from 1969 to 1970 and helped found the Business Roundtable; he was vice-chair of the Committee for Economic Development, and a member of the Council on Foreign Relations and other significant business groups. He has also been a member of the Public Advisory Committee on U.S. Trade Policy and the Industry Advisory Council of the U.S. Department of Defense. Borch belongs to many social clubs, including the Wee Burn Country Club and the Woodway Country Club, both in Darien, Connecticut; the Blind Brook Club in Port Chester, New York; the Augusta National Golf Club in Georgia; and the University Club of New York City.[54]

## Direct Corporate Involvement in Matters of State

Reginald H. Jones succeeded Borch as CEO and chair in 1972. Jones became the model representative of corporate America, being named in 1980 as the business executive most widely respected by his peers. The *New York Times Magazine* hailed Jones as "a new breed of businessman that may be good for General Electric—and for the country."[55] Being so widely respected, Jones was able to lead the business community in directions he believed in. The most distinctive direction was toward increased direct involvement in government decision making.

Jones chaired the Business Council in 1979, but more notable was his help in founding the Business Roundtable in 1972. The Roundtable, in contrast to other prominent business groups, placed greater emphasis in two important areas. The Roundtable was set up for the purpose of direct lobbying for corporate interests, to be done by chief executive officers themselves.[56] In the words of a *New York Times* article:

> The so-called superstars–Mr. Shapiro [of Du Pont], Mr. Jones [of GE], Mr. deButts [of AT&T] and Mr. Murphy [of General Motors]–pioneered an unusual era of business involvement in Government affairs. As founders of the Roundtable, they spoke in unison for the collective concerns of business and were heard–and listened to–by everyone who counted in Washington, from the President down.[57]

During Jones's tenure at GE, the nuclear weapons corporations combined forces to fight off a threat to their lucrative business. The government, in an attempt to hold war profiteering in line, set up the DOD Renegotiation Board. The board was intended to recoup excess profits made by the weapons contractors.

In the normal course of business, profits on nuclear weapons contracts are significantly higher than profits in the civilian sector.[58] Combined with cost-plus contracts, huge cost overruns and contractor fraud, the nuclear weaponmakers turn a tidy profit on their government contracts. The public and Congress were becoming increasingly outraged over weaponmaker profiteering.

In the early 1970s, Congress introduced several bills to strengthen the Renegotiation Board. The nuclear weapons industry, with the help of its trade associations, used intense lobbying to defeat all such legislation inimical to its interests. Finally, in 1979, the industry's efforts resulted in ultimate victory: Congress killed the Renegotiation Board.[59]

Reginald Jones, the consummate business leader and influential advocate of close business-government cooperation, had paved the way for his successor. In 1981, GE's legacy passed to John F. Welch, Jr., who assured his shareholders that the company's close relationship with the federal government would continue. In April, 1986, Welch said: "We work hand-in-hand with the government to try to establish policies that are good for this country and good for our enterprise."[60]

## GE: The Conjunction of Business, Government and Military Power

GE's Chief Executive Officer John Welch claims most vehemently, "We only do defense work at the behest of the government who awards the contracts."[61] In fact, 40 years of history, and GE's current extraordinary relationship with the federal government, suggest otherwise.

### What GE Says...What GE Does

GE is shaping policies and influencing decisions on war and peace—decisions that should properly be made by the American people and our elected representatives. General Electric has billions of dollars at stake in perpetuating the nuclear weapons build-up. For this reason alone, the company should remain far removed from policy making.

As Mr. Welch's previous statement shows, GE claims it keeps its distance. In various public statements issued in response to INFACT's Nuclear Weaponmakers Campaign, General Electric claims it does not set defense or foreign policy.

In a prepared release, the company said: "The number and kinds of arms needed by the U.S. aren't going to be determined by INFACT or GE, but by the U.S. Government."[62]

In fact, the number and kinds of arms needed to defend this country are indeed determined to a significant degree by GE. As described in the chapter on Research and Development, the ideas for new nuclear weapons systems—or a substantial change in nuclear weapons policy—is often first developed by R & D people at GE and then "sold" to the Pentagon.

In the fall of 1987, GE's CEO John Welch addressed the Harvard Business School and stated: "...when a contract is up for bid and we have the capability, we go out and do it"[63]—implying that GE simply competes for weapons contracts once the policy and budgetary decisions have been made.

In fact, General Electric is deeply embedded in the policy-making and decision-making processes long before the contracts are ever let for competition. As shown in the chapter on GE's role in the military-industrial complex, the company uses aggressive lobbying, Pentagon advisory committees, and the revolving door to ensure that important national security decisions are favorable to GE's interests. Competing for and winning the lucrative contracts is simply the final—and most visible—step in the long process.

## Creating Both the Supply and the Demand

It is now clear how General Electric shapes fundamental government policy on war and peace. GE's role as a prominent business force has been examined in some detail, as has GE's powerful role in the military-industrial complex. The careful and calculated steps GE has taken over the past 40 years to become so well positioned have been laid out.

**GE is a powerful leader in the worlds of business, government, and the military. Using its special relationship to the federal government, GE actively secures its lucrative nuclear weapons business.**

Within the intricate internal workings of the military-industrial complex, GE is a skilled and successful player in its never-ceasing efforts to influence nuclear weapons policies to ensure more contracts. Among other nuclear weapons contractors, GE is nearly unique.[64] Few other top weaponmakers have the stature and strength that GE has in the business community. None of the companies easily identified as weapons contractors—General Dynamics, McDonnell Douglas, Rockwell, Lockheed, Raytheon—are in GE's league.[65] Thus, GE has an incredible advantage over other weapons contractors in its efforts to shape decisions on war and peace.

On the other hand, in the larger context of U.S. transnational corporations, GE is also very powerful—ranking with IBM, AT&T, Exxon, and Du Pont.[66] Yet none of these transnational giants is as well placed as GE in the world of weapons contracting. Therefore, the avenues of access and influence available to weapons corporations can not be as well exploited by the other transnationals as they are by GE.[67] Although the other leading companies all have an interest in shaping national security decisions, GE's close relationship with this country's military apparatus gives the company additional clout among its transnational peers.

GE's substantial business clout, combined with the company's skilled manipulation of the more commonly recognized avenues of influence used by other weapons corporations, makes GE a powerful force in business, government, and the military. From this special leadership position, GE successfully *creates both the supply and the demand for more costly and deadly nuclear weapons*.

# Update 1989: Continued Efforts to Shape Nuclear Weapons Policies for Profits

## 13

Data show that General Electric continues to use PAC funds in order to buy influence on important weapons-procurement committees, to give out honoraria to influential congresspersons, to lobby hard for expensive weapons systems, and to take advantage of the revolving door. The following information represents the latest figures and background data documenting GE's role in the continued promotion of nuclear weapons.

## Political Action Committee Contributions and Honoraria

### PAC Contributions

GE, one of the largest users of PAC contributions, has steadily increased the total amount of contributions to federal candidates to gain preferential access to Congress [see pp. 69-71]. In 1985-86, GE gave a total of $243,100 to 280 candidates; in 1987-88, this figure rose to $370,445 to 340 candidates, a 52 percent increase. Of the $370,445, $85,800 went to elected officials who were members of defense-related committees. The following charts provide an update and more background data for Figure 10, p. 70. The charts show that GE has given PAC contributions strategically directed at key members of weapons committees (the Armed Services Committee and the Defense Appropriations Subcommittee).

### GE PAC Contributions to Federal Candidates (1979-1988)[1]

| Years | Dollars to Candidates | No. of Candidates | % Change from Previous Year | Dollars to Incumbents | % of Total | Dollars to Members of Defense Committees |
|---|---|---|---|---|---|---|
| 1979-80 | $133,875 | 291 | — | $98,500 | 73% | $38,650 |
| 1981-82 | $149,125 | 289 | 11% | $141,525 | 95% | $27,975 |
| 1983-84 | $204,375 | 288 | 37% | $185,065 | 91% | $70,325 |
| 1985-86 | $243,100 | 280 | 19% | $213,350 | 88% | $53,310 |
| 1987-88 | $370,445 | 340 | 52% | $340,810 | 92% | $85,800 |
| Totals | $1,100,920 | | | $979,250 | | $276,060 |

### Contributions to Defense Committee Members: Armed Services Committee and Defense Appropriations Subcommittee (1979-1988)[2]

ASC = Armed Services Committee
DAS = Defense Appropriations Subcommittee

| Years | Total $ to Members of Defense Comm. | House ASC | House DAS | Senate ASC | Senate DAS |
|---|---|---|---|---|---|
| 1979-80 | $38,650 | $7,300 | $4,700 | $11,375 | $15,275 |
| 1981-82 | $27,975 | $10,500 | $6,625 | $6,100 | $4,750 |
| 1983-84 | $70,325 | $18,150 | $16,750 | $17,400 | $18,025 |
| 1985-86 | $53,310 | $16,250 | $15,060 | $8,100 | $13,900 |
| 1987-88 | $85,800 | $36,600 | $23,000 | $12,750 | $13,450 |

### Honoraria

GE has also increased payments to legislators for speaker's fees, or honoraria [see pp. 71-72]. The following charts update and provide more background data for Figure 12, p. 72.

### GE Honoraria to House and Senate Combined Totals[3]

| | 1988 | 1987 | 1986 | 1985 | 1984 |
|---|---|---|---|---|---|
| Total No. of Recipients | 35 | 42 | 42 | n/a | n/a |
| Total Amount Given | $65,500 | $74,000 | $69,540 | $47,500 | $38,656 |
| Average Amount | $1,871 | $1,762 | $1,656 | n/a | n/a |
| No. of Recipients on ASC | 13 | 18 | 13 | n/a | n/a |
| No. of Recipients on DAS | 9 | 13 | 8 | n/a | n/a |
| Total No. on Defense Committees | 22 | 31 | 21 | n/a | n/a |
| % of Recipients that Are on Defense Committees | 63% | 63% | 50% | n/a | n/a |
| Total Amount Given to Legislators on Defense Committees | $39,500 | $52,000 | $32,000 | $36,500 | $22,500 |
| % of Total Amount Given to Members of Defense Committees | 60% | 70% | 46% | 77% | 58% |

The following two charts show GE honoraria given to specific House and Senate members in 1988.

### GE Honoraria Contributions to House Members, 1988[4]

ASC = House Armed Services Committee Member
DAS = House Defense Appropriations Subcommittee Member

| Name | Party | State | Amount | Date | Amount | Date | Member of |
|------|-------|-------|--------|------|--------|------|-----------|
| Aspin, Les | D | WI | $2000 | 2/25/88 | | | ASC |
| Buechner, Jack | R | MO | $1000 | 7/25/88 | | | — |
| Bustamante, Albert | D | TX | $1000 | 1/18/88 | | | ASC |
| Byron, Beverly | D | MD | $1000 | 3/26/88 | | | ASC |
| Coughlin, Lawrence | R | PA | $2000 | 5/19/88 | | | — |
| Davis, Robert | R | MI | $1000 | 1/18/88 | | | ASC |
| Dickinson, William | R | AL | $2000 | 3/15/88 | | | ASC |
| Dingell, John | D | MI | $2000 | 3/14/88 | | | — |
| Dyson, Roy | D | MD | $1000 | 3/14/88 | | | ASC |
| Foley, Thomas | D | WA | $2000 | 1/15/88 | | | — |
| Gray, William | D | PA | $2000 | 1/26/88 | $2000 | 2/26/88 | — |
| Leath, Marvin | D | TX | $1000 | 3/7/88 | | | ASC |
| Livingston, Bob | R | LA | $2000 | 5/6/88 | | | DAS |
| Lott, Trent | R | MS | $2000 | 1/26/88 | | | — |
| McCurdy, Dave | D | OK | $2000 | 3/31/88 | | | ASC |
| Michel, Robert | R | IL | $2000 | 1/24/88 | | | — |
| Mineta, Norman | D | CA | $2000 | 2/18/88 | | | — |
| Murtha, John | D | PA | $2000 | 2/18/88 | | | DAS |
| Roe, Robert | D | NJ | $2000 | 6/12/88 | | | — |
| Walker, Robert | R | PA | $1000 | 6/24/88 | | | — |
| Weldon, Curt | R | PA | $1000 | 4/5/88 | $1000 | 3/31/88 | ASC |
| Young, C.W. Bill | R | FL | $2000 | 1/20/88 | $2000 | 1/22/88 | DAS |

Total = 22 House Members for a total of $41,000

Twelve of the 22 House members who received honoraria from GE in 1988 were members of defense committees.

### GE Honoraria Contributions to Senate Members, 1988[5]

ASC = Senate Armed Services Committee Member
DAS = Senate Defense Appropriations Subcommittee Member

| Name | Party | State | Amount | Date | Member of |
|------|-------|-------|--------|------|-----------|
| D'Amato, Alfonse M. | R | NY | $2000 | 3/14/88 | DAS |
| Danforth, John C. | R | MO | $2000 | 1/15/88 | — |
| Dixon, Alan J. | D | IL | $2000 | 5/17/88 | ASC |
| Hollings, Ernest F. | D | SC | $2000 | 5/27/88 | DAS |
| Johnston, J. Bennett | D | LA | $2000 | 6/13/88 | DAS |
| Mitchell, George J. | D | ME | $2000 | 1/25/88 | — |
| Nunn, Sam | D | GA | $2000 | 2/26/88 | ASC |
| Rudman, Warren B. | R | NH | $2000 | 1/26/88 | DAS |
| Sasser, James R. | D | TN | $2000 | 3/16/88 | DAS |
| Shelby, Richard C. | D | AL | $2000 | 3/15/88 | ASC |
| Simpson, Alan K. | R | WY | $2000 | 2/17/88 | — |
| Stevens, Ted | R | AK | $1000 | 7/22/88 | DAS |
| Wilson, Pete | R | CA | $1500 | 6/7/88 | ASC |

Total = 13 Senators for $24,500

Ten of the 13 Senators that GE gave honoraria to in 1988 were members of defense-related committees.

## Lobbyists

GE has approximately 150 employees working out of its Washington Corporate Government Relations office–the largest lobbying office of all of the weapons contractors [see pp. 81-92]. As of June 28, 1989, GE had a total of 26 *registered* lobbyists.

### List of Active GE Registered Lobbyists as of June 28, 1989[6]

| Name | GE Division | Title |
|------|-------------|-------|
| Barrie, Robert W. | Washington Office | Mgr., Federal Legislative Rels. Opers. |
| Beach, Tina Marts | Washington Office | Mgr., Aircraft Engines Cong. Relations |
| Brown, Virginia W. | GE Mortgage Ins. | Government Relations Consultant |
| Campbell, John G. | Washington Office | Consultant |
| Canfield, Anne C. | Washington Office | Wash. Rep., Corporate Gov't Relations |
| Cook, K. Richard | Washington Office | Wash. Rep., Corporate Gov't Relations |
| Davis, John W. | Washington Office | Mgr., Aerospace Congressional Rels. |
| Dewey, Ballantine, Bushby, Palmer & Wood | GE Pension Trust | Law Firm |
| Forman, Sallie H. | NBC–Washington Office | Vice Pres., Government Relations |
| Freeman, Mary Ann | Washington Office | Mgr., Cong. & Industry Relations |
| Fried, Frank, Harris, Shriver & Jacobson | GE Nuclear (San Jose) | Law Firm |
| Hynes, Robert D. Jr. | NBC–Washington Office | None given |
| Ketchel, Robert M. | Washington Office | Mgr., Energy Projects |
| LaPlante, Clifford C. | Washington Office | Mgr., Cong. & Executive Office Rels. |
| Mahony, Terence P. | NBC–Washington Office | None given |
| McManus, William F. | Washington Office | Wash. Rep., Corporate Gov't Relations |
| Messick, Neil T. | Washington Office | Wash. Rep., Corporate Gov't Relations |
| Moliter, Robert M. | Washington Office | None given–Lobbies on medical matters |
| Neill & Co., Inc. | GE Industrial & Power | None given |
| Peter, Phillips S. | Washington Office | Vice Pres., Government Relations |
| Portnoy, David A. | Washington Office | Mgr., Civil Programs |
| Riley, Susan | Kidder Peabody | None given |
| Shelley, Zack H. Jr. | Washington Office | Mgr., Aerospace Congressional Relations |
| Thacher, Proffitt & Wood | GE Mortgage Insurance | Law Firm |
| Walton, John C. | Washington Office | Consultant |
| Wilkinson, David A. | Washington Office | Mgr., Civil Programs |

Since the first printing of this book, the following weapons-related lobbyists are no longer registered as active lobbyists for GE:

Harry Levine, Jr.
William Patterson
J.D. Williams
Heron, Burchette, Ruckert & Rothwell

GE has added the following weapons-related lobbyists since 1987:

John C. Walton
John W. Davis
John G. Campbell
David A. Portnoy
David A. Wilkinson

### Lobbying Report Forms

A recent trend has been for lobbyists to deliberately downplay their lobbying role on their reporting forms. This is how some weapons-related GE lobbyists now describe their activities:

Interested in laws that concern GE such as authorization and appropriation bills, and government procurement. Major activity will be reporting legislative activities of the government to the Company in order to determine the effect of such legislation on the operation of the Company. *A small percentage of time may be spent in activities directed toward influencing the passage or defeat of the language of specific legislation.* [Emphasis added.][7]

# The Revolving Door

The "revolving door," the hiring of former government personnel by GE and of former GE personnel by the government, continues to bring more influence, inside information, and weapons contracts to GE [see pp. 76-79]. Since 1985, GE has hired at least 170 people from the Pentagon to work with the company in its military work. Seventy percent of these employees are retired career military officers. Many had contracting responsibilities while at the Pentagon. Others were involved in planning, research, and development of weapons systems. These individuals have many important contacts and bring years of Pentagon experience to their new job at GE. They are very helpful to GE's nuclear weapons business.

**Record of People Hired by
GE 1985-1988 Who Are on File
at the Department of Defense (DOD)
(Went through the Revolving Door *and* Filed Form 1787)[8]**

|  | 1988 | 1987 | 1986 | 1985 | Totals |
|---|---|---|---|---|---|
| No. of People Hired by GE | 39 | 33 | 46 | 52 | 170 |
| No. of Retired Military | 28 | 24 | 31 | 36 | 119 |
| No. of Former Military | 5 | 1 | 2 | 1 | 9 |
| No. of Civilians | 6 | 8 | 11 | 12 | 37 |
| No. of Unknown | 0 | 0 | 2 | 3 | 5 |
| Hired from: |  |  |  |  |  |
| U.S. Air Force | 12 | 11 | 20 | 26 | 69 |
| U.S. Navy | 13 | 9 | 7 | 6 | 35 |
| U.S. Army | 5 | 7 | 7 | 5 | 24 |
| Defense Intelligence Agency | 1 | 1 | 1 | 1 | 4 |
| Office of Joint Chiefs of Staff | 0 | 0 | 0 | 2 | 2 |
| Def. Contract Audit Agency | 0 | 0 | 2 | 1 | 3 |
| Office of Asst. Secretary of Defense | 0 | 0 | 0 | 1 | 1 |
| CIA | 1 | 1 | 0 | 0 | 2 |
| Office of Secretary of Defense | 1 | 0 | 0 | 0 | 1 |
| Air Force Systems Command | 0 | 0 | 1 | 4 | 5 |
| Other Agencies | 6 | 4 | 8 | 6 | 24 |
| TOTAL (Same as above) | 39 | 33 | 46 | 52 | 170 |

## Other "Door Revolvers"

The following employment histories update pages 76-79 and exemplify how GE continues to take advantage of the revolving door to gain inside information and influence in the selling of weapons and weapons systems. These biographies came from Form 1787s filed by each individual at the Department of Defense.

**Daniel B. Denning** Date Left Department of Defense: January 19, 1987
Date Began Work with GE: March 29, 1988

Before joining GE, Denning was the Deputy Assistant Secretary of Defense-Senate Affairs. He worked out of the Office of the Secretary of Defense-Legislative Affairs (OSD-LA). He was responsible for liaison with the U.S. Senate on behalf of the Secretary and OSD elements.

In April 1988, Denning reported that he was the GE Division Vice President, Government Relations. On the report form, he describes himself as a Legislative Liaison with Congress and executive branch agencies relating to acquisition and retention of government services for contracts for GE. He works out of GE's Washington office. He is not a *registered* lobbyist for GE.[9]

**S.J. Pryzby** Date Left Department of Defense: September 1988
Date Began Work with GE: October 1988

Pryzby is a retired Navy Captain whose last job at the Pentagon was Director of Combat System Design Engineering. He was responsible for reviewing task instructions issued against an RCA omnibus contract and monitoring contract status.

Pryzby's title is "Manager, Advanced Planning" and he works for GE Government Services, based in Cherry Hill, NJ. According to his GE job description, he is "responsible for complex market research, capture planning, competitor analysis and development of Government Services Business. Responsible for field marketing, operating and support for all Government Services Operations including maintenance of existing business and development of new ... business." He also "develops, establishes and maintains effective market relationships with government officials and agencies, military commands and industrial users to enhance company image and acquaint potential customers with Government Services capability."[10]

**Daniel M. Littley, Jr.** Date Left Department of Defense: August 1, 1988
Date Began Work with GE: July 18, 1988

Littley is a retired Major who was a Ballistic Missiles Defense Plans Officer and was responsible for BMD Command and Control Concept Development. He also chaired the BMD C2 Working Group Mission Requirements and thus was involved in planning.

At GE, Littley is a "Systems Engineer" working at Falcon Air Force Base. He is "responsible for strategic wargaming development, definition, enablement and analysis ... and the development of a strategic defense system, Strategic Offensive Forces Interface Requirements Document and a National Military Command System IR & D."

Littley has much to offer GE in the way of inside information and/or insight on upcoming technology.[11]

**Thomas E. Cooper, PhD** Date Left Dept. of Defense: April 6, 1987
Date Began Work with GE: August 1, 1987

Thomas E. Cooper was one of several top-ranking Pentagon officials who deliberately left the Pentagon *before* April 16, 1987, when a new law would go into effect limiting where a former DOD person could go to work.[12] In some of the summer 1988 newspaper articles on the "Operation III Wind" procurement scam, Cooper was mentioned in terms of "the revolving door." He was cited by the *Christian Science Monitor* as an example of someone who failed to abide by the law and file the required forms with the DOD after he left.[13]

Cooper eventually *did* file (in July 1988–after the 1988 deadline). He blamed an "administrative oversight on the DOD's part" for this failure to file.

### Department of Defense Work Experience

Cooper was a high-ranking civilian at the Pentagon. From January 1983 until March 1987, he served as the Assistant Secretary of the Air Force for Research, Development and Logistics. Cooper was appointed to his first position by President Reagan and was confirmed by the U.S. Senate. From March 1987 until April 6, 1987, Cooper was Assistant Secretary of the Air Force for Acquisition. In his own words, Cooper claims that both positions

> . . . had essentially the same set of responsibilities, namely I was the senior Air Force civilian official responsible for the research, development, procurement and logistics activities of the United States Air Force and I served as the Air Force Acquisition Executive. I reported directly to the Secretary of the Air Force and derived my authority from him.[14]

Cooper was also the chairperson of the F-16 Multinational Fighter Program Steering Committee and was the senior *U.S. delegate to the NATO Advisory Group for Aerospace Research and Development.*

### Background

Cooper graduated from UC Berkeley in 1970, where he received a bachelor's degree in engineering-mathematics, and master's and doctoral degrees in mathematical engineering.

In 1977, he was appointed as a professional *staff member of the Armed Services Committee*, U.S. House of Representatives. During his tenure there he worked on a wide range of research, development, and acquisition issues. His responsibilities included strategic, tactical, space, and command, control, and communications programs. He also had responsibility for all intelligence-related issues.

He had extensive experience with industry, having worked with Procter and Gamble, Aerojet General, and the State of California, as well as serving as an engineering consultant to the Lawrence Radiation Laboratory, Livermore, CA; the Naval Weapons Center, China Lake, CA; and the Naval Weapons Laboratory, Dahlgren, VA.

### Cooper's Role at GE

Thomas Cooper's title at GE is Vice President, Aerospace Technology–Corporate Executive Office. Right after he was hired, Cooper described himself as having a wide-ranging set of responsibilities at GE with an initial focus on learning the company, its people and its many and varied businesses with a primary emphasis on the aircraft engine and aerospace businesses. He said he was to work on long-range technology plans, resource allocation, and international business strategies.

He has two offices: one in Fairfield, CT, at GE Corporate Offices, and the other in Washington, DC. Effective May 1, 1988, the GE Aerospace and Aircraft Engine offices in Washington, DC, reported to him. Cooper reports to the "GE Vice Chairman responsible for GE's Aerospace, Aircraft Engine and Technology programs." He has broad oversight responsibility for all of GE's major defense systems.

Cooper also admits that all of the Air Force-sponsored GE Aerospace and Aircraft Engine programs that currently fall under his broad areas of responsibility at GE are the responsibility of the Assistant Secretary of the Air Force for Acquisition–the job he left just before joining GE.[15]

# PART IV. NUCLEAR WEAPONS PROFITS AND THE HUMAN TOLL

GE has a long history of profiting from weapons production—from the company's earliest war production to GE's permanent war economy plan. With the dawn of the Nuclear Age, GE's role expanded to include shaping nuclear weapons policies for profits.

GE's benefits from nuclear weapons production are clear: GE grosses billions of dollars in nuclear weapons sales, and the company is now set to reap even more lucrative profits on Star Wars contracts.

But what are the benefits to the rest of the country—and the world? GE and other nuclear weaponmakers would have people believe that nuclear weapons increase security.

Yet nuclear weapons production puts millions of people—in this country and around the world—in deadly peril. Nuclear weapons mean that people are denied the most basic security of food, shelter and jobs. Nuclear weapons are weakening the U.S. economy, destroying the country's industrial competitiveness, and leaving an economic burden for our children to shoulder far into the future. Nuclear weapons poison the air, land, and water people depend on. And even though we are not yet fighting a nuclear war, the radiation from nuclear weapons is *killing people now*.

Nuclear weapons threaten our economy, our environment, our very lives. The only "security" from their production is for the nuclear weaponmakers themselves.

# GE's Nuclear Weapons Work

## 1

## The Overview

General Electric makes critical components to more nuclear weapons systems than any other company. It is involved in nearly every major nuclear weapons system. In fiscal years 1984–86, GE grossed at least $11,074,175,000 ($11 billion) from nuclear warfare systems.[1]

GE's work includes components for most first-strike weapons from the MX missile and the Trident submarine to the Stealth and the B-1 bombers.[2] GE also produces the neutron generator, the "trigger" for every U.S. hydrogen bomb.[3] And, in 1986, GE moved up to the position of third largest Star Wars contractor.[4]

Over the years, GE has been active in the full range of the nuclear weapons cycle from mining uranium and processing plutonium to producing bomb components and testing nuclear weapons. GE mined uranium when it owned the Pathfinder Mines Corporation.[5] From 1946 to 1964, General Electric ran the Hanford Nuclear Reservation, which processed plutonium. At the Pinellas plant in Florida, GE produces the "trigger" for nuclear bombs and special "triggers" for nuclear testing.[6]

GE not only produces nuclear weapons but it has been involved in researching and developing new weapons and weapon systems. In the 1950s, GE developed the neutron generator for the hydrogen bomb.[7] During the 1970s and 1980s, GE developed the multiple independently-targeted re-entry vehicle (MIRV).[8] A re-entry vehicle is what accurately carries a nuclear bomb to its target. A multiple re-entry vehicle acts like a "bus," dropping off its passengers—that is, nuclear bombs—at different destinations. As Randolph Ryan noted in the *Boston Globe*, "This invention is one main reason the number of strategic warheads has increased sharply in recent years."[9] In the 1980s, GE is now researching and developing Star Wars. As part of its research, GE is working on a nuclear power plant for space.[10]

## The Pinellas Plant

The Pinellas plant located near St. Petersburg, Florida, produces the neutron generator for all nuclear bombs. The neutron generator is about the size of a fist and is used to initiate the fission chain reaction within a nuclear weapon.[11] This is why it is often known as the "trigger" for the nuclear bomb.

General Electric built the Pinellas plant in 1956–57 at the request of the U.S. government. Shortly thereafter, the Atomic Energy Commission (AEC) exercised an option to purchase the plant.[12] Since that time, GE has run the plant under five-year contracts with the AEC and the Department of Energy (DOE). GE's current contract expires on September 30, 1988.[13]

The budget for the Pinellas plant has increased dramatically during the 1980s. In 1981, the budget was only $61.9 million. By 1986, the budget was $138.6 million. This is an increase of over 100 percent.[14] For fiscal years 1984-86, GE contracts for Pinellas totaled $362.2 million.[15]

At Pinellas, along with the neutron generator for nuclear bombs, GE produces special neutron generators and measurement devices for nuclear weapons testing.[16]

Radioactive materials used in work at Pinellas include tritium and plutonium-238.[17] According to the Department of Energy, the plant releases small quantities of radioactive substances from on-site exhaust stacks. Water containing tritium is filtered through soil at the plant, raising concerns

The Pinellas Plant where GE produces the neutron "trigger" for the nuclear bomb.
Source: *Nuclear Weapons Databook*, Volume III.
Natural Resources Defense Council.

about contamination of ground water. Radioactive materials are regularly shipped to and from the plant.[18]

## The Knolls Lab

When GE took over the management of the Hanford Nuclear Reservation in 1946, the deal was sweetened with a $20 million award to build an atomic research center on GE-owned land near Schenectady, New York.[19] The Knolls complex includes two other facilities as well—one in West Milton, New York, and one in Windsor, Connecticut. The complex is now known as the Knolls Atomic Power Laboratory. GE operates Knolls under contract with the DOE. The current contract expires on September 30, 1990.[20]

At the Knolls lab, GE is responsible for the research and development of nuclear reactors for the U.S. Navy's nuclear propulsion program. For example, at Knolls GE developed the nuclear reactors for the Trident ballistic missile submarine fleet.[21]

Much radioactive material is used at the Knolls lab. The nuclear reactors at Knolls use weapons grade uranium for fuel. In 1977, the Nuclear Regulatory Commission (NRC) cited the General Electric Knolls lab as one of the facilities in the U.S. which has lost weapons grade uranium or plutonium.[22]

## Star Wars

GE has been rapidly increasing its involvement in Star Wars. In fiscal year 1983, GE had just slightly over $3 million in Star Wars contracts. Out of the current top 20 Star Wars contractors, GE then ranked 17th. By fiscal year 1986, GE had over $200 million ($208.7 million) in Star Wars contracts. In 1986, GE ranked number three.[23] Merging with RCA put GE in a better position to lobby for Star Wars contracts due to RCA's electronics and laser work. Prior to the merger RCA had received few Star Wars contracts. It had none in fiscal years 1983-84 and $9.3 million in fiscal year 1985, compared to GE's $28.6 million in fiscal year 1985.[24]

General Electric's Star Wars contracts range from a systems architecture contract in which GE examined the feasibility of Star Wars, to a contract to develop a nuclear power plant for space.[25]

# General Electric's Nuclear Weapons-Related Work

The following tables break down GE's diverse nuclear weapons-related work by program and by geographic area.

## Department of Defense and Department of Energy Awards Fiscal Years (FY) 1984–86[26]

| Nuclear Capable Weapons | FY 1984-86 ($ stated in millions) Amount |
| --- | --- |
| Aegis Missile | $ 400,852,000 |
| Ballistic Missile Defense System | 29,366,000 |
| Minuteman Missile | 13,520,000 |
| MX Missile | 413,444,000 |
| Polaris Missile | 4,348,000 |
| Poseidon Missile | 11,663,000 |
| Tomahawk Missile | 19,495,000 |
| Trident Missile | 707,130,000 |
| Other | 29,782,000 |
| Subtotal Nuclear Capable Weapons | $1,629,600,000 |

| Nuclear Capable Delivery Vehicles | Amount |
| --- | --- |
| A-6 Intruder Attack Aircraft | $ 40,176,000 |
| AV-8 Harrier Aircraft | 55,320,000 |
| B-1 Bomber | 94,995,000 |
| Destroyer DDG-47 Aegis | 82,003,000 |
| F-4 Phantom II Fighter Aircraft | 12,975,000 |
| F-15 Eagle Fighter Aircraft | 28,051,000 |
| F-18 Hornet Fighter Aircraft | 1,817,156,000 |
| F-111 Fighter Aircraft | 163,985,000 |
| P-3 Orion Patrol Aircraft | 64,774,000 |
| SH-60 Seahawk Helicopter | 18,924,000 |
| SSN-Nuclear Submarine | 323,857,000 |
| SSN-688 Submarine | 492,205,000 |
| Trident Nuclear Submarine | 503,027,000 |
| Other | 23,606,000 |
| Subtotal Nuclear Capable Delivery Vehicles | $3,721,054,000 |

| Nuclear-Related Power Plants (Engines) | Amount |
| --- | --- |
| F-101 Engine | $ 243,637,000 |
| F-110 Engine | 2,683,337,000 |
| J-79 Turbojet Engine | 412,174,000 |
| TF-34 Turbofan Engine | 365,191,000 |
| Subtotal Engines | $3,704,339,000 |

| Nuclear Weapons-Related Electronic Systems | Amount |
| --- | --- |
| AN/SQS-53 Sonar | $ 290,857,000 |
| Defense Satellite Communication System (DSCS III) | 453,336,000 |
| Forward Scatter over the Horizon Radar | 143,559,000 |
| Seek Skyhook | 4,960,000 |
| Strategic Army Communication System (STARCOM) | 59,653,000 |
| Other | 113,925,000 |
| Subtotal Electronic Systems | $1,066,290,000 |
| Total Department of Defense | $10,121,283,000 |

| Department of Energy Contracts | Amount |
| --- | --- |
| Naval Nuclear Reactor Program (Knolls Atomic Power Laboratory) | $590,684,000 |
| Pinellas Plant Operation | 362,208,000 |
| Total Department of Energy | $952,892,000 |
| TOTAL DOD AND DOE NUCLEAR WEAPONS-RELATED WORK FY 1984–86 | $11,074,175,000 |
| GE DOD and DOE Nuclear Weapons-Related Work as a Percentage of Annual Sales | 11.8 percent |

The Trident submarine—capable of carrying close to 200 nuclear warheads.
Source: Department of Defense.

Test of the Tomahawk Cruise Missile.
Source: *Nuclear Weapons Databook*, Volume I.
    Natural Resources Defense Council.

### Geographic Breakdown of GE's Nuclear Weapons-Related Work in Fiscal Year 1986[27]

| State | Total Amount | All Locations | Partial listing |
|---|---|---|---|
| OH | $1,840,365,000 | Cincinnati<br>Cleveland<br>Evendale<br>Xenia | F-4 Phantom<br>F-16<br>F-100 Engine |
| MA | $982,838,000 | Fitchburg<br>Lynn<br>Pittsfield<br>Rowley<br>West Lynn<br>Wilmington | Nuclear SSN Submarine<br>Trident<br>Aegis<br>F-18 Hornet<br>Polaris |
| NY | $763,994,000 | Binghamton<br>East Syracuse<br>Johnson City<br>Niskayuna<br>Schenectady<br>Syracuse<br>Utica | Over-the-Horizon Radar<br>F-111<br>B-52 Strato Fortress<br>Trident |
| NJ | $498,537,000 | Camden<br>Moores Meadow<br>Moorestown<br>Mount Laurel<br>Princeton | Aegis<br>Satellite Communications<br><br>Trident<br>Tomahawk<br>Ballistic Missile Defense System |
| PA | $273,317,000 | Erie<br>King of Prussia<br>Lancaster<br>Philadelphia<br>Valley Forge<br>Warminster | MX Missile<br>A-6 Intruder<br>Defense Satellite Communications System (DSCS III)<br>S-3 Viking |
| FL | $130,136,000 | Cape Canaveral<br>Daytona Beach<br>Pinellas<br>Orlando | Seek Skyhook<br>F-16<br>Neutron Generator<br>F-18 Hornet |
| VT | $36,707,000 | Burlington | AV-8 Harrier<br>F-18 Hornet<br>A-7 Corsair<br>F-16 |
| Pacific Islands | $25,820,000 | Trust Territory | Ballistic Missile Defense System |
| VA | $20,187,000 | Dahlgren<br>Springfield | **DDG-47 Destroyer<br>Aegis** |
| KS | $14,698,000 | Arkansas City | J-79<br>TF-34 |
| KY | $4,898,000 | Madisonville | F-101 |
| DC | $1,823,000 | Washington, DC | Submarine<br>SSN-688<br>Trident |
| WA | $1,100,000 | Seattle | TF-34 Turbofan Engine |
| MD | $669,000 | Rockville | Poseidon |
| TX | $500,000 | Kelly Air Force Base | MX Missile |
| CA | $172,000 | Ontario | J-79 |
| OK | $84,000 | Tinker Air Force Base | F-16 |
| AK | $60,000 | Clear Missile | 474L BMEWS |

## Profits on GE's Nuclear Weapons Work

"Defense contractors are active participants and partners in a military-industrial establishment which possesses its own internal, largely self-generating dynamism, whose motive power is the drive for the above-average profit that can be made producing the weapons of war."
—United Auto Workers President Walter Reuther, 1969

Profits on GE's nuclear weapons work are very hard to measure. To see GE's profits for the corporation as a whole, one need only look at GE's annual report to its shareholders. GE's goal as a corporation is to maximize profits for its shareholders. Therefore, the company will show maximum profits in its annual report.

GE breaks out profit figures by its industry segments, but GE's military contracts are spread through several different segments. The company does not identify the profits it makes on its overall military work or its nuclear weapons work in particular. Therefore, it is not easy to see how much of our tax dollars are going towards GE's profits on nuclear weapons.

There has been much debate recently between Congress, the Pentagon, and weapons corporations regarding the level of profits on military work. If the weaponmakers show high levels of profit, then Congress may try to reduce their profits.

The office of the Secretary of Defense, the Navy, and the General Accounting Office (GAO) have all done studies of military contracts in recent years. The Secretary of Defense concluded profits were equitable between mili-

Open missile hatches for Trident missiles on the Trident submarine.
Source: *Nuclear Weapons Databook*, Volume I.
    Natural Resources Defense Council.

tary and commercial work.[28] The Navy issued a subsequent report charging that corporate profits on military work were actually 15 to 20 percent higher than commercial work.[29] More recently, the GAO reported that military contractors were 35 percent more profitable than commercial manufacturers during 1970–79 and *120 percent* more profitable during 1980–83.[30]

Why such differences? The methodologies do differ. The main problem, however, is that the weaponmakers just do not provide the data on weapons profitability. The question remains: How much did GE make on its $11 billion of nuclear weapons work, 1984–86?

# Unrestrained Weapons Spending
# Ruins the Economy

## 2

> *Worst of all, we are hooked on the drug of military spending as the way to create jobs. That is what the arms-makers tell us, and we have come to believe it. In fact, reliance on military production is sabotaging our ability to produce and compete in civilian goods.*[1]
> —Anthony Lewis, *The New York Times*

## GE and Jobs: An Example

Veteran GE employee Peter Beaton of Lynn, Massachusetts, found out on January 12, 1987, that he and 2,800 other GE workers in Massachusetts would soon be without jobs. Beaton was employed in GE's turbine division. "It hit us all like a bombshell. We knew bad times were coming, but nobody thought it would be this bad." In the case of Beaton and many of the other workers, GE had employed generations of their families. GE's role in the community was much more than just that of an employer.[2] The International Union of Electronic Workers (IUE) leadership in Lynn knew that GE had record sales for 1986, with double-digit earnings growth projected for 1987 and 1988.[3] Why then, did GE reduce the number of employees it has by 100,000 people between 1981 and 1985?[4]

GE's employment reductions can be attributed both to factors particular to the corporation and to overall trends in the U.S. economy. Chief Executive Officer John Welch established early on in his management of GE a policy of maintaining a number one or number two position in all of GE's business segments. If a division fails to come up to standards, the company will "fix, sell, or close" that division.

Some of the union leadership of the IUE in Lynn felt that GE chose not to upgrade the equipment at the Lynn factory and had made a decision not to compete in the international turbine market. GE is laying off workers at some of its unionized plants and hiring workers at non-union plants in the southern U.S. and in factories in developing countries. GE is the U.S.-based company with the third largest number of employees in Mexico's industrial belt. GE is a corporation on the run, moving plants and disrupting communities.

## Money Spent on the Military = Fewer Jobs

According to a recent analysis prepared for the Joint Economic Committee of Congress, military spending creates 6,400 *fewer* jobs per $1 billion than federal spending for health, education, or housing. This study examined a scenario of transferring $35 billion from the military to domestic programs. The study found that an additional 262,000 full-time jobs would be created by spending money on programs that meet human needs. Also, spending money on social programs would add $8 billion more in wages and salaries to the economy.[5]

From 1984 to 1986, General Electric received over $11 billion in federal tax dollars for nuclear weapons work.[6] Based on the job creation numbers calculated in the study prepared for Congress, if that $11 billion that went towards nuclear weapons had gone instead towards meeting human needs through federal spending on social programs, over 70,000 more jobs would have been created.

One reason there are fewer jobs created by increased military spending is that although the production of goods for the military does create some jobs, as does the production of anything, military production is considered capital intensive. In other words, more money goes towards equipment and machinery to produce the weapons than goes towards employing people.

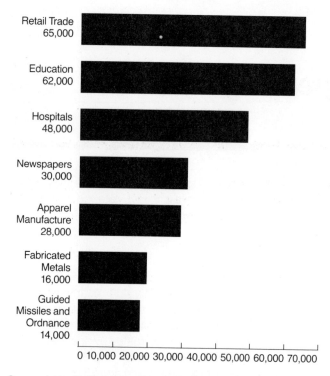

Source: Jobs with Peace. Figures from *The Empty Pork Barrel* by Marion Anderson, as calculated from U.S. Bureau of Labor Statistics data.

**Figure 17.** Jobs Generated by One Billion Dollars of Expenditure

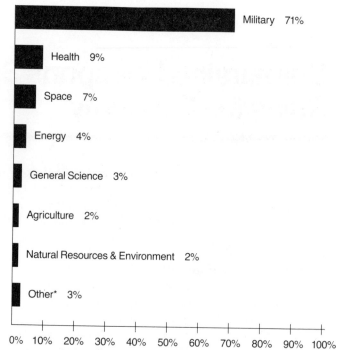

*Other includes Commerce (.5%), Transportation (.5%), International Affairs (.3%), Veteran's (.3%), and (.9%) divided among Education and Training, Labor, Justice, Housing and Urban Development, and other Social Services.

Source: Jobs With Peace

**Figure 18.** Federal Spending for Research and Development in 1987

Most of the work done by the weapons industry requires a high level of technical sophistication. Highly skilled, highly paid jobs are created by the aircraft, communications, missile, and computer industries that the Pentagon contracts with. These skilled specialists could easily be employed in other sectors doing civilian work. Blue collar workers who are most in need of employment are losing jobs and finding it increasingly difficult to find comparable work.

In late 1982, when overall unemployment reached 10.8 percent, unemployment for professional and technical workers was only 3.7 percent. Demand for engineers was so great that even though the economy was in a recession, their salaries continued to rise dramatically. At the same time, unemployment for laborers and machine operators was above 20 percent.

Independent researchers for the AFL-CIO Industrial Union Department revealed startling employment statistics at a 1986 conference.[7]

- From 1980 to 1984, 12 million breadwinners in the U.S. lost their jobs through plant closings and permanent layoffs. Almost half of those workers were unemployed for at least 6 months, and many were driven out of the labor force altogether.

- In terms of take-home pay, adjusted for inflation, U.S. workers are about 14 percent worse off than they were in 1973. Real earnings are lower today than they were in 1961.

- Only one-third of the unemployed receive unemployment payments, the lowest percentage receiving unemployment compensation since the system was created during the Great Depression of the 1930s.

## Competition in the World Market

Another factor to take into account when looking at jobs lost through the military build-up is that because the U.S. has concentrated so much of its technological research, development, and manufacturing into the military, we have become less competitive in other areas. In recent years, the U.S. has been flooded with foreign imports, resulting in hundreds of thousands of lost jobs in the industrial sector.

Research and development spending is an important influence on the competitiveness of a country's products in the international markets. R & D can improve competitiveness by reducing costs to manufacture and distribute products and by improving product quality and reliability.

To highlight this, it is interesting to examine the differences between R & D spending in the U.S. and the R & D spending in Japan and West Germany. The U.S., Japan, and West Germany devote almost exactly the same share of their gross national product to research and development. The major difference between the three countries, however, is the percentage that each devotes to military-related purposes.[8]

The U.S. spends over 70 percent of its publicly funded R & D on the military.[9] When the publicly funded R & D is combined with the independent R & D funds spent by weaponmakers, the total of funds going towards military R & D rises. In contrast, less than 4 percent of Germany's R & D funds and 1 percent of Japan's are military.[10]

Devoting such a high percentage of a country's R & D to the military decreases a country's competitiveness in the world. One way to measure this is to look at a country's trade deficit. The trade deficit compares a country's exports with its imports.

In 1983 the U.S. trade deficit reached 26 percent. In other words, the U.S. imported a lot more goods and services than it exported. In contrast, both West Germany and Japan had trade surpluses, 10 percent and 17 percent respectively. This means they both exported more products than they imported.[11]

Because both West Germany and Japan have put so much less money into the military, they have been able to develop lower cost and higher-quality products that they can sell in their countries and around the world, thereby improving their economies and providing jobs for their people.

The U.S., on the other hand, has devoted so much money to military R & D that the country has not been developing products that are competitive in the world markets. This means that jobs are lost in the U.S. as manufacturing gets cut back.

An argument often given for increased military R & D is that there will be benefits to the civilian economy through new technological advances. These technological advances are few, and come at a very high cost.

For example, solar cells for producing solar power have been developed in the U.S. for the military. The military requires very pure, very high-quality, and therefore, very expensive solar cells. In contrast, Japan has been researching a lower-cost solar cell that we now see on calculators and watches. These mass produced, low-cost solar cells are now providing many jobs in Japan.

Auth, Copyright 1987, *Philadelphia Inquirer*

## The Myth

The myth that massive military spending creates a strong economy is just that—a myth. A myth that has been used most effectively by the weapons industry in an effort to increase military spending.

As the military budget grew, so did the U.S. deficit. The United States now has the largest debt of any nation in the world. From 1980 to 1986, the U.S. debt doubled to over 2 trillion dollars.[12] Our children will be paying for the massive military budget into the next century.

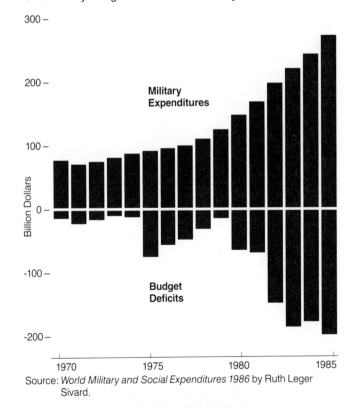

Source: *World Military and Social Expenditures 1986* by Ruth Leger Sivard.

**Figure 19:** Military Expenditures and the Budget Deficit of the Federal Government

# Basic Human Needs Denied

**3**

*Every gun that is made, every warship launched, every rocket fired signifies in the final sense, a theft from those who hunger and are not fed, those who are cold and are not clothed.*
— Dwight D. Eisenhower[1]

Since 1980, the U.S. has been engaged in the largest military build-up in its history. The annual budget authority for the military has more than doubled between 1980 and 1987. During those 7 years, $1.9 trillion was spent on the military.[2] In 1987, 55 percent of the federal budget was devoted to the military and military-related programs. About half of the military budget is spent developing and buying new weapons, with the rest going to personnel, operations, and the military portion of the national debt.[3]

Not surprisingly, GE's growth during this period has been quite healthy. With the Pentagon as the company's largest single customer, GE's sales to the U.S. government have doubled since 1980.[4]

This year you and your family will pay hundreds and more likely thousands of dollars in income taxes to the U.S. government.

For every $1 you pay in income taxes:

 **55¢ will go for military spending.**

 **2¢ will go for housing.**

 **2¢ will go for education.**

 **2¢ will go for food and nutrition.**

Source: Jobs with Peace

**Figure 20.** Distribution of a Federal Tax Dollar

## Human Need or Corporate Greed

In contrast to the 55¢ out of every federal tax dollar that goes to the military, only 2¢ goes for food and nutrition, 2¢ for education, and 2¢ for housing.[5]

Looking at the period 1982 to 1986, the military budget increased 38 percent. This contrasts sharply with programs that meet human needs. During this same time period, spending on our health *decreased* 8 percent, spending to educate our children *decreased* 14 percent, and spending to provide the people of this country with homes and shelter *decreased* 82 percent.[6]

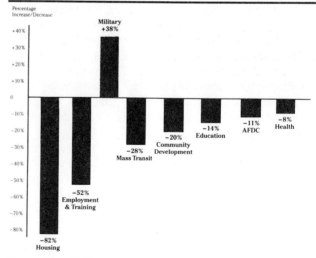

Source: Jobs with Peace

**Figure 21:** Federal Spending from 1982–86 (after inflation)

The U.S. ranks number one in the world both militarily and economically. We account for fully 30 percent of the world's military expenditures, yet occupy 7 percent of the world's land surface, and represent only 5 percent of the world's population. In spite of the number 1 ranking of the U.S. economically, among 142 countries it ranks 10th for education expenditures per capita, 10th for public health expenditures, 14th for the total number of people in our population with safe drinking water, and *17th for infant mortality*.[7]

| | RANK |
|---|---|
| ARMS EXPORTS | 1 |
| GNP | 1 |
| MILITARY EXPENDITURES | 1 |
| MILITARY TECHNOLOGY | 1 |
| MILITARY BASES WORLD-WIDE | 1 |
| NAVAL FLEET | 1 |
| NUCLEAR REACTORS | 1 |
| NUCLEAR WARHEADS AND BOMBS | 1 |
| LITERACY RATE | 4 |
| PERCENT SCHOOL-AGE IN SCHOOL | 6 |
| LIFE EXPECTANCY | 7 |
| PUBLIC EDUCATION EXPENDITURES PER CAPITA | 10 |
| PUBLIC HEALTH EXPENDITURES PER CAPITA | 10 |
| SCHOOL-AGE POPULATION PER TEACHER | 13 |
| PERCENT POPULATION WITH SAFE WATER | 14 |
| INFANT MORTALITY RATE | 17 |
| PERCENT WOMEN IN UNIVERSITY ENROLLMENT | 17 |
| POPULATION PER PHYSICIAN | 22 |

Source: *World Military and Social Expenditures 1986* by Ruth Leger Sivard.

**Figure 22.** US Rank Among 142 Countries

The $1.9 trillion spent on the military since 1980 has not added security to the lives of millions of Americans.

- Critical shortages of low-cost housing have resulted in the highest number of homeless people in the U.S. since the Great Depression—up to 3 million in 1986.
- The number of individuals living below the poverty threshold has increased from 29 million in 1980 to 33 million in 1986, about 14 percent of the population.
- Infant mortality rates in inner cities of the U.S. ranked as high as the rates in some of the poor countries of the Caribbean.
- In the U.S., the largest food-producing country in the world, an estimated 20 million people are without adequate nutrition on a regular basis.

- The share of total income going to the poorest 20 percent of the population dropped to 4.7 percent, the lowest in 25 years, while the share to the richest 20 percent increased to 42.9 percent.[8]

## Global Impact

Along with U.S. military growth, there have been increased military expenditures around the world. Military budgets of the world's governments have left millions of people without means to meet basic human needs, and without much hope of attaining real security—the security of a home, food, clean water, and adequate health care.

The world's military expenditures are now in excess of $1.7 million per minute,[9] and *every minute of every day, 30 children die from lack of food and inexpensive vaccines*. The number of people living in severe poverty is now one in five,[10] and the number of people suffering from chronic hunger, homelessness, curable disease, and illiteracy is growing.

## A DAY IN THE LIFE OF THE PLANET

TODAY WE SPENT...

over $2.5 billion on military weapons.

AND TODAY...

43,000 children died for want of adequate food and health care.

The weapons build-up, and the money devoted to it, has placed all the world's citizens in jeopardy. The human costs of our world's priorities can be seen not only in developing countries but in cities, towns, and farm regions across the United States.

# Radiation: The Deadly Legacy

**4**

*It's just that our people are dying is what it amounts to. Our next generation isn't even having a chance to be born.*

—Lacota Hardin, Women of All Red Nations
testifying at Radiation Victims Hearings, 1980

The first nuclear bombs were dropped by the U.S. on Hiroshima and Nagasaki, Japan, in August 1945. Hundreds of thousands of people were killed instantly; the longer term effects continue to kill thousands more. Since 1945, over one million women, men, and children in the U.S. have been the unknowing victims of deadly radiation from nuclear weapons production.

The National Association of Radiation Survivors estimates that at least 1,050,000 U.S. service personnel, uranium miners, employees of nuclear weapons labs and production factories, nuclear test site workers, and residents surrounding test sites and bomb factories have been exposed to damaging levels of radiation.[1] Thousands of people have suffered health effects associated with radiation exposure such as hypothyroidism; stomach, thyroid, skin, and lung cancer; leukemia; bone cancer; and birth defects in their children. From the beginning to the end of the nuclear weapons production cycle, whenever radioactive materials are involved, the potential exists for radioactive exposure far above levels deemed "acceptable" even by industry and government standards.

GE has been an active participant in every major step of the nuclear weapons production cycle—research, production, testing, and deployment—since its involvement in the research and production of the first bomb.

## Uranium Mining

One of the first steps in the nuclear weapons production cycle is the mining of uranium. For plutonium bombs, the uranium is then processed (enriched) into plutonium, which powers the bomb. Uranium is a naturally occurring mineral found in abundance in several areas of the world, including the American southwest. Fifty to eighty percent of U.S. uranium reserves are located on Native American land, and Native Americans have made up most of the workforce that mines and mills the uranium.[2]

The danger of radiation from uranium is not limited to people directly involved in the mining and milling. The leftover ore after the uranium is extracted is crushed and left unattended on the mining sites, creating health risks to all residents of the area. Radioactive gases continue to be released into the air, soil, and water supply. The Environmental Protection Agency has identified over 6,000 sites surrounding active or inactive uranium mills in 9 states. A study at one site in Fall County, South Dakota showed a cancer rate 50 percent higher than that of any other county in the state.[3]

Before the 1950s, lung cancer was virtually unheard of on the Navaho Reservation in the southwestern United States. Between 1965 and 1979, according to a study by Drs. Leon Gottlieb and LuVerne Hosen, 17 Navaho men were treated for lung cancer at the Shiprock, New Mexico Indian hospital. Sixteen were ex-uranium miners; 14 did not smoke. At Cameron, Arizona, an area of intensive uranium mining and milling during the 1950s and 1960s, the birth defects rate, according to physiologist Alan Goodman, is seven times the national average.

The miners of uranium, their families, and neighbors are the first victims of the nuclear weapons production cycle.[4] General Electric was involved in the mining of uranium through its wholly owned subsidiary Utah International and the Pathfinder Mines Corporation.[5]

---

**Wagoner Study of Uranium Miners**

Lung cancer was officially diagnosed among miners in 1879. Despite this long history of documentation, Dr. Joseph Wagoner has continued documenting deaths among uranium miners to convince the United States government that strong, enforced regulations are needed to protect all uranium miners.

| Lung Disease | Cases Observed* | Cases Expected* |
|---|---|---|
| Nonmalignant Respiratory Disease | 8/80 | 3.67/24.9 |
| Malignant Respiratory Disease* | 17/144 | 9.89/29.8 |

*Indian/white miners

---

# GE and Hanford

The Hanford Nuclear Reservation, in southeast Washington State, has produced much of the plutonium used for the U.S. nuclear arsenal. GE contracted with the Atomic Energy Commission (AEC) to manage and operate the facility from 1946 until 1964. From the first days of Hanford's operation, GE and the AEC claimed a high degree of safety for workers and residents in the area. Fred Schlemmer, AEC chief at Hanford, stated that it was "ten times as safe to work at Hanford as in an average chemical plant."[6] Contrary to the official line, accidents, spills, and sheer negligence have lead to massive radioactive contamination of the environment, animals, and people surrounding the facility.

June Casey attended Whitman College in Walla Walla, Washington, from 1949 to 1951. During the holiday break in December 1949, June went home to visit her family. Her mother's first look at June told her something was terribly wrong—she looked as if she had aged 50 years. June admitted she had been feeling quite sick and that her hair had been falling out in clumps. Her family took her immediately to the family doctor. The doctor found she had the most severe case of hypothyroidism he had ever seen, though she had never before had any significant health problems.

June began taking medication to improve her thyroid condition, though she lost all of her hair and has had to wear a wig ever since. This was the beginning of serious health problems that would plague June for the rest of her life. After she was married, she and her husband attempted to start a family. Her first pregnancy ended in a miscarriage, the second in a still birth. In 1969, June gave birth to a son, John, whose neurological system was damaged, causing him to shake uncontrollably throughout his childhood.

## Forty Years of GE/Government Coverup

June knows now that she could not have been living in Walla Walla at a worse time. On Mother's Day 1986, she was scanning the *Oakland Tribune* and came across an article about the Hanford Nuclear Reservation—just 50 miles from her college. *The article revealed information that had been concealed from the public for almost 40 years.* June felt this information finally began to explain her health problems.[7]

On December 2, 1949, an experiment was conducted at GE's Hanford facility, apparently to test monitoring techniques. In the experiment—called the "Green Run"—GE released a large volume of radioactive gas, iodine-131, into the atmosphere. The gas had a radioactivity measurement of 5,039 curies—hundreds of times greater than the amount of iodine-131 released in the nuclear reactor acci-

dent at Three Mile Island. Yet not a single person was warned of the planned release.

The gas spread a cloud of radioactivity 200 miles long and 40 miles wide over Washington and Oregon. In areas surrounding Hanford, tests on vegetation showed radioactive iodine levels 100 to 600 times above normal, and immediately outside the Hanford site, up to 1,000 times above normal.[8]

It was not until 1986, when this information was demanded through the Freedom of Information Act, that June and other residents of the Hanford area discovered that they had been intentionally exposed to deadly radioactivity by GE and the Atomic Energy Commission. Since then, June has found out that in the two years that she attended Whitman College, 489,000 curies of iodine-131 were released from Hanford. During GE's management of Hanford, *over a million curies of radiation were released from the Hanford facility.*[9]

---

### Johnson Study of Rocky Flats

Dr. Carl Johnson, former director of the Jefferson County Health Department, collected data on the cancer rates of the Coloradans living downwind of Denver's controversial Rocky Flats nuclear weapons plant. In a report released in February 1979, Dr. Johnson found that citizens living in areas contaminated by plutonium were suffering a cancer rate significantly higher than those living in nearby, uncontaminated areas.

| Cancer Type | Percent of Increase | |
| --- | --- | --- |
| | Women | Men |
| Lung | — | 34 |
| Leukemia | — | 40 |
| Lymphoma and Myeloma | 10 | 43 |
| Colon | 30 | 43 |
| Ovary | 24 | — |
| Testis | — | 140 |
| Tongue, Pharynx, Esophagus | 100 | 60 |

---

### Mancuso Findings at Hanford

In 1964, Dr. Thomas Mancuso was commissioned by the Atomic Energy Commission (forerunner of today's Department of Energy) to look into cancer rates among nuclear workers at the Hanford Nuclear Facility. He found a rate higher than expected, touching off a major controversy. His funding was terminated by the AEC before completion of the study; analysis of the data continues through independent financial sources. His latest findings are listed below.

| Cancer Type | Percent of Increase |
| --- | --- |
| All Cancers | 26 |
| RES Neoplasms | 58 |
| Bone Marrow | 107 |

---

# Nuclear Weapons Testing

## Testing in the Pacific

Atmospheric testing of nuclear weapons began less than one year after the bombings of Hiroshima and Nagasaki. "Operation Crossroads," the code name for the first test series, was intended to study the impact of existing weapons. The U.S. government chose the Bikini Islands for these first tests, evacuating the people who lived there. Operation Crossroads involved more than 42,000 service personnel, hundreds of civilian specialists, and several hundred test animals. Their purpose in attending the bomb tests was to assess both the impact of and damage from atomic explosions. Within hours after bomb explosions, unprotected service personnel were sent in to investigate and clean up ships and other equipment that had been within a few miles of the detonation. All of the equipment was, of course, covered with enormous amounts of radioactive fallout.

In 17 years of bomb testing in the Pacific Islands starting in 1946, at least 220,000 U.S. troops were exposed to atomic radiation. Not until the 1970s did the U.S. government conduct inquiries into the health effects of these tests on the people involved. In a report ordered by a bipartisan congressional investigative office, it was found that more than 17,000 military personnel were at high risk because of the tests.[10]

In 1954, the U.S. tested the first hydrogen bomb. This huge bomb, code named "Bravo," blanketed many inhabited islands downwind of Bikini with high levels of fallout.

The people of the Pacific Islands are still feeling the long-term effects of radiation exposure. Cancers, thyroid abnormalities, adverse birth outcomes, diminished immune response and shortened lifespan continue to affect the people there. Also affected are previously unexposed people who must now live in an environment that is still radioactive from the years of testing.[11]

## Nuclear Weapons Testing in the U.S.

In 1951, the government began looking for a site on U.S. soil to conduct atomic weapons tests. To move testing operations to U.S. soil would be more convenient to the government and less of a security risk. The Atomic Energy Commission claimed thousands of square miles in southern Nevada, 63 miles north of Las Vegas, and 112 miles east (upwind) from the town of Enterprise, Utah. Atmospheric testing of nuclear bombs began on January 27, 1951.[12]

One resident of Enterprise, Preston Truman, was born the same year testing began at the Nevada Test Site. As a young boy, he remembers watching the flash of the bombs light up the sky, and sometimes he could even hear the explosions. He also remembers that clouds would sometimes cover their farm—never imagining that the clouds contained lethal radiation.[13]

Preston was in high school when he was diagnosed with a form of cancer called lymphoma. Of the ten children who lived in the immediate area of Enterprise when he was growing up, only Preston lived past the age of 28 years. All the others have died from leukemia or cancer.[14]

In 1980, the Department of Defense circulated a press release stating that "...based upon research to date, the average exposure of atmospheric nuclear test participants [atomic veterans] is about one-tenth of the level that is generally agreed as an acceptable annual exposure for radiation workers."[15]

Several independently conducted studies have seriously disputed the government's reports. For example, the Lyon study of childhood leukemias reported in 1979 that the

American soldiers exposed to radiation at the Nevada test site. GE produced the "trigger" for the bomb.

Nuclear weapon test in the Pacific.
Source: Department of Energy.

childhood leukemia levels in the "downwind" region were *250 percent higher* during the time of the testing than levels either before or after the atmospheric testing.[16]

## Evidence Suppressed

In 1957, the Atomic Energy Commission issued a booklet to downwinders in Nevada and Utah called "Atomic Tests in Nevada." The pamphlet said, "You have been close observers of tests which have contributed greatly to building the defenses of our country and of the free world... Every test detonation in Nevada is carefully evaluated as to your safety before it is included in a schedule." Referring to research conducted to determine possible effects of the tests on people, the pamphlet assured "all such findings have confirmed that Nevada test fallout has not caused illness or injured the health of anyone living near the test site."

The AEC's misleading findings are disputed by a report issued 23 years later by the U.S. House of Representatives Subcommittee on Oversight and Investigations. This study revealed that "The Government's program for monitoring the health effects of the tests was inadequate and, more disturbingly, all evidence suggesting that radiation was having harmful effects, be it on the sheep or the people, was not only disregarded but actually suppressed."[17]

By the early 1950s, despite repeated assurances from the government, residents of Nevada and southern Utah could not ignore the terrifying truth. Ranchers witnessed the sudden, unexplained deaths of thousands of sheep; wildlife from birds to deer were thinning noticeably with each fallout cloud. And, most horrifying of all, people in one community after another began dying from diseases rarely seen before the tests: leukemia, lymphoma, acute thyroid damage, and many forms of cancer.[18]

## White House Shelves Report

One test conducted by a U.S. Public Health Service researcher in 1965 correlated radioactive fallout with an inordinately high leukemia rate among downwind Utah residents. An Atomic Energy Commission assistant gen-

eral manager told AEC commissioners that "researching such topics as downwind leukemia rates would pose potential problems to the commission: adverse public relations, lawsuits and jeopardizing the programs of the Nevada Test Site." The White House ended up shelving the report and blocking any follow-up research.[19]

## GE's Involvement in Nuclear Testing

Over the years, GE has made special neutron generators or "triggers" for the nuclear bombs used at the test sites. GE also produces special measurement devices for nuclear weapons testing. Both "products" are produced at the Pinellas plant in Largo, Florida.[20] For the Kwajalein test site in the South Pacific, GE manufactured the floating power plant.[21]

While GE ran the Hanford Nuclear Reservation it was producing plutonium for the nuclear weapons testing in both the Pacific Islands and Nevada. In the spring of 1953, after a test now known as "Dirty Harry," thousands of sheep began to die.[22] The Atomic Energy Commission held hearings on the deaths. Because of GE's role in producing plutonium, an envoy from GE came down from Hanford to take part in the hearings. When a local rancher described the mysterious illness of his sheep, the GE representative tried to deny that the illness was due to radiation. He told the rancher, "There is very little protein in corn and they could be low in protein."[23]

## Nuclear Wastes

According to Don Behm, environmental reporter for the *Milwaukee Journal* (1986):

> If you inhaled or swallowed a microscopic particle of plutonium, it could enter your bloodstream and be absorbed by your bone marrow. There, the particle's virtually endless supply of radiation would slowly destroy the body's ability to make new blood cells. A piece of plutonium the size of a pencil dot could cause lung cancer. A teaspoonful, divided into 5 billion parts, could be enough to injure every person on Earth.[24]

The amount of radioactive material that exists in the U.S. alone is a great deal more than a teaspoonful. Thousands of pounds of radioactive wastes are generated through the production of nuclear weapons each year.

The Department of Energy (DOE) is looking for a disposal site for 70,000 tons of radioactive waste generated from the processing of plutonium for nuclear weapons. It has not been easy to find a community in the U.S. willing to accept the risks involved. Currently, over one half of the country's radioactive wastes are stored in underground containers at the Hanford Nuclear Reservation in Washington.[25] This waste amounts to at least 55 million gallons of highly radioactive materials, by-products of the plutonium processing for use in nuclear warheads. The waste

---

**Caldwell Study of "Smoky" Veterans**

In 1980, Dr. Glyn G. Caldwell completed a study of participants of the August 31, 1957, "Smoky" nuclear test at the Nevada Test Site. Nine cases of leukemia have occurred among the approximately 3,200 test participants. The expected incidence of leukemia in this age group is 3.5.

| Leukemia Cell Type | Cases Observed | Cases Expected |
|---|---|---|
| All Types | 9 | 3.5 |
| Acute Myelocytic | 4 | 1.1 |
| Chronic Myelocytic | 3 | 0.7 |
| Hairy Cell | 1 | — |
| AML and CML | 7 | 1.8 |

---

Source for all boxed information: SANE and Nuclear Weapons Facilities Project.

is stored in containers, some of which are over 40 years old. These containers have been leaking radioactive materials into the soil, groundwater, and the nearby Columbia River at least since 1963, during the time GE managed the plant.

According to the DOE's own studies, the soil directly surrounding the facility contains an average of 84 micrograms of plutonium deposits per acre. To put this in context, the most intensive plutonium contamination of the soil at Nagasaki after the atomic bomb was dropped was measured at 2,500 micrograms per acre at the epicenter, ranging down to 66 micrograms 1 mile away.[26] Several years ago, the Federal Water Pollution Agency named the Columbia River the most radioactively contaminated river in the world.[27]

## GE Applies Pressure to Limit Liability

When the government first embarked upon its effort to develop nuclear energy, GE strongly supported the passage of the Price-Anderson Act. This act is a federal law originally passed by Congress in 1957. Even though the government's own estimates of the potential losses from a nuclear accident range from $7 billion to $280 billion in property damages alone, the act set limits far below this.[28]

The Price-Anderson Act states that a company is not responsible for any liability beyond the $700 million pool for nuclear power plants or the $500 million for nuclear weapons facilities. The nuclear utilities pay into the $700 million pool while taxpayers alone are responsible for the $500 million. In other words, the act *completely exempts* corporations from any liability to the public from accidents at nuclear weapons facilities. This is true even if the accident is caused by a company's negligence or disregard for established safety standards. Even though corporations hold contracts for nuclear weapons facilities worth at least $90 billion, their risk is not one penny.[29]

Demands for liability protection came early from the nuclear industry. General Electric began work on its first large commercial nuclear power plant near Morris, Illinois in 1955. Two years later, GE Vice President Francis McCune testified before Congress that GE would not continue to build nuclear power plants unless the company could be protected from the legal and financial risks of a major accident.[30] The Price-Anderson Act was enacted soon thereafter.

Since 1957, Price-Anderson has been up for renewal and amendments three times. GE played a significant role each time, threatening to pull out of nuclear programs unless the legislative protection continued at levels deemed acceptable to the company.[31]

For example, in 1987 Congress was considering a proposal to increase contractor liability as part of extending the Price-Anderson Act. Phillips Peter, the head of GE's Washington lobbying office, sent a letter to at least one key senator. His letter stated, "Developments in Congress with respect to extension of the Price-Anderson Act, however, create grave concern over our ability to continue in this role [as a government contractor on nuclear programs]."[32]

One of these congressional developments referred to in the letter from Peter was an amendment put forth by Senator Howard Metzenbaum of Ohio. This amendment would hold federal nuclear contractors accountable for accidents caused by their gross negligence or willful misconduct. In 1986, the amendment was defeated in committee by a vote of 2-17. In 1987, it lost by only one vote.[33]

The *Washington Post* reported that just two weeks after that vote, the DOE's nuclear contractors gathered in a secret meeting with David Rossin, the DOE's assistant secretary of nuclear energy, "in an effort to head off the liability provisions."[34]

This last minute effort has been preceded by years of targeted PAC contributions. A study of PAC contributions by the nuclear industry, done by the U.S. Public Interest Research Group (U.S. PIRG), looked carefully at the Metzenbaum Amendment vote on federal contractor negligence. The study found that supporters of the nuclear industry position received more than three times as much in PAC contributions as those who had voted against the industry position. The 10 Senators who voted against contractor liability had received an average of $76,851, while the remaining 9 had received an average of $23,593, during the period of January 1981 through December 1986.[35]

In the U.S. PIRG study, utilities with ownership in nuclear reactors, reactor and component manufacturers, architect-engineering firms, equipment vendors, uranium companies, and trade associations all made PAC contributions. Forty-three of them had given over $100,000 in PAC contributions from 1981 through 1986. General Electric ranked number 4 with $665,250 in PAC contributions.[36]

## Isn't It Time?

From uranium mining at the Pathfinder Mines, to plutonium production at Hanford, to nuclear bomb trigger production at Pinellas, General Electric has been involved in all phases of nuclear weapons development. By its intensive lobbying efforts on the Price-Anderson Act, GE recognizes the extensive public risk of nuclear weapons development. Isn't it time GE took responsibility for the suffering and death that radiation brings into people's lives?

# PART V. YOU CAN MAKE A DIFFERENCE: BOYCOTT GE!

*Boycotts chip away at the structure of social justice. They are a concrete way for us to channel our resources consistent with our ethical principles. It's time to bring home this message–of corporate responsibility–to the nuclear weapons industry and directly to General Electric.*
—Loretta J. Williams, Ph.D., Director of Social Justice, Unitarian Universalist Association

In a democracy, the people and their elected representatives should be making the life and death decisions about national security. The American people should be determining U.S. policy on the nuclear weapons build-up, the results of which so drastically affect all our lives.

Yet, as this special report makes painfully clear, the nuclear weapons industry, with General Electric at the forefront, is *not* simply filling government orders or reflecting the will of the people; the corporations are *not* simply doing a patriotic duty by providing for the national "defense." Rather, they vigorously and effectively promote the "need" for more and more deadly weapons and then produce these weapons at public expense for private profit. People suffer greatly as a result.

An independent nationwide poll commissioned by INFACT in July of 1987 revealed the clear majority opinion of the American people on the issue of continued nuclear weapons production. Eighty percent of the people in the U.S. feel that this country already has enough nuclear weapons. Roughly half of those felt we actually have too many. The will of the people is clear, yet the nuclear weapons race rages on.[1]

Through the Nuclear Weaponmakers Campaign, INFACT's proven experience and expertise with transnational corporations contribute a critical missing piece in the overall effort to stop the nuclear weapons build-up. By campaigning for corporate accountability in the nuclear weapons industry, INFACT complements the work of other organizations whose focus is on legislative change, improved U.S.-Soviet relations and the impact of an increasingly militarized economy.

At the same time, INFACT's campaign provides an essential perspective in the ongoing dialogue to redefine this country's national security. To talk about new visions of security, we must talk about transnational corporations and their role in building a peaceful world. To talk about the future, we must work today to give people the skills, the tools, and the hope needed to forge a new vision. INFACT's focus on the transnational nuclear weaponmakers, combined with intensive grassroots organizing, are two critical components of a collective vision for a secure world without a nuclear weapons build-up.

## Redefining America's National Security

A new definition of national security will be forged from a combination of many factors, and INFACT's campaign is shaping and changing the way America thinks: How we think about nuclear weapons production, how we understand corporate influence gone amuck, how we have tolerated the subversion of our democratic ideals and institutions, and how corporations must change to make peace possible.

A new national security will evolve from the current cultural, political, and economic context in which Americans operate. INFACT's Nuclear Weaponmakers Campaign speaks to the following issues necessary to define this new vision:

- Information is power. An informed populace is necessary to participate fully in the national debate on security. In order to build a new vision, people must understand how the current system works—or does not work—and must determine what should be changed. Right now, most people in this country do not know the powerful role corporations play in shaping national security decisions, nor do people know the mechanisms by which the influence is exerted.

- National security means people feeling secure that nuclear war can be averted and that the air they breathe, the water they drink, the environment in which they live and work are all free from nuclear contamination. This feeling of security begins with knowledge, and information critical to our health and safety has been systematically withheld.

- Any new vision of national security must also include the reallocation of our country's productive resources to products and services useful to and needed by the people. This means corporations like GE providing the resources and working together with the employees, unions, and communities affected by nuclear weapons production to develop alternatives.

- A new vision of security must be broadened to include the concept of global security. The deadly capacity of the world's nuclear weaponry and the dire prediction of nuclear winter make our destiny an even more common one. Since security is increasingly understood to be economic in nature, we are all linked by worldwide economic forces. Given the state of current technologies, the people of the world can communicate instantly. Recognizing that people in this country are intimately and inextricably connected with people in other parts of the world, we must expand our definition of security to be global.

- Finally, true security requires empowerment—people really taking control of their own lives and taking responsibility for the planet. Empowerment includes the fundamental belief that change *can* happen, that we *can* do things differently. The Nestlé campaign proved that hundreds of thousands of people working together can change the behavior of even the most powerful transnational corporations. This is the heart of INFACT's grassroots organizing.

## Taking Action: The GE Boycott

The nuclear weapons corporations can and must be held accountable to the people whose lives they are endangering—that is all of us. The goals of INFACT's Nuclear Weaponmakers Campaign—to stop the production of nuclear weapons, to reduce corporate influence over government decisions and policies that promote nuclear weapons, and to create a climate that no longer supports nuclear weapons production as an acceptable business activity—are ambitious ones. But by focusing massive grassroots pressure on the leader of the nuclear weapons industry, we can take a very concrete step toward achieving those goals. We can challenge GE to live up to its public claim to "bring good things to life."

Because the root of the problem is economic—that is, fueled by the corporate profit motive—consumers have a very powerful tool for change. GE's nuclear weapons work accounts for about 11.8 percent of the company's overall sales. This means GE can be convinced that its own self-interest lies in stopping its nuclear weapons work rather than risking other lucrative business segments. Most of us cannot vote with GE's board members on the future course of the company, but we can *all* "vote with our pocketbooks" by choosing to withhold our business from GE until the company stops endangering our lives.

On June 12, 1986, INFACT launched the GE Boycott. The boycott is the principal strategy behind the goals of the Nuclear Weaponmakers Campaign. It is a way to build broad-based economic pressure to directly counter the profits of the nuclear weapons "business" and to send a clear message to the corporate leader, GE, that people will not support the company's continued promotion and production of nuclear weapons.

By February of 1987, the first 100,000 people had already signed the boycott pledge, and the signatures were delivered to GE offices across the country, spelling out the boycotters' demands for GE to

1) Stop all nuclear weapons work

2) Stop interfering with government decision making on war and peace

3) Stop all direct marketing and promotion of nuclear weapons

4) Implement peace conversion plans in consultation with employees and affected communities.

By July of 1987, a nationwide poll commissioned by INFACT showed two million people boycotting GE because of GE's nuclear weapons work—that is 1 in 100!

That same poll revealed that a majority of Americans are opposed to the continued nuclear weapons build-up. The GE Boycott gives all of us who want to stop the arms race something concrete to *do* about it.

From the millions who are making a point of buying another brand of lightbulb to the doctor who cancelled a half-million-dollar purchase of GE medical equipment, people across the country are sending a clear, strong message to this leader of the nuclear weapons industry.

## What Can *You* Do?

As the campaign grows, people are joining and challenging GE in many different and *creative* ways.

- INFACT activists in Florida, where GE makes the neutron trigger for nuclear bombs, responded to GE's advertisement—"We're not satisfied until you are"—by calling the tollfree GE Answer Center (1-800-626-2000) to express their dissatisfaction with the MX, the B-1 bomber, the Trident submarine, and other GE "products." Ford Slater, GE's Special Issues Manager, called back personally from corporate headquarters in an attempt to defend the company's position.

- Students at Brown University and the University of Minnesota are focusing on GE recruiters on campus, making sure during each visit by GE that their fellow students—potential GE employees—know about the kinds of things GE *really* brings to life.

- John Law, a San Francisco area architect and developer, used GE appliances exclusively in his buildings for more than 30 years. He joined the boycott, immediately changed the specifications for appliances in his apartment building, and wrote to the company. He is now encouraging his colleagues to do the same.

- Other peace and justice groups are working actively on the campaign. For example, Seattle Women's Action for Nuclear Disarmament (WAND) and Women's International League for Peace and Freedom (WILPF) chapters have joined together to sign up GE boycotters and educate people on where to find alternative products.

- Many religious organizations are putting the strength of their constituencies behind the campaign. The United Methodist Southern New England Conference recently endorsed the campaign. The conference will encourage its members to sign the GE boycott petition. And the conference as a whole will notify GE's management to convert their nuclear weapons facilities and will set up a fund to financially assist employees doing GE's nuclear weapons work who leave their positions for moral or other reasons.

Many diverse organizations, local and national, religious and secular, have endorsed the Boycott and are spreading the word through their membership—from the Social Responsibilities Round Table of the Minnesota Library Association to national Church Women United; from the student body of Macalester College in St. Paul, Minnesota, to Northern California Interfaith Center for Corporate Responsibility. Many prominent activists and celebrities have also joined the campaign—from anti-nuclear activist Dr. Helen Caldicott to singer/TV personality Gloria Loring to labor organizer Victor Reuther. These groups and individuals are united by a common desire for peace and justice, and by a willingness to work for it.

## Boycott GE!

So what can *you* do? Join the boycott, and start by spreading the word. Encourage your friends to join the boycott. Share this book. Look around you to see how GE impacts on your community—consumer outlets, manufacturing plants, weapons facilities—and where the opportunities lie for you to have the greatest influence on GE. Have a block party to sign your neighbors onto the Boycott, and then start a local INFACT Action Committee. Visit your local retailers to talk about stocking alternative brands. Expand to other neighborhoods, churches, schools, stores....The opportunities to influence GE are unlimited.

Perhaps you know GE shareholders who would be interested in helping move the company out of the nuclear weapons business. Or GE employees with similar concerns. Some activists have even taken the Boycott through the local political channels—Democratic districts in Wisconsin and Washington State have already endorsed.

Those are only a few ideas. You will probably come up with many other constructive ways to help build the Boycott, once you start talking to people and looking around. And however you decide to get involved, whether you have questions, comments, or new ideas, whether you need materials or just inspiration, please contact the INFACT office nearest you. We want to hear from you.

PEGGY POWELL

Just remember that you *can* make a difference. When you join INFACT's Nuclear Weaponmakers Campaign and the GE Boycott, you have the power of hundreds of thousands of concerned people working with you. Your participation *will* make a difference.

Reflect for a moment on this delightful folk tale.

> "Tell me the weight of a snowflake," a coal-mouse asked a wild dove.
>
> "Nothing more than nothing," was the answer.
>
> "In that case I must tell you a marvelous story," the coal-mouse said. "I sat on the branch of a fir, close to its trunk, when it began to snow, not heavily, not in a raging blizzard, no, just like in a dream, without any violence. Since I didn't have anything better to do, I counted the snowflakes settling on the twigs and needles of my branch. Their number was exactly 3,741,952. When the next snowflake dropped onto the branch—nothing more than nothing, as you say—the branch broke off."

Having said that, the coal-mouse flew away.

The dove, since Noah's time an authority on the matter, thought about the story for a while and finally said to herself: "Perhaps there is only one person's voice lacking for peace to come about in the world."

So make your voice heard. Let GE know that you will not stand for its continued subversion of the democratic process. Let the company know that its promotion of nuclear weapons and interference with national security decision making must stop, that profit is *not* an acceptable motive for endangering our lives. And let your friends and neighbors know that they, too, must speak out.

With the effort and commitment of every individual who chooses peace, we can and will change the activities of the weapons corporations that threaten the very survival of our planet. Join us!

# Notes

## PART I.
## Notes on Chapter 1: Saga of the B-1

1. *Congressional Record*, December 11, 1971, p. S21437; quoted in John Woodmansee et al., *The World of a Giant Corporation* (Seattle: North County Press, 1975), p. 34.

2. National Resources Defense Council, Inc., *Nuclear Weapons Databook*, vol. 1, *U.S. Nuclear Forces and Capabilities*, by Thomas B. Cochran, William M. Arkin, and Milton M. Hoenig (Cambridge, MA: Ballinger Publishing Company, Harper & Row, 1984), pp. 31 and 156.

3. David Wood, "B-1 Symbolizes Power of Military-Industrial Complex," *Los Angeles Times*, July 10, 1983, part 6, p. 8.

4. "Low-Level Flights of B-1 Are Halted," *New York Times*, December 4, 1987, p. B7.

5. Brandywine Peace Community, *Bulbs to Bombs: GE and the Permanent War Economy* (Swarthmore, PA: 1986), p. 30.

6. *World of a Giant Corporation*, p. 28; see also *Encyclopedia Americana* (Danbury, CT: Grolier Inc., 1986), s.v. Department of Defense.

7. Ad taken out by Citizens for Peace with Security, *Washington Post*, June 30, 1969.

8. *Commercial Banks and Their Trust Activities: Emerging Influence on the American Economy*, vol. 1, Staff Report for Subcommittee on Domestic Finance, Committee on Banking and Currency, 90th Congress, 2nd Session, July 8, 1968, p. 78 (generally referred to as the "Patman Report"); cited in The GE Project, "Who Wants the B-1?" (Cambridge: GE Project, early 1970s), p. 33. See also *Spectrum 3*, Computer Directions Advisors, Inc., Silver Springs, MD, June 30, 1987, p. 310.

9. *World of a Giant Corporation*, p. 28; see also *Commercial Banks*.

10. Ibid., p. 31.

11. *Nuclear Weapons Databook*, p. 156.

12. *Bulbs to Bombs*, p. 30.

13. *Wall Street Journal*, June 8, 1970, p. 4; cited in "Who Wants the B-1?" p. 22.

14. Investor Responsibility Research Center, *The Nuclear Weapons Industry*, by Kenneth A. Bertsch and Linda S. Shaw (Washington, DC: 1984), p. 176.

15. *Bulbs to Bombs*, p. 30.

16. "B-1 Symbolizes Power," p. 9.

17. Gordon Adams, *The Politics of Defense Contracting: The Iron Triangle* (New Brunswick, NJ: Council on Economic Priorities, 1981), pp. 190-191.

18. Ibid., pp. 192-193.

19. "B-1 Symbolizes Power," p. 8.

20. Ibid., p. 9.

21. *World of a Giant Corporation*, p. 28.

22. Philip J. Simon, *Top Guns: A Common Cause Guide to Defense Contractor Lobbying* (Washington, DC: Common Cause, 1987), p. 33; see also "B-1 Symbolizes Power," pp. 8-9.

23. "B-1 Symbolizes Power," pp. 8-9.

24. Ibid., p. 8.

25. Ibid., p. 9.

26. Ibid.

27. Investor Responsibility Research Center, *Stocking the Arsenal: A Guide to the Nation's Top Military Contractors*, by Linda S. Shaw, Jeffrey W. Knopf, and Kenneth A. Bertsch (Washington, D.C.: 1985), p. 42.

28. Anne Edwards, *Early Reagan: The Rise to Power* (New York: William Morrow and Company, Inc., 1987), pp. 451 and 476.

29. "No Flak from Jones over a B-1 Bomber," *New York Times*, February 1, 1981.

30. *Nuclear Weapons Industry*, p. 176; see also, *Stocking the Arsenal*, p. 42.

31. "GE Gets Work for $1.58 Billion from Air Force," *Wall Street Journal*, July 23, 1984, p. 7; and "GE Awarded Balance of B-1B Engine Work," *Cincinnati Post*, July 24, 1984.

32. GE Annual Report, 1982, pp. 24 and 27.

33. "B-1 Symbolizes Power," p. 9.

34. For a good chronology of the B-1 bomber developments and its costs, see "B-1 Symbolizes Power," p. 9. For 1987 figures, see *New York Times*, December 4, 1987, p. B7.

35. "B-1 Symbolizes Power," p. 9; and Fred Kaplan, "B-1 Study Reflects a Failure of Oversight," *Boston Globe*, April 5, 1987, p. 10.

36. "GE Awarded Balance of B-1B Engine Work." See also subsequent exchange in letters to the *Cincinnati Post* editor, August 9, September 14, and September 26, 1984. See also "GE Gets Work for $1.58 Billion," *Wall Street Journal*, p. 7.

37. "B-1 Study Reflects Failure," p. 10.

38. Ibid., p. 10.

39. "Inquiry on Bomber Focuses on Birds," *New York Times*, September 30, 1987, p. A19.

40. "Low-Level Flights," December 4, 1987, p. A1.

41. "B-1 Symbolizes Power," p. 8.

42. *Nuclear Weapons Industry*, p. 176; see also *Bulbs to Bombs*, p. 30.

43. "Rockwell Scrambles to Extend Life of B-1," *Los Angeles Times*, June 1, 1986, part 4, p. 7.

## PART II:
## Notes on Chapter 1: The Company Profile

The following sources produced by General Electric are used throughout this chapter:

GE Annual Report, 1986.

*Notice of 1987 Annual Meeting of Share Owners: Proxy Statement.*

*GE Opportunities*, 1986-87.

Form 10-K for fiscal year 1986.

1. "General Eclectic," *Forbes*, March 23, 1987, p. 75.

2. "*Number one*" corresponds to such phrases in GE literature as "number one position," "the leading," and "number one rank." "*Leading*" corresponds to phrases like "a leading," "one of the largest," etc.

3. "General Eclectic," p. 75.

4. Ibid., p. 77.

5. Ibid., pp. 74-75.

6. "Jack Welch: How Good a Manager?" *Business Week*, December 14, 1987, p. 94.

7. Ibid.

8. Ibid., p. 93.

9. "General Electric to Sell Consumer Electronics Lines to Thomson SA for Its Medical Gear Business, Cash," *Wall Street Journal*, July 23, 1987, p. 3.

## Notes on Chapter 2: Behind GE's Public Relations

1. "The Human Costs of GE's Decision," *Chicago Sun-Times*, October 4, 1987, p. 7.

2. Town of East Hampton, NY, Petition before the Federal Communications Commission, July 7, 1986, p. 3.

3. Ibid., p. 2.

4. "GE Guilty in Federal Bribe Case," *Chicago Tribune*, February 12, 1981.

5. "Payments by U.S. Defense Contractors to South Korean Firm Are Investigated," *Wall Street Journal*, October 2, 1985.

6. "Firm's Aides Accused of Paying Kickbacks to Get Defense Jobs," *Wall Street Journal*, May 5, 1986.

7. "GE Finds Defective Parts in Jet Engines," *Boston Herald*, April 7, 1987.

8. U.S. Senate, Committee on the Judiciary, Subcommittee on Administrative Practices and Procedures, "False Claims Reform Act," Senate hearing 99-452, September 17, 1985, p. 50.

9. Ibid., p. 51.

10. Ibid., pp. 50-51.

11. "Ex-Foreman Sues GE Charging Government Was Improperly Billed," AP wire, Cincinnati, November 5, 1984.

12. "U.S. Attorney Asks to Intervene in Suit Filed against GE," *Wall Street Journal*, December 1984.

13. "Ex-Foreman Sues GE."

14. "Ex-GE Worker Can Probe Claim," *Cincinnati Post*, October 4, 1986, p. 28.

15. "General Electric Admits Falsifying Billing on Missile," *New York Times*, May 14, 1985.

16. Ibid.

17. Ibid.

18. Ibid.

19. Ibid.

20. Brandywine Peace Community, *Bulbs to Bombs: GE and the Permanent War Economy* (Swarthmore, PA: 1986), pp. 37-38.

21. "On Probation," *Defense Week*, April 22, 1985, p. 3.

22. Ibid.

23. "General Electric Admits Falsifying," May 14, 1985.

24. "GE Can't Get Charges Dismissed," *Cincinnati Enquirer*, September 9, 1986.

25. Ibid.

26. "A Nuclear Cloud Hangs over GE's Reputation," *Business Week*, June 15, 1987, p. 32.

27. "GE Internal Data Show Firm Hid Flaws in Reactor Design, Zimmer Owners Claim," *Wall Street Journal*, February 24, 1986, p. 5.

28. "A Nuclear Cloud," p. 32.

29. "GE, 3 Utilities Settle Nuclear Plant Suit," *Investor's Daily*, November 23, 1987.

30. "Coverup Charged on Danger at 39 U.S. Nuclear Plants," *San Francisco Chronicle*, May 20, 1986.

31. "NRC Says Flaw May Pose Hazard at Pilgrim," *Boston Globe*, July 14, 1987, p. 1; "Pilgrim and Millstone, Two Nuclear Plants, Have Disparate Facts," *Wall Street Journal*, July 28, 1987, p. 1.

32. "A Nuclear Cloud," p. 32.

33. "After $2 Million in Repairs, GE Not Sure It Will Use N-plant," *San Jose Mercury News*, August 11, 1984, p. 2B.

34. "General Electric Target of 2 Suits by Power Firms," *Wall Street Journal*, January 28, 1976.

35. "Coverup Charged on Danger."

36. "GE, Whose Plants Spilled PCB's, Sees Signs of Natural Breakdown," *New York Times*, June 9, 1987.

37. "Swimmers: Don't Go Near the Housatonic," *Berkshire (MA) Eagle*, July 27, 1987.

38. "Upstate Residents' Water Worries Help Move G.E. to Accord," *New York Times*, May 13, 1986.

39. "The Best and Worst of American Business: Taking Stock," *Mother Jones*, June 1985, p. 37.

40. "GE Sees Signs of Natural Breakdown."

41. Town of East Hampton, NY, Resolution adopted July 7, 1986.

42. "Best and Worst of Business," p. 37.

43. "Taxation and Accounting," *Daily Tax Report*, Bureau of National Affairs, Inc., Washington, DC, April 17, 1986, G-4 (No. 74).

44. "The Toxic Waste Battle Is Boiling Over," *Business Week*, August 3, 1987.

45. "Jack Welch: How Good a Manager?" *Business Week*, December 14, 1987, p. 93.

46. GE Annual Report, 1986, p. 2.

47. "GE vs. Labor: Heading for 'One of the Biggest Fights Ever,'" *Business Week*, December 14, 1987, p. 102.

48. "Last Day at Iron Plant Marked by Mock Funeral," *UE News*, March 22, 1982.

49. "News of Layoffs Dulls G.E. Centennial in Schenectady," *New York Times*, November 26, 1986, p. B-1.

50. "The Human Costs of GE's Decision," *Chicago Sun-Times*, October 4, 1987, pp. 1 and 7.

51. Ibid., p. 1.

52. Ibid., p. 7.

53. "GE vs. Labor," p. 102.

54. Ibid., p. 103.

55. Ibid. The union election was held on December 18, 1987, and the IUE won.

## Notes on PART III: GE Shaping Nuclear Weapons Policies for Profits

1. President Dwight D. Eisenhower's farewell radio and television address to the American people, January 17, 1961; reprinted in pamphlet by Council for a Livable World, Boston, 1981.

2. Ibid.

3. Gordon Adams, *The Politics of Defense Contracting: The Iron Triangle* (New Brunswick, NJ: Council on Economic Priorities, 1981), p. 15.

4. Fred Kaplan, "Has the U.S. Heeded Ike's 1961 Warning?" *Boston Globe*, January 12, 1986, pp. 89-91.

5. "A Year of Pain and Promise: The Fortune 500 Largest U.S. Industrial Corporations," *Fortune*, April 27, 1987, pp. 364-365.

6. "General Eclectic," *Forbes*, March 23, 1987, pp. 75-76.

7. Defense Industry Organization Service, "Table 1: Top 100 Defense Department Contractors, FY 1986," Washington, DC.

8. "Top Ten Military Contractors: 1986," *Recon*, Fall 1987, p. 9.

9. Investor Responsibility Research Center, *The Nuclear Weapons Industry*, by Kenneth A. Bertsch and Linda S. Shaw (Washington, DC: 1984), pp. 172-73.

10. It is notable that the interests of the nuclear weapons industry sometimes diverge from the interests of the larger business community. So, for example, this country's current massive federal budget deficit is of serious concern to business as a whole, yet it is the bloated military budget that is one of the direct causes of the imbalance. While many business leaders call for weapons reductions, the nuclear weapons contractors persist in their efforts to expand the military budget. The following quote exemplifies this split:

" 'What the hell is their [the Reagan Administration's] agenda?' fumes one service-company lobbyist about the administration. 'They care more about the defense budget than they do about the deficit.' "

Source of quote: *Fortune*, "Business to the White House: You Blew It," October 28, 1985.

Comparison of GE to other top weapons contractors in terms of overall business position:

| Company | Sales | S.H.E. | Net | MV Amt. |
|---|---|---|---|---|
| 1) GE | #6 | #6 | #5 | $47.9 billion |
| 2) McDonnell-Douglas | #23 | #46 | #61 | 3.2 billion |
| 3) Rockwell | #24 | #42 | #26 | 7.7 billion |
| 4) Lockheed | #30 | #68 | #44 | 3.4 billion |
| 5) General Dynamics | #36 | #107 | #443 | 3.3 billion |
| 6) Raytheon | #48 | #66 | #46 | 5.8 billion |

S.H.E. = Shareholder Equity
Net = Net Income
MV Amt. = Market Value
Source of table: "A Year of Pain and Promise: The Fortune 500 Largest U.S. Industrial Corporations," *Fortune*, April 27, 1987, pp. 364-65.

12. Defense Industry Organization Service table. IBM, for example, was #19 DOD contractor in 1986; Exxon, #36; ATT, #25; Du Pont was not among the top 100 DOD contractors in 1986.

# Notes on Chapter 2: GE Board Connections

1. James Keith Louden, quoted in "Directors Feel the Legal Heat," *New York Times*, December 15, 1985.

2. "Cathcart to Head Kidder Peabody," *Chicago Sun-Times*, May 15, 1987, p. 65.

3. GE, *Notice of 1987 Annual Meeting of Share Owners: Proxy Statement*, pp. 14-15.

4. "The Quiet Billionaire," *Forbes*, December 31, 1984, p. 148.

5. "Can Jack Welch Reinvent GE?" *Business Week*, June 30, 1986, p. 65.

6. Ibid.

7. "Reginald Jones Plans April 1 Retirement From GE: John Welch Will Succeed Him," *Wall Street Journal*, December 22, 1980.

8. Drawn from facsimile of sketch by Welch in "General Electric—Going with the Winners," *Forbes*, March 26, 1984, p. 106.

9. "G.E. Says Merger May Take a Year," *New York Times*, December 13, 1985; GE Annual Report, 1986.

10. "GE + RCA = Powerhouse Defense Contractor," *Business Week*, January 27, 1986, p. 116.

11. "General Electric Is Stalking Big Game Again," *Business Week*, March 16, 1987, p. 113.

12. Defense Industry Organization Service, *General Electric Company Organization Chart* (Washington, DC: Carroll Publishing Company, Summer 1987).

13. *Who's Who in America*, 1986-87.

14. *1986 Aerospace Industries Association Annual Report* (Washington, DC: AIA, 1987), p. 1.

15. *GE Organization Chart*.

16. "Out for a 'Helluva Good Time,' " *Fortune*, January 12, 1981, p. 15.

17. "Building a Life after Citicorp," *New York Times*, April 21, 1985; "Citicorp after Wriston," *Fortune*, July 9, 1984.

18. "Citicorp after Wriston."

19. "Citicorp's Conservative Rebel," *New York Times*, December 22, 1980, Business section, p. 1.

20. Ibid.; "Wriston Rules Out Job as Fed Chief," *New York Times*, March 11, 1983; "Citicorp after Wriston"; "Building a Life after Citicorp."

21. Abrecht and Locker, eds., *CDE Stock Ownership Directory* (New York: Corporate Data Exchange); cited in John Woodmansee, "1986 GE Directors as a Group," unpublished paper, May 1986.

22. John Woodmansee et al., *The World of a Giant Corporation* (Seattle: North County Press, 1975), p. 30.

23. Ibid.

24. "Keeping the Faith," *Forbes*, May 20, 1985, p. 44.

25. "The Wealth and Aura of Morgan," *New York Times*, April 10, 1983, p. 1.

26. "Keeping the Faith," p. 44.

27. Ibid.

28. "Wealth and Aura of Morgan," p. 1.

29. "The Elite Welcome Reagan, Who Offers Toast to the City," *New York Times*, December 10, 1980.

30. *Who's Who*.

31. "Why Griffiths Is Out as RCA Chairman," *Business Week*, February 9, 1981, p. 72.

32. "Getting a Handle on Energy," *Time*, March 31, 1980.

33. Ibid.

34. "A Peacemaker Comes to RCA," *Fortune*, May 4, 1981, p. 140.

35. "Bradshaw Assumes the Helm at RCA," *New York Times*, July 1, 1981, Business section, p. 1.

36. "RCA's Bradshaw Planning to Retire after Sale to GE," *New York Times*, December 13, 1985, p. 2.

37. "RCA Head Reassures Holders," *New York Times*, May 5, 1982, Business section, p. 1.

38. "Talks That Led to GE-RCA Pact Started Casually," *Wall Street Journal*, December 13, 1985, p. 18.

39. Ibid.

40. "RCA Employees, in Upheaval over Plan for GE to Buy Firm, Fear for Their Jobs," *Wall Street Journal*, December 20, 1985.

41. "GE + RCA," p. 116.

42. " 'He Is Exasperated with People about Half the Time,' " *Time*, October 29, 1979, p. 29.

43. *Who's Who*.

44. "Joint Chiefs Dissent on Carter-Brown Military Budget," *New York Times*, May 30, 1980.

45. "Military Chief Denies Making Offer to Resign If Reagan Wins Election," *New York Times*, June 5, 1980.

46. "Joint Chiefs' Head Retained by Reagan," *New York Times*, February 10, 1981.

47. "No Flak from Jones over a B-1 Bomber," *New York Times*, February 1, 1981.

48. *Air Force Magazine*, April 1987, p. 120.

49. Survey of *Air Force Magazine* ads 1980-1987: many GE ads appear in the most prominent space of all, the inside front cover.

50. "Industrial Associates of the Air Force Association: Partners in Aerospace Power," one-page display, *Air Force Magazine*, April 1983.

51. "Nuclear Freeze Called Unsound U.S. Strategy," *New York Times*, April 29, 1982.

52. "Soviet Buildup near Iran Tested Carter," *New York Times*, August 28, 1986, p. A3.

53. "Jones Seeks Reorganizing Joint Chiefs," *Aviation Week & Space Technology*, February 22, 1982, p. 25.

54. "Jones Urges Global Strategic Doctrine," *Aviation Week & Space Technology*, February 16, 1981, p. 98.

55. "General Electric Company: 1986 Annual Meeting of Share Owners," Transcript of GE annual meeting, Kansas City, MO, April 23, 1986, p. 28.

56. "Ties of Attorney General to Chief," *New York Times*, January 30, 1984.

57. "Reagan Designates Eight to Fill Posts at Cabinet Level," *New York Times*, December 12, 1980, pp. 1 and A28.

58. "Attorney General: William French Smith," from article on Reagan cabinet choices, *U.S. News & World Report*, December 22, 1980, p. 15.

59. "Lawyer a Possibility for Attorney General Post," *New York Times*, October 31, 1980.

60. "Letter from Washington," *National Review*, July 24, 1981, p. 817.

61. "Smith Issues Rules for Naming Judges," *New York Times*, March 7, 1981.

62. "Reagan Revolution Takes Firm Hold at Justice," *U.S. News & World Report*, April 26, 1982, p. 24.

63. "Smith's Term: Vast Change under a Conservative," *New York Times*, January 23, 1984, p. A16.

64. "U.S. Agencies to Get Greater Discretion on Releasing Files," *New York Times*, May 4, 1981, p. 1.

65. "Attorney General Outlines Campaign to Rein in Courts," *New York Times*, October 30, 1981, p. 1.

66. "A Politician Called Smith," *The Nation*, April 10, 1982, p. 429.

67. "Smith Talk Today Raises Questions," *New York Times*, August 4, 1984.

68. "What's News," *Wall Street Journal*, November 1, 1984, p. 1.

69. "Growth of a Coast Law Firm," *New York Times*, September 14, 1982, Business section, p. 1.

70. "Reagan Cabinet Choice Is in Club for Men Only," *New York Times*, December 28, 1980.

71. "The Backlash against Corporate Raiders," *Wall Street Journal*, November 12, 1986.

72. "A Corporate Lobby Pulls Its Punches," *Wall Street Journal*, July 23, 1986.

73. "Building a New Empire out of Paper," *New York Times*, August 12, 1984.

74. "Appointment of 44 Members of the President's Task Force on Private Sector Initiatives, and Designation of Chairman," *Public Papers of the President*, 1981, pp. 1107-1108.

75. "Cathcart to Head Kidder Peabody," *Chicago Sun-Times*, May 15, 1987, p. 63.

76. "Hillman: Pittsburgh's High-Rolling Recluse," *Business Week*, January 21, 1985, p. 74.

77. "Tycoon's Travails: Pittsburgh Billionaire Finds Venture Capital a Rough Game to Play," *Wall Street Journal*, September 17, 1986, p. 1.

78. Ibid.

79. From 1940 to 1965; source: GE Annual Report, 1976.

80. "Scott Faces Stiff Competition," *New York Times*, March 30, 1981, Business section, p. 1.

81. "Tax Leasing Is Supported by Executives," *New York Times*, March 19, 1982.

82. The tax laws regarding leasing are crucial to the profits of the GE Credit Corporation and other GE operations.

83. "Cluett, Peabody & Co.'s Henley Takes a Dim View of Suitor's Qualifications," *Wall Street Journal*, October 24, 1985, p. 16.

84. "U.S. Urged to Keep Tight Reins," *New York Times*, May 12, 1980, pp. D1 and D9.

85. "Henley Takes Dim View," p. 16.

86. "Goodyear Plans Charge in Period of $150 Million," *Wall Street Journal*, November 25, 1986, p. 12.

87. "Tax Code Changes That Hurt Business," *New York Times*, November 1, 1985.

88. Robert S. McIntyre, "The Failure of Corporate Tax Incentives," *Multinational Monitor*, October/November 1984, p. 4.

89. *National Cyclopedia of American Biography*, s.v. Richard Thomas Baker.

90. "Notes on People: First Woman Named to State Financial Control Board," *New York Times*, June 20, 1980.

91. Ibid.

92. Referred to on the board as "private" members. "3 on State Panel Challenge Budget for New York City," *New York Times*, May 12, 1982, p. A24.

93. Ibid.

94. *Who's Who*.

95. Frank H. T. Rhodes, "The Role of the Liberal Arts in a Decade of Increased Technology," *Vital Speeches of the Day*, June 15, 1984, pp. 532-534.

96. Frank H. T. Rhodes, "To Gain a Market Edge" (guest column), *New York Times*, November 2, 1985.

97. "Cornell Graduates 4,300," *New York Times*, June 3, 1985.

98. *Who's Who*.

99. Ibid.

## Notes on Chapter 3: Ultimate Connection

1. "Top Ten Military Contractors: 1986," *Recon*, Fall 1987, p. 9.

2. "Rockwell Scrambles to Extend Life of B-1," *Los Angeles Times*, June 1, 1986, Business section, p. 1.

3. GE Star Wars contracts, fiscal years 1983-86, data from Council on Economic Priorities, New York.

4. Michio Kaku and Daniel Axelrod, *To Win a Nuclear War: The Pentagon's Secret War Plans* (Boston: South End Press, 1987), pp. 242-43.

5. Ibid., p. 228.

6. Ibid., p. 227.

7. Garry Wills, *Reagan's America: Innocents at Home* (Garden City, NY: Doubleday & Company, Inc., 1987), p. 257.

8. Anne Edwards, *Early Reagan: The Rise to Power* (New York: William Morrow and Company, Inc., 1987), pp. 451-53.

9. Ronnie Dugger, *On Reagan: The Man & His Presidency* (New York: McGraw-Hill Book Company, 1983), p. 12; Laurence Leamer, *Make-Believe: The Story of Nancy and Ronald Reagan* (New York: Harper and Row, 1983), p. 186.

10. *Reagan's America*, p. 283.

11. Ibid., p. 280.

12. *Early Reagan*, p. 459.

13. *Reagan's America*, p. 280.

14. Ibid., pp. 280-81.

15. *Make-Believe*, p. 188.

16. *Reagan's America*, pp. 284-85.

17. Ibid., pp. 287-88.

18. "Attorney General: William French Smith," *U.S. News and World Report*, December 22, 1980, p. 15; "Reagan Revolution Takes Firm Hold at Justice," *U.S. News and World Report*, April 26, 1982, p. 24.

19. "Wriston Rules Out Job as Fed Chief," *New York Times*, March 11, 1983; "Building a Life after Citicorp," *New York Times*, April 21, 1985, p. 1.

20. Hedrick Smith, Adam Clymer, Leonard Silk, Robert Lindsey, and Richard Burt, *Reagan, the Man, the President* (New York: Macmillan Publishing Co., Inc., 1980), pp. 122-23.

21. *To Win a Nuclear War*, p. 231.

22. Thomas B. Edsall, "The GE Lobby: Bringing Goodies to Life," *Washington Post Magazine*, May 13, 1985, pp. 6-7.

23. Robert S. McIntyre, "The Failure of Corporate Tax Incentives," *Multinational Monitor*, October/November 1984, p. 4.

## Notes on Chapter 4: Business Policy Groups

1. "How to Win in Washington," *Fortune Magazine*, March 27, 1978, p. 53.

2. *Encyclopedia of Associations*, 22nd ed., 1988, p. 1370.

3. Grant McConnell, *Private Power and American Democracy* (New York: Alfred A. Knopf, Inc., 1966), pp. 276-77.

4. Ibid., pp. 277-78.

5. Ibid., p. 277.

6. Ibid., pp. 277-78.

7. *The Business Council: 1987* (Washington, DC: The Business Council, 1987).

8. John Woodmansee et al., *The World of a Giant Corporation* (Seattle: North County Press, 1975), p. 28; Business Council executive membership list, 1933.

9. Business Council executive membership lists, 1933-79.

10. "Business Roundtable Wages Vicious War on People," *The Service Union Reporter*, January 1981.

11. *Encyclopedia of Associations*, 22nd ed., 1988, p. 1370.

12. G. William Domhoff, *Who Rules America Now? A View for the 1980's* (New York: Simon and Schuster, 1983), p. 135.

13. G. William Domhoff, *The Powers that Be: Processes of Ruling Class Domination in America* (New York: Vintage Books, Random House, 1978), pp. 79-80.

14. "The New Face of Business Leadership," *New York Times*, May 22, 1983.

15. "The Business Lobby's Wrong Business," *New York Times*, December 20, 1981.

16. *The Powers That Be*, pp. 80-81.

17. A. Lee Fritshler and Bernard H. Ross, *How Washington Works* (Cambridge, MA: Ballinger Publishing Company, Harper & Row, 1987), p. 4.

18. *Business Council: 1987*; "Who's in Charge—Six Possible Contenders," in *The Almanac Special Collection*, p. 83.

19. *The Business Roundtable*, Membership list (New York: The Business Roundtable, June 1987).

20. "An Elite Group on U.S. Policy Is Diversifying," *New York Times*, October 30, 1982, pp. 29-30.

21. *Encyclopedia of Associations*, 21st ed., 1987, p. 1359.

22. "Who's In Charge"; *Council on Foreign Relations: Roster of Current and Former Members* (New York: CFR, roster current as of December 31, 1986).

23. *The Powers That Be*, pp. 65-66.

24. "Who's in Charge," p. 85.

25. Compare CFR membership list with list of Stimson Committee members in Richard C. Hewlett and Oscar E. Anderson, Jr., *The New World, 1939/1946*, vol. 1, *A History of the United States Atomic Energy Commission* (University Park, PA: The Pennsylvania State University Press, 1962), pp. 344-45.

26. *The Powers That Be*, p. 66; "Who's in Charge," p. 86.

27. *The Powers That Be*, p. 101.

28. Ibid., p. 66.

29. "Who's in Charge," p. 87.

30. Ibid.

31. *Council on Foreign Relations: Annual Report, July 1986—June 1987* (New York: CFR, 1987), pp. 124-25.

32. "Who's in Charge," p. 7; *CFR Roster*, pp. 1 and 28.

33. *CFR Annual Report*, pp. 74, 76, and 102.

34. *Who's Who in America*; *The Rand Corporation: 1985-1986* (Santa Monica: Rand Corporation, 1986).

35. "National Academy of Engineering to Elect Welch Council Chairman," *Chemical and Engineering News*, April 7, 1986, p. 13.

36. "GE's Political Savvy Scores in Washington Marketplace," *Washington Post*, April 13, 1985, p. A1.

## Notes on Chapter 5: Influential Social Ties

1. "Bastion of the Powerful," *Los Angeles Times*, May 26, 1987, p. 21.

2. *Walking Bohemia's Home*, publication of the Bohemian Grove Museum Committee, cited in literature of the Bohemian Grove Action Network, Occidental, CA.

3. "Bastion of the Powerful," p. 21.

4. G. William Domhoff, "Politics among the Redwoods: Ronald Reagan's Bohemian Grove Connection," *The Progressive*, January 1981, p. 32.

5. G. William Domhoff, *The Bohemian Grove and Other Retreats: A Study in Ruling Class Cohesiveness* (New York: Harper and Row, 1974), p. 31.

6. G. William Domhoff, *Who Rules America Now? A View for the 1980's* (New York: Simon and Schuster, 1983), p. 48.

7. "Henry Kissinger, the Bohemian Grove, and Central America: The Mandalay Camp Connections," Santa Rosa, CA; and Kerry Richardson's Report #4, Bohemian Grove Action Network, September 1987. Membership and guest information used throughout this chapter comes from the BGAN.

8. *The Bohemian Grove*, p. 35; and data provided by the Bohemian Grove Action Network.

9. *Who Rules America Now?*, p. 70.

10. G. William Domhoff, *Who Rules America?* (Englewood Cliffs, NJ: Prentice-Hall, Inc., 1967), p. 26.

11. *Who's Who in America*, 1986-87.

12. Ibid.

13. Speech given by John F. Welch at the Harvard Business School, Cambridge, MA, October 28, 1987.

## Notes on Chapter 7: R & D

1. Center for Defense Information (CDI), *The Weapons Bazaar*, produced by Arthur Kanegis (Washington, DC: CDI, 1985), Transcript, p. 11.

2. Investor Responsibility Research Center, *The Nuclear Weapons Industry*, by Kenneth A. Bertsch and Linda S. Shaw (Washington, DC: 1984), p. 78.

3. Philip J. Simon, *Top Guns: A Common Cause Guide to Defense Contractor Lobbying* (Washington, DC: Common Cause, 1987), p. 65.

4. Ibid., p. 68.

5. Brandywine Peace Community, *Bulbs to Bombs: GE and the Permanent War Economy* (Swarthmore, PA: 1986), p. 30.

6. Ibid., p. 17.

7. Ibid., p. 19.

8. Ibid., pp. 18-19.

9. GE Star Wars contracts, fiscal years 1983-86, data from Council on Economic Priorities, New York.

10. Gordon Adams, *The Politics of Defense Contracting: The Iron Triangle* (New Brunswick, NJ: Council on Economic Priorities, 1981), p. 98.

11. Ibid., p. 99.

12. Ibid., p. 95.

13. Rosy Nimroody, "Star Wars: The Economic Fallout," *CEP Research Report* (Council on Economic Priorities), November/December 1987, p. 4.

14. GE Annual Report, 1986, p. 26.

15. *Top Guns*, p. 7.

16. Jobs with Peace Campaign (JwP), Fact Sheet No. 4, "Investing in Our Future: Better Weapons or a Better Life?" (Boston: JwP, January 1987).

## Notes on Chapter 8: Creating the Climate

1. Center for Defense Information (CDI), *The Weapons Bazaar*, produced by Arthur Kanegis (Washington, DC: CDI, 1985), Transcript, p. 17

2. Michio Kaku and Daniel Axelrod, *To Win a Nuclear War: The Pentagon's Secret War Plans* (Boston: South End Press, 1987), p. 315.

3. "On Making a Better Warhead," *New York Times*, February 26, 1987.

4. Carla Johnston, *Basic Facts on the Nuclear Age* (Boston: New Century Policies, 1983), p. 21.

5. Fred Kaplan, "Just How Much Do Soviets Spend?" *Boston Globe*, March 3, 1985.

6. Ibid.

7. Max M. Kampelman, Introduction to *Alerting America: The Papers of the Committee on the Present Danger*, ed. Charles Tyroler, II (Washington: Pergamon-Brassey's International Defense Publishers, 1984), p. xviii.

8. Ibid., p. xix; see also *Encyclopedia of Associations*, 22nd ed., 1988, p. 1358.

9. *Alerting America*, pp. vii and xvii.

10. Ibid., p. 7; see also House of Representatives, Office of the Clerk, lobbying report #01260029, 3rd quarter, 1987.

11. "Committee on the Present Danger: Members of the Board of Directors Appointed to the Administration" (Washington, DC: CPD, November 3, 1987), p. 3.

12. Ibid., p. 6; *Alerting America*, p. xxii; John Woodmansee et al., *The World of a Giant Corporation* (Seattle: North Country Press, 1975), p. 65.

13. *Alerting America*, p. xvi. Updated information confirmed by CPD Washington Office, January 25, 1988.

14. Ibid., p. ix; Robert Scheer, *With Enough Shovels: Reagan, Bush and Nuclear War* (New York: Vintage Books, 1983), p. 41.

15. "CPD: Members of the Board," pp. 1-5.

16. "U.S. Public Attitudes toward Arms Control, INF and the Summit," CPD poll, November 24, 1987.

17. Ibid.

18. "Public Attitudes toward the U.S.-Soviet Military Balance, the Strategic Defense Initiative and Central America," CPD poll, November 30, 1987.

19. *Weapons Bazaar* script, pp. 18-19.

20. Gordon Adams, *The Politics of Defense Contracting: The Iron Triangle* (New Brunswick, NJ: Council on Economic Priorities, 1981), pp. 186-87.

21. Ibid.

22. *Air Force Magazine*, September 1987, vol. 70, no. 9., p. 132.

23. Ibid., p. 203.

## Notes on Chapter 9: PACs and Honoraria

1. Philip J. Simon, *Top Guns: A Common Cause Guide to Defense Contractor Lobbying* (Washington, DC: Common Cause, 1987), p. 35.

2. Campaign finance data, Federal Election Commission (FEC), Public Disclosure Division of the Office of Public Records, Washington, DC, January 6, 1988.

3. Gordon Adams, *The Politics of Defense Contracting: The Iron Triangle* (New Brunswick, NJ: Council on Economic Priorities, 1981), p. 107.

4. "As Campaign Costs Skyrocket, Lobbyists Take Growing Role in Washington Fund-Raisers," *Congressional Quarterly*, May 17, 1980, p. 1333; quoted in *The Iron Triangle*, p. 112.

5. "PACs a Menace to Democracy," *Boston Globe*, September 1, 1985.

6. *Top Guns*, p. 37.

7. "Some Donors See Chance of Shaping Senate," *USA Today*, October 31, 1986, p. 8A.

8. *Top Guns*, pp. 36-37.

9. Ibid.

10. "In the War on PAC's," *New York Times*, May 23, 1986, p. A16.

11. FEC data, 1983-84; *Congressional Yellow Pages 1984*, p. 1349.

12. *Top Guns*, p. 69.

13. "NBC Head Proposes Staff Political Contributions," *New York Times*, December 9, 1986, pp. A1 and C26.

14. Ibid., p. C26.

15. Ibid.

16. *Business Week*, March 9, 1987, pp. 70-71.

17. *Top Guns*, p. 38.

18. Ibid., p. 39.

19. Ibid., p. 41.

20. Ibid.

21. Ibid.

22. "Lobbyists Who Pay Lawmakers $1,000 an Hour Have Found an Effective Way to Communicate," *Wall Street Journal*, June 25, 1986, p. 64.

23. Ibid.

24. Ibid.

25. *Top Guns*, p. 42.

26. Ibid.

27. "House Members Pressing to Curb Special Interests Gifts," *New York Times*, September 26, 1979; quoted in *The Iron Triangle*, p. 112.

## Notes on Chapter 10: Formulating Policy

1. Gordon Adams, *The Politics of Defense Contracting: The Iron Triangle* (New Brunswick, NJ: Council on Economic Priorities, 1981), p. 165.

2. Grant McConnell, *Private Power and American Democracy* (New York: Alfred A. Knopf, Inc., 1966), p. 259.

3. Ibid.

4. Ibid., p. 260.

5. Ibid., pp. 261-64.

6. *The Iron Triangle*, p. 165.

7. Ibid., p. 166.

8. Ibid.

9. Ibid., pp. 166-67; *Defense Science Boards: A Question of Integrity*, Report no. 98-580, 27th Report by the Committee on Government Operations (Washington, DC: U.S. Government Printing Office, 1983), pp. 2-3.

10. *Defense Science Boards*, p. 3.

11. Ibid., p. 1.

12. Ibid., p. 3.

13. Ibid., pp. 4-5.

14. Ibid., pp. 5-6.

15. Ibid., pp. 7-8.

16. Ibid., pp. 10 and 12.

17. Ibid., p. 16.

18. Brandywine Peace Community, *Bulbs to Bombs: GE and the Permanent War Economy* (Swarthmore, PA: 1986), p. 37.

19. Office of Technology Assessment, *Strategic Defenses: Ballistic Missile Defense Technologies* (Washington, DC: U.S. Government Printing Office, 1985; reprint Princeton, NJ: Princeton University Press, 1986), p. v.

20. Diana Roose, "Top Dogs and Top Brass: An Inside Look at a Government Advisory Committee," pp. 53 and 56.

21. This chart was compiled from the following sources:

Final FY 1986 update, Reports control no. 0304-

GSA-XX, Government Service Accounting (GSA) Office —DOD Advisory Committees.

1984 advisory committee information and final FY 1985 update, Office of the Assistant Secretary of Defense.

*Top Dogs and Top Brass*, pp. 53 and 56.

GE Annual Reports, 1979-86.

*General Electric Monogram*, January/February 1973.

*General Electric Monogram*, January/February 1974.

*The Iron Triangle*, p. 63.

Defense Industry Organization Service, *General Electric Company Organization Chart* (Washington, DC: Carroll Publishing Company, Summer 1987).

John Woodmansee et al., *The World of a Giant Corporation* (Seattle: North County Press, 1975), pp. 27-28.

*Strategic Defenses*.

Denise M. Allard and Donna Batten, eds., *Encyclopedia of Governmental Advisory Organizations*, 6th ed., 1988-89 (Detroit: Gale Research Company).

Descriptions of the advisory committees are from *Encyclopedia of Governmental Advisory Organizations*.

In dates column on the chart in the text, "present" means appearing on most recent printouts of DOD advisory committees, received fall of 1987. Date ranges shown may represent only part of an individual's committee term in certain cases.

22. *The Iron Triangle*, pp. 82-83.

23. "With New Curb on Life after Government, More Officials Leave," *New York Times*, March 24, 1987.

24. *The Iron Triangle*, p. 77.

25. Ibid., p. 78.

26. Ibid.

27. "New Curb," March 24, 1987.

28. Ibid.

29. "No Flak from Jones over B-1 Bomber," *New York Times*, February 1, 1981.

30. "Dr. Paine Resigns as Head of NASA," *New York Times*, July 29, 1970.

31. John Woodmansee et al., *The World of a Giant Corporation* (Seattle: North County Press, 1975), p. 27.

32. Ibid.

33. Ibid.

34. Ibid.

35. Ibid.

36. *GE Monogram*, March-April 1972, p. 26.

37. "The Space Station Launching a Thousand Contracts," *Business Week*, November 23, 1987, pp. 126-127.

38. "NASA Picks Space-Station Main Builders," *Wall Street Journal*, December 2, 1987, p. 4.

39. *World of a Giant Corporation*, p. 28.

40. Ibid.

41. Ibid.

42. Ibid., pp. 28 and 64.

43. Ibid., p. 28.

44. Bob Adams, "'Revolving Door' Seen as Open to Conflict," *St. Louis Post-Dispatch*, April 19, 1983.

45. Ibid.

46. Ibid.

47. Ibid.

## Notes on Chapter 11: GE's DC Operations

1. George G. Troutman, then a GE Defense Department lobbyist in Washington, DC; quoted in "How the Weapons Lobby Works in Washington," *Business Week*, February 12, 1979, p. 128.

2. Defense Industry Organization Service, *General Electric Company Organization Chart* (Washington, DC: Carroll Publishing Company, Summer 1987).

3. Philip J. Simon, *Top Guns: A Common Cause Guide to Defense Contractor Lobbying* (Washington, DC: Common Cause, 1987), p. 25.

4. Gordon Adams, *The Politics of Defense Contracting: The Iron Triangle* (New Brunswick, NJ: Council on Economic Priorities, 1981), p. 132.

5. "A Year of Pain and Promise: The Fortune 500 Largest U.S. Industrial Corporations," *Fortune*, April 27, 1987, p. 364.

6. *Top Guns*, p. 26.

7. Thomas B. Edsall, "The GE Lobby: It Brings Goodies to Life," *Washington Post*, May 13, 1985, p. 6.

8. "Top Ten Military Contractors: 1986," *Recon*, Fall 1987, p. 9.

9. *Who's Who in America*.

10. Ibid.

11. "The GE Lobby," p. 7.

12. Ibid., p. 6.

13. *Top Guns*, p. 66.

14. Lobbyists' reports, U.S. House of Representatives, Office of Records and Registration, Longworth House Office Building, Washington, DC, 1986-87.

15. Ibid.

16. Ibid.

17. Names from lobbyists' reports; affiliations from *Top Guns*, p. 67.

18. John M. Barry, "How GE Beat UT for Huge Engine Contract," *Dun's Business Month*, April 1984, p. 40.

19. *Top Guns*, p. 67; "NASA: Space Contractors Named," *Los Angeles Times*, December 2, 1987.

20. John Woodmansee et al., *The World of a Giant Corporation* (Seattle: North County Press, 1975), p. 65.

21. Paraphrased from Gordon Adams, *The Politics of Defense Contracting: The Iron Triangle* (New Brunswick, NJ: Council on Economic Priorities, 1981), p. 132. The company was Boeing, reporting in 1975 to the Defense Contract Audit Agency.

22. *Top Guns*, p. 29.

23. Phyllis S. McGrath, *Redefining Corporate-Federal Relations: A Report from the Conference Board's Division of Management Research* (New York: The Conference Board, 1979), p. 15; quoted in *The Iron Triangle*, p. 131.

24. *The Iron Triangle*, p. 134.

25. In particular the "hunting lodge scandals" of the mid-1970s, in which Pentagon officials received free goose-hunting trips from large contractors like Rockwell and Northrop. Source: "Arms Lobby Works in Secret to Gain Clout," *St. Louis Post-Dispatch*, April 17, 1983.

26. "How the Weapons Lobby Works," p. 128.

27. *Top Guns*, p. 29.

28. "How the Weapons Lobby Works," p. 135.

29. Ibid., p. 130.

30. Congressional hearings dated 1981 through 1986.

31. Information for this case history from the official transcripts of the hearings, published by the House of Representatives, May 24, 1983 and October 8-10, 1985.

32. In 1983, the Subcommittee on Energy Research and Production, and the Subcommittee on Space Science and Applications; in 1985, the Subcommittee on Energy Research and Production.

33. GE Star Wars contracts, fiscal years 1983-86, data from Council on Economic Priorities, New York.

34. *Redefining Corporate-Federal Relations*, p. 35; quoted in *The Iron Triangle*, p. 134.

35. This case history is based largely on two sources: "How GE Beat UT"; and "The GE Lobby: It Brings Goodies to Life."

36. "How GE Beat UT," pp. 40-44.

37. GE contracts, fiscal years 1982-85, Military Spending Research Services (MSRS) data, Middleburg, VA, 1986.

38. "Printouts Reveal Lockheed, Military Worked in Tandem," *St. Louis Post-Dispatch*, April 20, 1983.

39. "Accounts of Cargo Plane Lobbying Clash," *St. Louis Post-Dispatch*, April 20, 1983.

40. Ibid.

41. "Printouts."

42. "Accounts."

43. "Printouts."

44. *The Iron Triangle*, p. 156.

45. Ibid.

46. *The Iron Triangle*, pp. 156-57.

47. "Defense Activities: White House Budget Briefing," *National Defense*, May-June 1987, p. 111.

48. *The American Defense Preparedness Association*, Pamphlet (Arlington, VA: ADPA, 1988).

49. *The Iron Triangle*, p. 159.

50. ADPA pamphlet.

51. *American Defense Preparedness Association: Corporate Member Washington Offices, 1988*, Annual directory (Arlington, VA: ADPA, 1987), pp. iii and 12.

52. "Strategic Defense Division," *National Defense*, October 1985.

53. "Partners in Preparedness: Corporate Members 1987," *National Defense*, May-June 1987, pp. 196 and 266.

54. *Encyclopedia of Associations*, 21st ed., 1987, p. 438.

55. *Annual Report and Directory: NSIA* (Washington, DC: National Security Industrial Association, January 1, 1987), pp. 4-5.

56. Ibid., pp. 18-19.

57. Ibid., pp. 4-5.

58. Ibid., pp. 12-19, 21-43, 51-59, and 78.

59. *Encyclopedia of Associations*, 22nd ed., 1988, p. 550.

60. "Grand Jury Probe Jars the Close-Knit World of Electronic Warfare," *Wall Street Journal*, March 20, 1985, p. 1.

61. *Encyclopedia of Associations*, 22nd ed., 1988, p. 550.

62. "Convention Report," *Electronic Defense*, November/December 1978, pp. 57-58.

63. "AOC Affairs," *Electronic Warfare*, June 1978, p. 92.

64. "1988 AOC Directory," *Journal of Electronic Defense*, January 1988, pp. 11-12 and 15.

65. "Grand Jury Probe," p. 1.

66. Ibid.

67. *Encyclopedia of Associations*, 21st ed., 1987, p. 466.

68. Membership list, *Air Force Magazine*, April 1983.

69. *Air Force Magazine*, survey of ads 1980-1987.

70. *Air Force Magazine*, March 1983, March 1984, March 1985, March 1986, and April 1987.

71. "An AFA Almanac 1987," *Air Force Magazine*, September 1987, p. 203.

72. *Encyclopedia of Associations*, 21st ed., 1987, p. 29.

73. *1986 Aerospace Industries Association Annual Report* (Washington, DC: AIA, 1987), p. 4; *Aerospace Industries Association of America, Inc.: Organization and Functions*, Pamphlet (Washington, DC: AIA, January 1, 1987).

74. *Encyclopedia of Associations*, 21st ed., 1987, p. 29.

75. *1986 AIA Annual Report*.

76. *Encyclopedia of Associations*, 21st ed., 1987.

77. Ibid., p. 236.

78. "GE's Political Savvy Scores in Washington Marketplace," *Washington Post*, April 13, 1985.

## Notes on Chapter 12: War Economy

1. Milton Moskowitz, Michael Katz, and Robert Levering, eds., *Everybody's Business Almanac–The Irreverent Guide to Corporate America* (San Francisco: Harper & Row, 1980), pp. 176-77. See also, "GE Capsule History," *General Electric Monogram*, March/April 1972, p. 11.

2. *GE Monogram*, pp. 11-12.

3. *Everybody's Business*, p. 177.

4. John Woodmansee et al., *The World of a Giant Corporation* (Seattle: North County Press, 1975), p. 30.

5. Ibid.

6. *Everybody's Business*, p. 178.

7. *The National Cyclopedia of American Biography*, s.v. Gerard Swope; *GE Monogram*, p. 12.

8. *Council on Foreign Relations: Roster of Current and Former Members* (New York: CFR, roster current as of December 31, 1986).

9. *Cyclopedia of American Biography*, s.v. Gerard Swope.

10. *World of a Giant Corporation*, p. 30.

11. Jerry De Muth, *G.E.: Profile of a Corporation* (Ann Arbor, MI: The Radical Education Project, 1967), p. 507.

12. *World of a Giant Corporation*, p. 31.

13. *Profile of a Corporation*, p. 507.

14. Ibid.

15. *World of a Giant Corporation*, p. 31.

16. *Profile of a Corporation*, p. 507.

17. Many authors of this time period designated GE's Charles E. (Edward) Wilson with this nickname to distinguish him from Charles E. (Erwin) Wilson of General Motors. GM's head was dubbed "Engine Charlie," and he was Eisenhower's Secretary of Defense.

18. *Everybody's Business*, p. 178.

19. *GE Monogram*, p. 14.

20. Investor Responsibility Research Center, *The Nuclear Weapons Industry*, by Kenneth A. Bertsch and Linda S. Shaw (Washington, DC: 1984), p. 169.

21. John N. Ingham, *Biographical Dictionary of American Business Leaders* (Westport, CT: Greenwood Press, 1983), s.v. Charles Edward Wilson.

22. G. William Domhoff, *Who Rules America* (Englewood Cliffs, NJ: Prentice-Hall, 1967), pp. 118-19.

23. *GE Monogram*, p. 14.

24. *Nuclear Weapons Industry*, p. 171.

25. *Biographical Dictionary*, s.v. Charles Edward Wilson.

26. John Woodmansee, "GE's Electrifying Struggle to Get Its Hands on the Atom," *CALC Report* (Clergy and Laity Concerned), October 1987, p. 7.

27. Ibid.

28. Bruce Catton, *The Warlords of Washington* (New York: Harcourt, Brace and Company, 1948), pp. 244-46.

29. For text of Wilson's speech see "For the Common Defense: A Plea for a Continuing Program of Industrial Preparedness," *Army Ordnance*, March-April 1944, pp. 285-88.

30. Although Wilson did not use the words "permanent war economy" in this speech, he did use phrases such as "permanent preparedness" and clearly argued for continuing governmental support for research and production of war goods. Most authors discuss this speech in terms of Wilson advocating a "permanent war economy" and credit Wilson for coining that term. See: *Who Rules America?*, p. 122; Sidney Lens, *The Day Before Doomsday* (New York: Doubleday & Co., 1977), p.53; John H. Swomley, Jr., *American Empire* (New York: Macmillan Co., 1970), pp. 43-45; Richard J. Barnet, *Roots of War* (Middlesex, England: Penguin Books, 1972), p. 164; Tristram Coffin, *The Passion of the Hawks* (New York: The Macmillan Co., 1964), p. 162.

31. "For the Common Defense," pp. 286-87.

32. Ibid., p. 287.

33. *Encyclopedia of Associations*, 21st ed., 1987, p. 466; *America Defense Preparedness Association: Corporate Member Washington Offices, 1988*, annual directory (Arlington, VA: ADPA, 1987), pp. iii and 12; *National Defense*, May/June 1987, p. 32.

34. Richard C. Hewlett and Oscar E. Anderson, Jr., *The New World, 1939/1946*, vol. 1, *A History of the United States Atomic Energy Commission* (University Park, PA: The Pennsylvania State University Press, 1962), pp. 90-91 and 322-25.

35. Ibid., p. 325.

36. Ibid., pp. 90-91.

37. Ibid., pp. 528 and 534.

38. Ibid., p. 629.

39. "New Research Set on Atomic Power," *New York Times*, November 10, 1946.

40. "GE to Run Hanford Atom Plant," *New York Times*, June 5, 1946; "Electrifying Struggle," p. 7.

41. "Production to Assure World Peace: Toil and Sweat to Avert Blood and Tears," *Vital Speeches of the Day*, October 1-15, 1951, p. 456.

42. *GE Monogram*, p. 14; *Profile of a Corporation*, p. 512.

43. Investor Responsibility Research Center, *The Nuclear Weapons Industry*, by Kenneth A. Bertsch and Linda S. Shaw (Washington, DC: 1984), p. 69.

44. Ibid.

45. *World of a Giant Corporation*, p. 27.

46. Ibid.

47. *Everybody's Business*, pp. 178-179.

48. *World of a Giant Corporation*, p. 64.

49. *Cyclopedia of American Biography*, s.v. Ralph Jarron Cordiner.

50. *GE Monogram*, p. 19; *World of a Giant Corporation*, p. 23.

51. Ibid., pp. 23-26.

52. Ibid., p. 26.

53. Ibid., p. 20.

54. *Cyclopedia of American Biography*, s.v. Fred J. Borch.

55. "GE's Jones Is No. 1," *Wall Street Journal*, August 21, 1980; *Everybody's Business*, p. 180.

56. "The New Face of Business Leadership," *New York Times*, May 22, 1983, pp. 1 and 8-9.

57. Ibid., p. 1.

58. See: "Pentagon Study Explores Profits for Contractors," *New York Times*, March 18, 1985; "Profits Soar in Build-up: As Firms Cash In, Questions Crop Up," *Washington Post*, April 1, 1985; "U.S. Weapons Makers Ring Up Healthy Profits," *New York Times*, April 9, 1985; and "Defense Contracts Yield Higher Profits Than Private Work, Navy Study Says," *Wall Street Journal*, November 29, 1985.

59. *Nuclear Weapons Industry*, p. 75.

60. Comments by John F. Welch, Jr., "General Electric Company: 1986 Annual Meeting of Share Owners," Transcript of GE annual meeting, Kansas City, MO, April 23, 1986, p. 74.

61. Speech given by John F. Welch at the Harvard Business School, Cambridge, MA, October 28, 1987.

62. Letter from Ford C. Slater, GE, Manager of Special Issues Planning and Communications, to Palo Alto Coop, CA, June 30, 1987.

63. Welch's speech at Harvard.

64. The one company that is arguably comparable to GE's stature in the business community *and* is a top 10 DOD contractor is General Motors. It should be noted that GM moved into a prominent contractor position in 1986, through the acquisition of Hughes Aircraft. Prior to this purchase, GM ranked #17 in 1985; #23 in 1984 and 1983; #26 in 1982 and 1980; and #27 in 1981. Compare that to GE's consistent placement in the top 10 DOD contractors; in fact, GE has been in the top 5 for six of the past seven years. (Source: "Top Ten Military Contractors: 1986," *Recon*, Fall 1987, p. 9.) Thus, GE's ability to exploit the government access afforded to nuclear weapons contractors is much greater than GM's.

65. Comparison of GE to other top weapons contractors in terms of overall business position:

| Company | Sales | S.H.E. | Net | MV Amt. |
|---|---|---|---|---|
| 1) GE | #6 | #6 | #5 | $47.9 billion |
| 2) McDonnell-Douglas | #23 | #46 | #61 | 3.2 billion |
| 3) Rockwell | #24 | #42 | #26 | 7.7 billion |
| 4) Lockheed | #30 | #68 | #44 | 3.4 billion |
| 5) General Dynamics | #36 | #107 | #443 | 3.3 billion |
| 6) Raytheon | #48 | #66 | #46 | 5.8 billion |

S.H.E. = Shareholder Equity
Net = Net Income
MV Amt. = Market Value
Source: "A Year of Pain and Promise: The Fortune 500 Largest U.S. Industrial Corporations," *Fortune*, April 27, 1987, pp. 364-65.

66. "The Fortune 500."

67. Defense Industry Organization Service, "Table 1: Top 100 Defense Department Contractors, FY 1986," Washington, DC. IBM, for example, was #19 DOD contractor in 1986; Exxon, #36; ATT, #25; Du Pont was not among the top 100 DOD contractors in 1986.

## Notes on Chapter 13: Update 1989

1. These tables were compiled by comparing lists of members of the Armed Services Committee and the Defense Appropriations Subcommittee to printouts of the "Federal Election Commission Committee Index of Candidates Supported/Opposed (Index D)," available from the Federal Election Commission Office, Washington, DC. The printouts were specifically for GE's two PACs: the "Non-Partisan Political Support Committee for General Electric Company Employees" and the "Non-Partisan Political Support Committee for Kidder-Peabody Employees."

2. Ibid.

3. Data for 1986, 1987, and 1988 was compiled from individual financial disclosure forms. The "Senate Public Financial Report" documents are from the Senate Office of Public Records, Washington, DC and the "Ethics in Government Act–Financial Disclosure Statement" documents are from the House Office of Records and Registration, Washington, DC.

Figures for 1985 and 1984 from Philip J. Simon, *Top Guns: A Common Cause Guide to Defense Contractor Lobbying* (Washington, DC: Common Cause, 1987), p. 70.

Note: The totals are likely understated since elected officials who retire or lose their seat are not required to file a disclosure form for their last year in office. Hence, it is possible that GE gave to some Senators and House members whose term ended in 1988 and thus have no record on file for that year. This is true for each of the years.

4. Ibid.

5. Ibid.

6. Information comes from reports ("Report Pursuant to Federal Regulation of Lobbying Act") filed by registered lobbyists at House Office of Records and Registrations, Washington, DC.

7. This passage was on the report forms of GE lobbyists David A. Portnoy and David A. Wilkinson, both filed in June 1989 at the House Office of Records and Registrations, Washington, DC.

8. Information compiled from review of separate form 1787s filed by individuals and by GE at the Standards of Conduct Office at the Pentagon, Washington, DC (1987-1988).

These numbers are likely underestimates. According to a U.S. General Accounting Office study, 70 percent of former Pentagon personnel who are required by federal law to report their employment with defense contractors to the Pentagon fail to do so. See Simon, *Top Guns*, p. 21.

9. Information describing an individual's work experience at the DOD and current GE work experience taken from form 1787 filed by individuals and by GE at the Standards of Conduct Office at the Pentagon.

10. Ibid.

11. Ibid.

12. "With New Curb on Life After Government, More Officials Leave," *New York Times*, March 24, 1987.

13. " 'Revolving Door' Spins Without Close Attention—Moves from Pentagon to Private Sector Often Go Unrecorded," *Christian Science Monitor*, July 11, 1988, p. 1.

14. From form 1787 which Cooper himself filed at the Standards of Conduct Office at the Pentagon.

15. Ibid.

# PART IV.
## Notes on Chapter 1: GE's Nuclear Weapons

1. GE nuclear weapons-related DOD and DOE contract totals, fiscal years 1984-86, Military Spending Research Services (MSRS) data, Middleburg, VA, 1987.

2. Ibid.

3. *Capsule Review of DOE Research and Development and Field Facilities*, U.S. Department of Energy, Office of Energy Research, Office of Field Operation Management (Springfield, VA: National Technical Information Service, September 1986), p. 93.

4. Council on Economic Priorities: *Star Wars: The Economic Fallout* (Cambridge, MA: Ballinger Publishing Company, Harper & Row, 1987).

5. GE Annual Report, 1980, p. 19.

6. *DOE Facilities*, p. 93.

7. Investor Responsibility Research Center, *The Nuclear Weapons Industry*, by Kenneth A. Bertsch and Linda S. Shaw (Washington, DC: 1984), p. 172.

8. Brandywine Peace Community, *Bulbs to Bombs: GE and the Permanent War Economy* (Swarthmore, PA: 1986), p. 19.

9. "War and Peace in the Nuclear Age," *The Boston Globe*, October 17, 1982, p. 12.

10. GE Star Wars contracts, fiscal years 1983-86, data from Council on Economic Priorities, New York.

11. National Resources Defense Council, Inc., *Nuclear Weapons Databook*, vol. 3, *U.S. Nuclear Warhead Facility Profiles*, by Thomas B. Cochran, William M. Arkin, Robert S. Norris, and Milton M. Hoenig (Cambridge, MA: Ballinger Publishing Company, Harper & Row, 1987), p. 81.

12. Ibid.

13. *DOE Facilities*, p. A-4.

14. *Nuclear Weapons Databook*, p. 81.

15. MSRS data.

16. *DOE Facilities*, p. 93.

17. *Nuclear Weapons Databook*, p. 81.

18. Brandywine Peace Community, *Bulbs to Bombs: GE and the Permanent War Economy* (Swarthmore, PA: 1986), p. 24.

19. Richard C. Hewlett and Oscar E. Anderson, Jr., *The New World, 1939/1946*, vol. 1, *A History of the United States Atomic Energy Commission* (University Park, PA: The Pennsylvania State University Press, 1962), pp. 629 and 635; and "New Research Set on Atomic Power," *New York Times*, November 10, 1946.

20. *DOE Facilities*, p. A-2; *The Nuclear Weapons Industry*, p. 175.

21. *The Nuclear Weapons Industry*, p. 175.

22. *Bulbs to Bombs*, p. 25.

23. *Star Wars: The Economic Fallout*.

24. Ibid.

25. GE Star Wars contracts, fiscal years 1983-86, data from Council on Economic Priorities, New York; *CEP Newsletter*, December 1987, p. 4.

26. GE nuclear weapons-related DOD and DOE contract totals, fiscal years 1984-86, MSRS data. Please note: these figures are stated in millions of dollars. Some small inconsistencies may result from rounding the figures. Exact total is: $11,074,175,000.

27. GE nuclear weapons-related DOD contracts, geographic breakdown, fiscal year 1986, MSRS data. Please note: the nuclear weapons examples listed are spread throughout the state. The examples do not necessarily match the city locations on the same line.

28. "Defense Firms, Facing Budget Squeeze, to Fight Plan for Agency to Measure Profits," *Wall Street Journal*, January 21, 1987, p. 48.

29. Ibid.

30. U.S. General Accounting Office, "Government Contracting: Assessment of the Study of Defense Contractor Profitability," December 1986, p. 1.

## Notes on Chapter 2: Unrestrained Weapons Spending Ruins the Economy

1. Anthony Lewis, "The Military-Industrial Complex," *New York Times*, November 21, 1985.

2. Bruce Butterfield, "Nobody Thought It Would Be This Bad," *Boston Globe*, January 13, 1987, p. 12.

3. "GE to Cut 1950 Workers from Lynn Plant," *Boston Herald*, January 13, 1987, p. 1.

4. GE Annual Report, 1985, p. 32.

5. Barry Bluestone and John Havens, "Reducing the Federal Deficit Fair and Square," prepared for the Joint Economic Committee of the U.S. Congress, January 1986; cited in Jobs with Peace Campaign (JwP), Fact Sheet No. 5., "The Choice Is Ours... More Military Spending or More Jobs" (Boston: JwP, January 1987).

6. GE nuclear weapons-related DOD and DOE contract totals, fiscal years 1984-86, Military Spending Research Services (MSRS) data, Middleburg, VA, 1987.

7. "IUD Delegates Set Agenda for Jobs, Peace," *The Machinist*, November 13, 1986.

8. "Military R & D Depletes Economy's Might," *Wall Street Journal*, August 21, 1986.

9. FY 1987 Enacted Budget, U.S. Office of Management and Budget; and "Federal R & D Funding by Budget Function, FY 1985-87," National Science Foundation, March 1986; both sources cited in Jobs with Peace Fact Sheet No. 4, "Investing in Our Future: Better Weapons or a Better Life?" (Boston: JwP, January 1987).

10. "Military R & D Depletes Economy's Might."

11. Ibid.

12. The National Disarmament Program, American Friends Service Committee (AFSC), *Briefing Paper: The Facts As We See Them* (Philadelphia: AFSC, March 5, 1986), p. 2.

## Notes on Chapter 3: Basic Human Needs

1. Dwight D. Eisenhower, April 1953, quoted in Jeanne Larson and Madge Micheels-Cyrus, *Seeds of Peace: A Catalogue of Quotations* (Philadelphia: New Society Publishers, 1986), p. 62.

2. "The Pentagon Prepares for Nuclear War," *The Defense Monitor* (Center for Defense Information), vol. 16, no. 4, 1987, p. 3.

3. FY 1987 Budget of the U.S. Government and FY 1987 Mid Session Review of the Budget, Office of Management and Budget, and Military Spending Research Services (MSRS) data; both sources cited in Jobs with Peace Campaign (JwP), Fact Sheet No. 2, "55% of Your Federal Income Tax Dollar Goes to the Pentagon" (Boston: JwP, January 1987).

4. Philip J. Simon, *Top Guns: A Common Cause Guide to Defense Contractor Lobbying* (Washington, DC: Common Cause, 1987), p. 65.

5. Jobs with Peace Fact Sheet No. 2.

6. Department of Defense data, December 1986; "The Republican Record, FY 1982-86," prepared for the American Federation of State, County and Municipal Employees by Fiscal Planning Services, September 1986; and Low Income Housing Information Service, housing figure from data in FY 1987 Budget of the U.S. Government; all cited in Jobs with Peace, Fact Sheet No. 3, "Winners & Losers: Federal Spending from 1982-86" (Boston: JwP, January 1987).

7. Ruth Legar Sivard, *World Military and Social Expenditures: 1986* (Washington, DC: World Priorities, 1986), p. 47.

8. Ibid., p. 51.

9. Ibid., p. 7.

10. Ibid., p. 5.

## Notes on Chapter 4: Radiation

1. "Survivors Find Shelter from Nuclear Shadow," *Oakland Tribune*, June 24, 1986.

2. National Committee for Radiation Victims, *Invisible Violence*, proceedings of the National Citizens' Hearings for Radiation Victims, April 10-14, 1980, Washington, DC, p. 18.

3. Ibid.

4. "Uranium Plagues the Navajos," *Sierra* magazine.

5. GE Annual Report, 1980, p. 19.

6. Hanson W. Baldwin, "New Atomic Capitol," *New York Times Magazine*, July 30, 1950, p. 19.

7. June Casey's statement at GE's Annual Meeting, Montgomery, AL, April 22, 1987.

8. "1949 Hanford Event Raises Health Problems," *The Oregonian*, March 12, 1986, p. B-1.

9. June Casey's statement.

10. Richard L. Miller, *Under the Cloud: The Decades of Nuclear Testing* (New York: The Free Press, Macmillan, Inc., 1986), pp. 75-78; "GAO Disputes Radiation Study on First A-Tests," *New York Times*, December 5, 1985, p. A22.

11. Glenn Alcalay, "Bombed, Robbed, Relocated, Irradiated by U.S., France," *The Guardian*, November 25, 1987, p. 10.

12. Statement by Janet Gordon at press conference, on occasion of GE's Annual Meeting, Montgomery, AL, April 22, 1987.

13. *Invisible Violence*, pp. 4-5.

14. Harvey Wasserman and Norman Solomon with Robert Alvarez and Eleanor Walters, *Killing Our Own: The Disaster of America's Experience with Atomic Radiation* (New York: Dell Publishing Co., Inc., 1982), p. 59.

15. Ibid., p. 34.

16. Janet Gordon's statement.

17. *Killing Our Own*, pp. 66-67.

18. Ibid., p. 64.

19. Ibid., p. 65.

20. *Capsule Review of DOE Research and Development and Field Facilities*, U.S. Department of Energy, Office of Energy Research, Office of Field Operation Management (Springfield, VA: National Technical Information Service, September 1986), p. 93.

21. Investor Responsibility Research Center, *The Nuclear Weapons Industry*, by Kenneth A. Bertsch and Linda S. Shaw (Washington, DC: 1984), p. 178.

22. *Killing Our Own*, p. 73.

23. Ibid., p. 79.

24. Don Behm, "The Warhead Legacy," *Milwaukee Journal*, August 1986; quoted in "Editorial: Satan Swindled Us Again," *Fishing Facts*, April 1987, p. 6.

25. "Hanford," *Greenpeace Disarmament*, Winter 1986/87.

26. Hanford Education Action League (HEAL), *Blowing in the Wind: Radioactive Contamination of the Soil around the Hanford Nuclear Reservation*, report produced by HEAL, Spokane, WA, p. 1.

27. John Woodmansee, "GE's Electrifying Struggle to Get Its Hands on the Atom," *CALC Report* (Clergy and Laity Concerned), November/ December 1978.

28. Keiki Kehoe, *Unavailable at Any Price: Nuclear Insurance* (Washington DC: Environmental Policy Center, 1980), pp. 2-5.

29. "What Is the Price-Anderson Act," flyer produced by the Price-Anderson Campaign, Washington, DC, 1987.

30. Testimony of Francis K. McCune of General Electric, hearings before the Joint Committee on Atomic Energy, 85th Congress, 1st Session (1957), pp. 148 and 156-161; *Unavailable at Any Price*, p. 4.

31. Letter from P. S. Peter to an anonymous U.S. Senator, May 1, 1987.

32. Ibid.

33. "Price-Anderson Goes to the Wire," article from the Price-Anderson Campaign, P.O. Box 15391, Washington, DC 20003, 1987.

34. Ibid.

35. U.S. Public Interest Research Group (U.S. PIRG), "Nuclear Power Industry PACs Gave Over $17 Million to Congress and Candidates," press release, Washington, DC, July 25, 1987.

36. Ibid.

# Index

## "I wondered why somebody didn't do something...then I realized that I am somebody."

**Here's what some of our supporters from around the country are doing to spread the GE Boycott:**

*From Sonoita, Arizona, June 8, 1987:*

"I am willing to do what I can ... as seen in the "Letter to the Editor" that went out in the mail today. If you have any brochures I could pass out, or stickers that I could paste on GE products at local stores, I'd be pleased to use them well."

*From Kansas City, Missouri, June 11, 1987:*

[Letter to the Editor, *Kansas City Star/Times*] "The GE Boycott uses the positive force of consumer choice to change the way our nation's major nuclear weaponmaker does business."

*From Piedmont, California, June 17, 1986:*

"I bought a $450 dishwasher...and told 3 retailers why I wouldn't buy GE."

*From Buffalo, New York, June 19, 1986:*

"...I am twelve years old. My parents received your letter about the G.E. boycott in the mail on June 12. I think it is a great idea and want to help. Do you think you could send me more stickers, etc., so that I could help spread the word about the boycott...I intend to write an article about the boycott for my school newspaper next fall."

*From Eaton, Pennsylvania, Oct. 27, 1986:*

"I have (for almost 1 year) and will continue to boycott General Electric and their products. Please send me any literature on this subject. I am only 16, but have attended GE protests at their Valley Forge location. Keep me updated."

*From San Jose, California, Dec. 5, 1986:*

"As an electrician, we use GE products every day. But there are other manufacturers that can be used in almost every case. I want to put together a flier designed to be mailed to all other electrical contractors in my area."

*From Downers Grove, Illinois, Dec. 17, 1986:*

[Letter to Apple Computer, Inc.] "I have recently decided to cancel my Apple Card ... and want you to be aware that I am doing this because the card is issued and administered through General Electric Credit Corporation."

*From Wilton, New Hampshire, Mar. 11, 1987:*

"I now realize my Zayre credit card is GECC [GE Credit Corporation]—I am tearing it up and returning it."

*From New York, New York, Dec. 15, 1986:*

[Letter to Morningside Heights Consumers Cooperative] "In one hour's time during the afternoon of December 4, 1986, Morningsiders for Reversing the Arms Race collected 228 signatures in the buildings of Morningside Gardens. The signers pledged not to buy General Electric products.

"Since those who signed are all presumably customers of the Coop Supermarket, which sells General Electric light bulbs only, they must now go elsewhere to buy electric light bulbs.

"Therefore, we request, as a service to the community, that the Coop Supermarket add another brand of light bulbs to its stock."

**To find out how you can help build the GE Boycott, write or call the INFACT office nearest you:**

**National Offices:**

*INFACT National Office*
256 Hanover Street
Boston, MA 02113
(617) 742-4583

*INFACT National Field Campaign*
P.O. Box 3223
S. Pasadena, CA 91031
(818) 799-9133

**Regional Campaign Centers:**

*INFACT – Northern California*
2414 B Telegraph Avenue
Oakland, CA 94612
(415) 272-9522

*INFACT – Southern California*
5338 Monte Vista Street
Los Angeles, CA 90042
(213) 255-0287

*INFACT – Upper Midwest*
3732 4th Avenue S, #1
Minneapolis, MN 55409
(612) 822-6024

*INFACT – Illinois*
5249 North Kenmore
Chicago, IL 60640
(312) 769-0401

*INFACT – Pennsylvania*
RD #4, Box 592
Boyertown, PA 19512
(215) 369-1636

*INFACT – New England*
25 Huntington Avenue, Rm #306
Boston, MA 02116
(617) 266-7173

*INFACT – Northwest*
P.O. Box 20729
Broadway Station
Seattle, WA 98102
(206) 325-8482

*INFACT – International*
P.O. Box 80013
Minneapolis, MN 55408
(612) 920-8716

# BOYCOTT GE UNTIL THEY ARE NUCLEAR–WEAPONS FREE.
## Don't buy these products:

### LIGHTING
GE Soft-White and MISER Lightbulbs
GE Extension Cords
GE Electric Lamps
GE Batteries
GE Car Headlights
Flip Flash II, Flash Bar II
Magicubes

### APPLIANCES
GE Microwave Ovens
GE Ranges
GE Refrigerators
GE Freezers
GE Washers
GE Dryers
GE Dishwashers
GE Disposals
GE Air Conditioners
GE Dehumidifiers
GE Heat Pumps

### MEDICAL SYSTEMS
GE CT Products
GE X-Ray Equipment
GE Magnetic Resonance Scanners
GE Ultrasound Equipment
GE Nuclear Medical Products

### SERVICES
GE Capital (GE Credit Corporation)
GE Information Services

### CONSTRUCTION
GE Wiring
GE Controls
GE Switches
GE Motors
GE Caulking
Silicone II Home Pro Sealants

or any other product that carries
the GE, Hotpoint, or RCA label

The GE Boycott Pledge has been signed by over 170,000 people from all 50 states and more than 40 different countries. An independent poll taken in July 1987 revealed that *two million* consumers in the U.S. are already boycotting GE! To let GE know of your commitment to boycott their products until they are nuclear weapons free, please copy and sign the pledge. Ask your friends and family to sign, too. Then return to INFACT and we'll deliver them along with thousands more to GE's Chief Executive Officer.

**To:** **John F. Welch, Jr., Chief Executive Officer**
**General Electric Company**

The nuclear weapons build-up must be stopped! GE's production and promotion of more costly and deadly nuclear weapons threatens the survival of people all over the world. Your company's influence over government decisions on nuclear weapons seriously undermines democracy in this country. GE's nuclear weapons work results in tremendous profits for GE but leads to poverty and death for millions of people as precious resources are devoted to preparation for war instead of to peacemaking and human needs. Therefore...

## I pledge to boycott all GE products and services until:

- **GE stops all nuclear weapons work;**

- **GE stops promoting the nuclear weapons build-up to the government and the public;**

- **GE redirects its resources to peaceful production.**

|  | *Name* | *Address* | *City/State/Zip* |
|---|---|---|---|
| 1. | | | |
| 2. | | | |
| 3. | | | |
| 4. | | | |
| 5. | | | |
| 6. | | | |
| 7. | | | |
| 8. | | | |
| 9. | | | |
| 10. | | | |
| 11. | | | |
| 12. | | | |
| 13. | | | |
| 14. | | | |
| 15. | | | |
| 16. | | | |
| 17. | | | |
| 18. | | | |
| 19. | | | |
| 20. | | | |